RUSSIA

CLASS AND POWER 1917-2000

MIKE HAYNES

BOOKMARKS PUBLICATIONS

London & Sydney

Russia: Class and Power 1917-2000 — Mike Haynes
First published 2002
Bookmarks Publications Ltd, c/o 1 Bloomsbury Street, London WC1B 3QE, England
Bookmarks, PO Box A338, Sydney South, NSW 2000, Australia
Copyright © Bookmarks Publications Ltd

ISBN 1 898876 87 8

Design by Noel Douglas (noel@freemachine.net)
Typeset by Dave Turley
Printed by Bath Press

Bookmarks Publications Ltd is linked to an international grouping of socialist organisations:
Australia: International Socialists, PO Box A338, Sydney South
Austria: Linkswende, Postfach 87, 1108 Wien
Britain: Socialist Workers Party, PO Box 82, London E3 3LH
Canada: International Socialists, PO Box 339, Station E, Toronto, Ontario M6H 4E3
Cyprus: Ergatiki Demokratia, PO Box 7280, Nicosia
Czech Republic: Socialisticka Solidarita, PO Box 1002, 11121 Praha 1
Denmark: Internationale Socialister, PO Box 5113, 8100 Aarhus C
Finland: Sosialistiliitto, PL 288, 00171 Helsinki
Germany: Linksruck, Postfach 304 183, 20359 Hamburg
Ghana: International Socialist Organisation, PO Box TF202, Trade Fair, Labadi, Accra
Greece: Sosialistiko Ergatiko Komma, c/o Workers Solidarity, PO Box 8161, Athens 100 10
Holland: Internationale Socialisten, PO Box 92025, 1090AA Amsterdam
Ireland: Socialist Workers Party, PO Box 1648, Dublin 8
New Zealand: Socialist Workers Organization, PO Box 13-685, Auckland
Norway: Internasjonale Socialisterr, Postboks 9226 Grønland, 0134 Oslo
Poland: Pracownicza Demokracja, PO Box 12, 01-900 Warszawa 118
Spain: Izquierda Revolucionaria, Apartado 563, 08080 Barcelona
United States: Left Turn, PO Box 445, New York, NY 10159-0445
Zimbabwe: International Socialist Organisation, PO Box 6758, Harare
For more information visit www.istendency.org

CONTENTS

PREFACE

I have been thinking of writing this book for a long time. I was finally provoked by someone I have never met. I was asked to read a long manuscript by Goretti Horgan on Ireland. Having read much on that subject, I did not look forward to it. When I finally plucked up courage I was transfixed. Every page seemed to sparkle because Goretti avoided simply recycling old arguments and familiar facts. It was not that the arguments were not there – they appeared with new life and force, illustrated by a wealth of things I did not know, because she allowed what she wrote to grow out of them but not be bound by them. This, I thought, was the way I should try to approach Russia. I wanted to stand on what had been done in the past but not be limited by it. If I have not detailed the origins of every argument this is not because I do not recognise my debts. They are there, but the tribute that is paid is my attempt to build beyond the foundations.

Whether I have succeeded or not is not for me to say. But this work would have been the worse without the help of many people. Pete Rooney made my work easier by passing on a mass of material. Similarly I have been fortunate to work with Rumy Husan on the general transition in Eastern Europe. I have benefited from the help of many Russians, especially those whose work has forced them to share my company. They patiently allowed me to discuss much with them, and they tolerated what sometimes seemed my strange lines of argument. I will not embarrass them by naming them. Suffice it to say that I learned much, and my greatest pleasures were when I felt my argument was making sense to them. Emma Bircham began work on this book and Dave Waller took over at an early stage. Both commented on it and shared many of my enthusiasms, if not all of them. Marcie Haynes, Ian Birchall and Chris Harman also made detailed comments on drafts from which I have benefited, and which have saved me from error. A special word of thanks must go to Pete Glatter. By good fortune I was asked to help supervise his doctoral work on Russia, some of which has since appeared in print, and hopefully more of which will follow. He came late to academic life with a wealth of experience, and quickly gained an enviable command of Russian. I have often depended on him for help. This book is not only the better for the care with which he worked on the manuscript and the suggestions he made – some of its argument leans heavily on discussions we have had over several years. Usually I have felt myself resisting his views, only to see that he was right. The one argument that I continued to resist was his suggestion that this was not the book to write on Russia. I hope he now feels that in this instance I was right. But, if I am, much is due to his continuing help. Needless to say, none of those mentioned above share responsibility for the faults that remain.

Finally, all authors have a problem over what to call Russia in the 20th century. Formally from the 1920s to 1991 it was the Soviet Union or the USSR, but essentially from 1928 onwards it was an empire under the control of Moscow – Russia writ large. This was one reason why it broke up in 1991. After 1928 there were no genuine 'soviets' in the sense that there had been in 1917. I have not rigidly avoided the terms 'Soviet Union' and 'USSR'. It would be too complex to do so – especially in quotations. But I have tried to minimise their use to better reflect the real situation.

Transliterating from Russian is rarely error free or consistent. I have kept older forms for the best known names but tried to follow modern practices for less familiar ones.

The seriousness of the internationalism of 1917 was reflected in the design of early banknotes. Count the languages

1 INTRODUCTION

This book is an attempt to settle accounts with the history of the Soviet Union. In 1917 a first revolution in February overthrew the Russian Tsar, and then in October a second revolution brought the Bolshevik Party to power. The Bolsheviks were committed to changing Russia, and to inspiring an international revolution that would help build a world free of inequality, war and class conflict. Yet within a decade most of the revolutionary generation were marginalised, and the revolution turned on its head. Under Stalin Russia re-emerged as a Great Power. The regime called itself 'socialist' and 'communist', it built statues to Marx and Lenin, but in its internal organisation it remained undemocratic and repressive. Externally Russian actions blocked or hindered the possibility of wider social change. This not only helped to set the pattern of the history of the 20th century, but it also trapped the larger part of the international left, who identified themselves more or less critically with the Soviet Union and its satellites. Here, they believed, was a system superior to capitalism – even if parts of it deserved sharp criticism – and here were, at least, some elements of the future. The collapse of the Soviet system in Eastern Europe in 1989 destroyed these illusions. It seemed to many as if a new epoch had arrived. What they imagined to be some form of socialism had turned to dust – 'capitalism' and 'the West' had won. In the United States Francis Fukuyama had already declared that the days of the great ideological challenges to liberal capitalism were over. The alternatives had been defeated and history, as the story of a battle between grand alternatives, was over. The future now lay with the global market and multinational firms under the benevolent eye of the US, the only remaining superpower. The US president, George Bush Sr, speaking to the International Monetary Fund in September 1990, said: 'Today leaders around the world are turning to market forces to meet the needs of their peoples... The jury is no longer out. History has decided'.[1] Then in 1991 the Soviet Union itself disintegrated after a failed coup in August that year. The rout of the system was complete. 'History will record [that] the 20th century essentially ended on 17 August...to 21 August 1991,' Boris Yeltsin later said.[2]

The disorientation of the international left was real. Communist parties collapsed, or reformed as Social Democratic parties. But rarely has such an apparent epochal shift had such a short life. Within a few years, across the globe, new waves of protest began to merge into an anti-globalisation and anti-capitalist movement. This movement was astonishingly broad. Churches challenged the debt mechanisms of the global economy. Environmentalists took on the great polluters. Consumers worried about the power of the great corporations to modify food or to profit from medicines desperately needed by the poor. The challenges are also deep – here is a world where the basic mechanisms seem out of control, where the few ride roughshod over the wishes of the many even when they have received clear expression in democratic elections. The word 'anti' is a strong one. It does not suggest equivocation – it stands for *against, opposed to*. It reflects the strength of feeling – sometimes moral, sometimes theorised – that there is something fundamentally wrong with a world order that gives so much to so few, but denies the most basic things to so many. Perhaps no calculation of the 1990s more clearly expressed this than that of the 1996 United Nations Human Development Report: 'Nearly 90 countries are worse off economically than they were 10 years ago... the gap in per capita income between the industrial and developing worlds tripled from 1960 to 1993, from US$5,700 to US$15,400... Today the net worth of the world's 358 richest billionaires is equal to the combined income of the poorest 45 percent of the world's population – 2.3 billion people'.[3]

But 'anti-globalisation' and 'anti-capitalism' are also terms of weakness, for they are both negative – you know what you are against, but what are you for? It is this question that makes the issue of the Soviet Union one that continues to have such contemporary political importance. Standing stark in the middle of any discussion of a possible better world is the history of the USSR. While the Eastern Bloc existed, sooner or later any discussion of an alternative to Western capitalism led there. 'Doesn't this show where revolution leads, especially when centralised parties take control?' the sympathetic would ask. For the hostile it was simpler to shout: 'Get back to Russia' to still criticism of the societies in which they lived. The biggest argument for Western capitalism seemed to be the Russia of Stalin and his successors. If this was what social-ism was like, who would want it? Not a lot of people who lived there, it seemed. One old joke in Russia asked: 'Is it possible to build socialism in one country? Answer: it is – but it is better to live in another country.' The joke gives the lie to the image of the Russians as stereotypical Communists – emotionless, obe-dient, and capable of anything in the name of 'progress'. But it confirmed the idea that there was something fundamentally wrong with the nature of Russia as a society of the future.

And so there was. But some were still attracted because of illusion. Others were attracted because of power. The tanks and rockets that rolled through Red Square on the great holidays were certainly impressive, and they helped to legitimise the system for many on the left. And in the Cold War the dominant view was that you either had for be 'for Washington' or 'for Moscow'. That an alternative anti-Stalinist tradition existed on the left that denied Russia the title socialist was seen as no more than an annoying quirk. It counted for little and was best ignored.

Then in 1989-91, when it all began to collapse, the vision of Russian power no longer legitimised anything. 'I have seen the future and it works,' the American journalist Lincoln Steffens famously said after a visit to Russia at the time of the civil war. But it is clear now that it did *not* work. Its failure was dragged out, but finally became complete in 1991. Triumphalism in the West grew to a crescendo. Western capitalism had proved itself the only viable sys-tem, and people in Eastern Europe were rushing towards it. It was time to give up illusions. But even at this early stage it seemed a bit more complicated to those who looked. People in the former Eastern Bloc were certainly rejecting the old, but they seemed less than enthusiastic about the new. Instinctively many recognised the limitations of the 'transition':

> As she contemplated today's recycled Communists, who miraculously have discovered the virtues of pluralism, one Polish lady gave me the following definition of her erstwhile homeland's governments throughout this cen-tury: 'Same shit, different flies!'[4]

How we make sense of the failure of Russia is therefore important for the pol-itics of the future as well as our understanding of the past. Clearing away illu-sions helps us not only to move forward, but it helps to see how we should move forward. Not least it shows the danger of identifying an alternative world with a reliance on state power from above to solve our problems. There is a dif-ference between amnesia and memory. Amnesia is about forgetting, and some of the left would prefer to forget Russia. Memory is about retaining and analysing the past so that it can help inform our present and our future.

All the best accounts of the history of Russia link past, present and future, but they do it in quite different ways. Take the example of some of the ways it operates in the conservative-liberal dismissal of the whole history of Russia between 1917 and 1991 as one great totalitarian nightmare inspired by an ideological crusade to create a new utopia. The word totalitarian is not a bad word – ironically, left wing critics of Stalin's Russia in the 1930s were some of the first to use it. But *totalitarianism* as a theory – seeking to explain everything from the top down in terms of leadership, ideology and repression – is something quite different. This argument was made by Western conservatives in the Cold War as part of the attack on the possibility of radical social change. It was taken up by penitent former Communists who recoiled from their earlier allegiances and who, rejecting the arguments of those on the left who had always doubted Russia's claims to be socialist, adopted the arguments of the other side. More disturbingly, the same path was followed by leading commentators and politicians in Russia after 1990-91. At first sight their blanket condemnation of Soviet Russia as an example of 'totalitarianism' seemed radical, but its implications are profoundly conservative both in terms of history and present and future politics.

Totalitarian theory to a large extent inverts the discredited Soviet regime's own image of itself. Soviet ideology stressed the positive role of leadership, the way in which the mantle was passed from Lenin to Stalin and on to the next generation, the role of the security forces, etc. Totalitarian theory identifies the same features but denounces them. The theory too is about continuity. It equates the Russia of Lenin to that of Stalin, Khrushchev and Brezhnev, through to the early Gorbachev, as if the era from 1917 onwards was all of a piece. Because of this, the theory finds it hard to explain change save in terms of the top-down actions of leaders, which themselves have no coherent explanation. Moshe Lewin, one of the best historians of the Soviet Union, memorably dismissed 'totalitarianism' as a theory for being 'itself "totalitarian" in its empty self-sufficiency – it did not recognise any mechanism of change in the Soviet Union and had no use for a shadow of some historical process'.[5] Despite the popularity of the theory after 1991, in its classical formulation it disavowed the possibility of internal change, not least because it placed so much emphasis on the centrality of repression and the consequent inability of society (the atomisation of the mass of the population) to organise against the regime. 'The totalitarian regime...dies when power is wrenched from its hands,' said Merle Fainsod in an account that for many set out the essence of the totalitarian approach to Soviet Russia.[6] These weaknesses led many Western commentators to move away from this theory in the 1970s and 1980s.

Yet when the Soviet Union disintegrated the stock of totalitarian theory rose. In the West historians such as Martin Malia and Richard Pipes seized the opportunity to restate and develop the argument in their historical writing.[7] Inside Russia too the ideas were widely taken up. One notable example was Dimitry Volkogonov, a Soviet general turned historian. Volkogonov had a disreputable past as a regime propagandist and military adviser, at home and abroad. But he now claimed that his archive-based explorations of Soviet history, which culminated in a portrayal of it in terms of totalitarian theory, were an attempt to atone for his past sins as a loyal but misguided servant of the regime. However, totalitarian theory allows him to try to achieve not so much atonement as absolution. If the regime was as all-powerful as he claims then he, as much as anyone else, was a victim of it. Indeed in his last book, completed just before he died, he said that 'all of us, from the General Secretary down to the rank and file Communists, were victims of the Bolshevik intolerance of everything that contradicted the Soviet religion of Leninism'.[8] Here the superficial radicalism of his exposé and wholesale condemnation of the Soviet past dissipates completely. What this argument effectively does is to legitimise the way in which Volkogonov personally, and Russia's rulers more widely, sought to shift from their positions in the old order to ones in the new order. Yes, of course, the argument says, the old regime was barbaric, repressive and brutal, and yes, of course, we helped to run it, but what choice did we have? We were all victims, and let him who is without sin throw the first stone. Indeed, in these distorted terms, the more repressive the image of the past, the greater the degree of absolution totalitarian theory offers *in the present* to the changelings who shifted their loyalty from old to new.

But there was a choice. Some made different choices to those of Volkogonov. He is forced, for example, to embarrassingly admit that he was an author of attacks on Solzhenitsyn when the latter tried to expose the real scale of repression. We do not share Solzhenitsyn's analysis of Russia, but any account of the history of Russia has to record the way that he and other dissidents courageously made a stand and suffered for it in a way that Volkogonov and others did not. Victimiser and victims were not alike, and totalitarian theory is the worse for allowing this blindness.

But totalitarian theory can do more than offer a conservative absolution of the role many played in the old order. Totalitarianism has also proved useful as a cover for Western policy. Although the West had proclaimed itself the friend of the Russian people against their leaders, once these same leaders had broken with the 'totalitarian past' the Russian people had to take second place to *realpolitik*. The West began to give more support to Gorbachev. Yeltsin and Putin, no less products of the old system, were to be treated even more generously. Gorbachev, said Mrs Thatcher in 1987, was a man she could do business with.[9] The US and British governments backed Gorbachev against independence movements seeking to break away from the USSR. In March 1990, two months after the shooting of protesters in the Baltic states, Douglas Hurd, the British foreign secretary, chose the Ukrainian capital of Kiev to give 'a clear signal of continued Western support for Soviet president Mikhail Gorbachev in his struggle to contain nationalist and ethnic pressures'.[10] In May 1990 an aide to President Bush (Sr) was reported as saying: 'We're not going to cancel the summit just because Lithuanian housewives can't heat their coffee on Saturday morning'.[11] In fact Lithuanians were trying to declare their independence after enormous demonstrations for a small country of less than 4 million people. On one occasion 200,000 had taken to the streets in the capital, Vilnius. When Gorbachev was swept away the Western politicians, American and British in particular, became even more enthusiastic cheerleaders for Boris Yeltsin.[12] Then when Putin came to power in 2000 the West just as quickly switched to him, effectively abandoning the real democrats in Russia. The British prime minister, Tony Blair, even electioneered for Putin.[13]

Totalitarianism as a theory has one more advantage. What unites many versions of totalitarian theory today is their emphasis on 'utopia' – the idea that the original sin of Bolshevism was its attempt to impose a new ideal of equality and justice on the world by force. One prominent account of Soviet history by two historian exiles was even entitled *Utopia in Power*.[14] We shall argue later that this argument profoundly misunderstands the difference between the nature of Stalinism as an ideology and the ideas that arose in the revolution itself. Far from being inspired by a radical utopia, Stalinism was a profoundly conservative and class-ridden doctrine. But the important thing here is that this attack on 'utopia' is used to disqualify any idea of radical change in a different direction to that taken in 1991. Indeed, by undermining the validity of questioning the inevitability of power and privilege, this argument helps to legitimise the ill-gotten gains of those who have succeeded in riding the wave of the transition. Criticism of their consolidation of power, their ostentatious wealth, in the name of justice and morality, becomes a stepping stone to a new barbarism. Grigorii Yavlinsky, perhaps the leading figure of post-Soviet liberalism, made exactly this argument, possibly without realising the full implications of what he was saying: 'The idea of social justice is one of the most dangerous political ideas there has ever been. It has been proved over and over again that the struggle for social justice ends horrifically'.[15] It is difficult to think of a more splendid argument by which the 10 percent of winners could discourage potential criticism that might engage the majority of losers in the 1990s.

No history of the Soviet Union can therefore be innocent. Each has implications that need to be understood. Our own argument will have four main steps – each of them controversial in their own terms – so it will be as well to set them out explicitly here.

The first is that Soviet history is not about continuity but *discontinuity*. There was a genuine workers' revolution in 1917, which degenerated into something else. This involves both an argument about 1917 itself and the possibility of alternative outcomes. The contrast between the hopes and aspirations of 1917 and what came later, the way that Stalin's terror was in part directed against the memory of 1917 and those who carried it, has always been a formidable stumbling block to those who believe there was a simple and logical progression 'from Lenin to Stalin'. In his bitter history of Stalin, Anton Antonov-Ovseyenko, the son of a leading Bolshevik killed in 1937 by Stalin's regime, whose mother committed suicide in Stalin's prison camps, and who himself spent his youth behind the wire, denounced Stalin as furiously as Volkogonov or Pipes, but with quite different implications:

> My father, the revolutionary Vladimir Antonov-Ovseyenko, fought against the Tsarist regime, took part in the October insurrection, and commanded several battalions in the civil war. He did not do this so that a filthy criminal could entrench himself in the Kremlin. Stalin murdered my father, just as he murdered thousands of other revolutionaries.[16]

The alternative that Vladimir Antonov-Ovseyenko and other revolutionaries originally fought for did not come about. But this was not something that was implicit in 1917. It arose from the situation that followed, when the revolution was left isolated in a Russia that was wrecked by a bitter civil war. It is here that we will find the beginnings of the real process of degeneration. As Peter Sedgwick once said, rejecting the idea that Stalinism can be traced back to an ideological logic deriving from Lenin's first writings: 'The "objective" social circumstances of Russia's revolution and civil war contain the sufficient conditions for the collapse of the mass revolutionary wave, without any recourse to causal factors stemming from the "subjective" deficiencies of Lenin's early formulations'.[17]

This is not to say that there was no relationship between what went before and what came later. Since the Stalin regime emerged out of the degeneration of the revolution, elements of it obviously link back. The point is that these were not predetermined. There was no logic intrinsic to the revolution that explains why Stalinism developed as it did. Victor Serge, an oppositionist close to Trotsky who was himself imprisoned for a period, expressed this relationship well when he wrote:

> It is often said that 'the germ of all Stalinism was in Bolshevism at its beginning'. Well, I have no objection. Only Bolshevism also contained many other seeds — a mass of other seeds — and those who lived through the enthusiasm of the first years of the victorious revolution ought not to forget it.[18]

To extend the analogy, to see why one seed flourished and others did not, we have to look at the ground in which they fell, and how they were fed and watered.

But to say that the revolution degenerated poses the question of what it degenerated into. In Chapters 4 to 8 we will argue that the Stalinist regime developed not as any form of socialism, degenerate or otherwise, nor as some peculiar form that was neither capitalist nor socialist. It was as a variant of 20th century capitalism, a form of bureaucratic state capitalism. This argument is not new. Elements of a theory of state capitalism were developed in the 1930s. After the

Second World War Tony Cliff, in a then little noticed work, set out what we believe is the most coherent theory of Russia in these terms.[19] But the theory has often been treated with disdain by critics who argue that it rests upon a misunderstanding of both the Soviet Union and the nature of capitalism. This is a criticism that we are happy to face head on. The argument that Soviet Russia developed into a form of bureaucratic state capitalism necessarily says something both about the specific nature of that society and the wider nature of capitalism. To say that Soviet Russia was capitalist is to argue that the basic features of capitalism – competition, exploitation, alienation, class, etc – were to be found there. In particular we will suggest that it was the competition which existed between Soviet Russia and the other capitalist powers, partly economic but crucially also military, that provides the core explanation for the pattern of Soviet development. Other theories are noticeably silent on this issue of the dynamic of Soviet development. Conventionally, for example, accounts of the workings of the system have spoken of 'planners' preferences', and then proceeded to explore the difficulties in realising them. But an obvious question is why the planners preferred what they preferred. The same problem arises with any account that starts by trying to isolate the internal nature of the system. The result is rather as if we are observers standing on a road bridge. In the distance, coming out of the sun, we see a group of cars approaching. As they get nearer we notice their differences – the cars are going at different speeds, some struggling to catch up and overtake. Some are clearly better designed and built, some have smoke coming out of their exhausts, and as they come closer we catch the sound of different engine whines. It is obvious also that the cars are performing differently. As they pass beneath us we look and try to discuss what we have seen, and marvel at the different performances, yet no one seems interested in asking a basic question – why are they racing, and all racing in the same direction?

But the argument goes beyond this. Soviet Russia was not merely capitalist – it was 'state capitalist' in the sense that the basic capitalist features were expressed through state property rather than private property considered in a narrow legalistic sense. Indeed, the argument goes a step further in characterising the system as 'bureaucratic state capitalist' to reflect the highly rigid, ossified and bureaucratic nature of the central internal mechanisms of the system. The historical evidence for each of these arguments – issues of dynamic, exploitation, ideology, class, and so on, can be found in what follows, and it is up to readers to decide how convincing they find them. But our argument also implies that capitalism is more complex than other accounts allow.

Any national form will contain specific elements, but we want to suggest that much of what is deemed to be unique to the Soviet system turns out on investigation to be an extension, a more intensive form, of elements present in modern capitalism as a whole. Here, too, much writing on the Soviet Union depends upon a caricature of modern capitalism. 'The Soviet Union was not capitalist,' the conventional argument runs, 'because capitalism is about...' and then follows a list or an analysis of capitalism in a model form which, if it ever existed historically, long ago disappeared. Take the central question of the state. Throughout its history capitalism has depended on the state to create the essential structures within which it develops. But it has also depended on the role of the state as a direct producer, an owner of factories and plants. Capitalism exists as a world of competing businesses and states which continually interact with one another. As the system has developed this state element has become more important. In the extreme case of war, capitalism becomes essentially a system of competing state war economies. Greater or lesser degrees of 'state capitalism' have therefore always been part of the system. Bertram D Wolfe was only slightly exaggerating when he said that *before the revolution* 'the Russian state became the largest landowner, the largest trader, the largest owner of capital in Russia, or in the world. The needs of its huge armies made it the largest customer for private industry as well. This brought into being the world's largest apparatus of bureaucracy'.[20] This makes a nonsense of the argument that socialism is essentially about 'state control', and that state control is somehow in contradiction with capitalism. Indeed, this was an argument that was explicitly opposed by Marx and Engels, and by the Bolsheviks in 1917, for they saw socialism as a rejection of wartime state capitalism. But this strand of analysis was not developed, and the radical understanding of capitalism was the poorer for it.

As the 20th century developed this failure to analyse the central role of the state in capitalism the world over became even stranger, for the role of the state continued to grow, as data collected by Angus Maddison reveals:

TABLE 1. GOVERNMENT EXPENDITURE AS A PERCENTAGE OF GDP AT CURRENT PRICES, 1913-99[21]

	1913	1938	1950	1973	1999
United States	8.0	19.8	21.4	31.1	30.1
United Kingdom	13.3	28.8	34.2	41.4	39.7
Germany	17.7	42.4	30.4	42.0	47.6
France	8.9	23.2	27.6	38.8	52.4
Holland	8.2	21.7	26.8	45.5	43.8
Japan	14.2	30.3	19.8	22.9	38.1
AVERAGE	**11.7**	**27.7**	**26.7**	**36.9**	**41.9**

So, far from always struggling against this rise, 'private capital' was often happy to support it. In 1946 one Conservative British politician bluntly said: 'My idea is that when things are not going so well the state should come in, but when things are going well the state should keep out. In other words, it is a policy determined by the state of trade in the country'.[22] Even today, after two decades of supposed 'rollback' of the state under the impact of globalisation, its economic role remains enormous in the heartlands of modern capitalism.

To make sense of this dynamic of state capitalism we also need an idea of capitalism as a global system, where the forms of competition include not only the competition of goods but state and military competition. This argument was made by Nikolai Bukharin in his *Imperialism and World Economy*, where he charted the central role of militarism and its relationship to interstate competition in modern capitalism. He was not alone in making these connections but, perhaps more than any other theorist, he foresaw the ways in which forms of competition would shift in the next century.

These insights are therefore important not only for the specific way in which we will argue Soviet Russia developed, but the general pattern of capitalist development. Indeed, it is in the military sectors of modern capitalism that we can see many of the elements mistakenly believed to be both unique to the Soviet Union and incompatible with 'capitalism'. Had commentators had more courage, and analysed these elements more systematically as part of the normal functioning of capitalism, this might have worked to the benefit of our understanding of both the Soviet Union and the wider world. The radical economist Howard Sherman, for example, pointed out in the early 1970s, again without following the implications through:

> The US Defence Department is the largest planned economy in the world...outside of the USSR. It spends more than the net income of all US corporations. By 1969 it had 470 major and 6,000 lesser installations, owned 39 million acres of land, spent $80 billion per year, used 22,000 prime contractors and 100,000 sub-contractors, thus directly employing in the armed forces and military production about 10 percent of the US labour force.[23]

The implications extend in one other important direction. If we are correct in our analysis of Soviet Russia, then it follows that the disintegration of the system in 1991 and the subsequent transition did not involve as radical a change as many accounts suggest. For us 1991 represents a combination of political revolution with a change in the *form* of capitalism – a shift away from the state towards more market forms. The political revolution, which allowed a degree of democracy and therefore created the possibility of independent organisation, was a huge gain whose significance should not be minimised. But the idea of the shift in the form of capitalism is, we would suggest, the key to what is otherwise the great puzzle of the transition – the quite astonishing continuity of rule at the top. Those accounts that stress the non-capitalist nature of Soviet Russia stumble on explaining how capitalism could then emerge, run by the same groups who ran the old system. How could it be that so much of the old order, so many of its personnel, simply converted to the new system if what was involved was such a qualitative change in the nature of the most basic social relationships? This was entirely unexpected and unpredicted. Listen, for example, to Olga Kryshtanovskaia, writing as head of elite studies at the Sociological Institute of the Russian Academy of Sciences. Here she describes just one part of this conversion:

> A ministry would be abolished, and in its ruins a business concern would be created in the form of a joint-stock company (same building, same furniture, same personnel); the minister would resign; the controlling parcel of shares would pass into the hands of the state, the rest would be distributed among the leadership of the ministry; as a rule, the second or third figure in the abolished ministry would become the head of the concern.[24]

This is not an account of a social revolution equivalent to a concentrated shift from feudalism to capitalism, or capitalism to socialism. It is not a change that bears any comparison with 1789 or 1917 or Stalin's counter-revolution of 1928-29. It is a description of something much more limited, though Kryshtanov-skaia, like others, fights shy of drawing out the full implications of what she so graphically describes. We, however, need be less inhibited.

The transition has caused widespread economic and social collapse in Russia, a collapse of which ordinary Russians have been victims, as they were victims of the old regime. But the conversion of power at the top has led not only to the leaders of the old order being able to consolidate their grip in a new form, but also to their being able to acquire vast personal wealth while beneath them tens of millions live out impoverished and shortened lives.

This could only happen because of the identification of the old regime with socialism. This narrowed the vision of social change so that only two alternatives appeared to exist – to go back to the old order or to attempt to remould the system to a form closer to Western capitalism. The result was little short of catastrophic for the mass of the population, as they were subject to a new top-down ideological experiment that has been justly called 'market Stalinism'.

Undoing the damage of the old order and the new is a formidable task. It cannot begin without getting the history of Russia in the last century right. It is to this task that this book aims to contribute. It does not take the form of a theoretical treatise. Such treatises exist, reflecting the way in which the critical left has tried to deal with the big questions of Russian history in the past century. There is also a substantial literature in journals debating the merits of different theoretical positions, to which this author has made minor contributions.[25] No study of the Soviet Union can ignore this literature, and at various points we will refer to it because our understanding of the past has to be under-pinned by 'theory'. But 'theory', even in more elegant forms than is usually found in debates on the Russian question, is only a means to understand the real pattern of events. It only begins to live when it helps unravel the real his-tory that is the concern of this book.

Our aim is not to cover every aspect of the Soviet past. What follows is more a series of historically based essays on some of the central themes of the Soviet experience. Our aim is to try to demonstrate the superiority of the approach that we think is correct by showing how it informs and illuminates the histo-ry of what has happened. The next chapter therefore tries to identify the true radical essence of the revolution. Chapter 3 analyses the process of degenera-tion of the revolution between 1918 and 1928. Chapter 4 considers the crucial question of the dynamic of the Stalin and post-Stalin regimes, and the conse-quent pattern of development. Chapter 5 explores the changing scale, nature and function of repression. Chapters 6 and 7 take up the issue of social class, looking first at the issue of the ruling class and then at the role of the working class. Chapter 8 then takes up the question of the transition of the 1990s.

Petrograd waiters demonstrating for better conditions and to assert their dignity in 1917. The main banners say:

2 REVOLUTION

Revolutions change people in quite astonishing ways. They are so astonishing that they are often hard to believe. We live in regimented worlds, with the limits of change constantly before us. Moments of radicalisation – strikes, demonstrations, popular protests – can give us an inkling of the changes that can occur. But then we are pulled back into the world we know. But revolutions, and especially great revolutions, involve seismic shifts. They involve sustained mobilisations that require a real leap of imagination to understand. The result is both inspirational and discomforting.

Such was the revolution that began in Russia on 23 February 1917.[1] Onto the streets of the capital Petrograd, with its 2.4 million strong population and its 400,000 factory workers, came striking women from the textile factories. Tension had been rising, but more experienced socialists were lukewarm about the women using International Women's Day as the occasion for a strike. 'Not a single organisation called for strikes on that day,' Trotsky recalled in his great *History of the Russian Revolution*. 'What is more, even a Bolshevik organisation, and a most militant one – the Vyborg [district] committee, all workers – was opposing strikes.' On the day, still doubting, the various left wing organisations responded a little more positively. 'Once there is a mass strike, one must call everybody into the streets and take the lead,' said Vasilii Kayurov, a Bolshevik who encouraged this response.[2] But the reality was that it was the leaders who were running to catch up with the led.

The strike met an immediate response. Later figures have an air of spurious accuracy, but they give us a sense of scale. On 23 February 128,000 workers struck. On 24 February 214,000 were on strike, and on 25 February 305,000. It was more or less the same on 26 February, and then from 27 February numbers rose to around 390,000. Not all were factory workers, but the general strike in the factory districts was more or less complete. Late on 26 February small groups of soldiers from the huge military garrison began to disobey orders. The next day troops were ordered to fire on crowds, and many refused. Perhaps 70,000 went over to the side of the protesters. On 28 February it was 127,000, and then 170,000 on 1 March.[3] As the troops switched allegiance the Tsarist monarchy, which had celebrated its 300th anniversary in 1913, collapsed.

Casualties in these February days were considerable. One account estimates that 433 were killed and 1,214 wounded. The police in particular had fired on the crowds. Some policemen and other figures of authority were killed in retaliation. Some policemen were beaten. Their actions in opening fire and the way they were seen as visible agents of the Tsarist state now rebounded on them.[4] But the new Russia was born in celebration. As news of the Petrograd events was telegraphed across the country, as trains carrying papers arrived, there was a near-universal rush to pledge loyalty to the new government. The old authorities collapsed, and ecstatic crowds joined symbolic marches or enormous public meetings to mark the change.

It seemed as if Russian society had become dislocated and moved a huge distance to the left. The right had largely disappeared. All that counted was the liberal centre and, above all, the left. One of the clearest measures of this came later in November 1917, when Russians voted in elections to create a Constituent Assembly. The Constitutional Democrats, many of them radical liberals in European terms but now the 'right' in Russian terms, managed to get only 5 percent of the vote, and the bourgeois-landowner parties 13 percent in total. The Mensheviks – fiery socialists compared with many in the West – secured only 3 percent. The Socialist Revolutionaries, with most of its members splitting towards an alliance with the Bolsheviks, got 44 percent, and the Bolsheviks, the most radical party, secured 25 percent.[5] The vast majority of Russians (even where they voted for national-based parties) voted for some kind of socialism, and most voted for a more rather than less radical version.

This shift was there in February. The collapse of Tsarism carried away the legitimacy of much else. To be credible you had to make a visible gesture to the new mood. One of the new socialist papers noted that 'the yellow boulevard press calls itself "non-party socialist". The financial newspapers reinvent themselves by adopting the protective colour of "realistic socialism", while the banks try to protect themselves by raising the red banner of the revolution over their buildings.' It is an image worth pausing on as a measure of the change. You wake up one morning and see the most reactionary newspapers proclaiming some sort of allegiance to socialism, even though it is not your socialism. The financial papers proclaim it too. And above you see, over the impressive banks, monuments to the stability of the system, red flags fluttering in the wind.

New possibilities opened up everywhere. 'Let's renounce the old world', said a line in the Workers' Marseillaise, one of the most popular songs in 1917. The Internationale, whose words few knew in February, was increasingly heard. All the parties of the left sang it. People were reaching out to a new future. It was not just a Russian future. The word 'international' appeared everywhere in 1917. It is there in the photographs on the banners of the crowds, some of them crudely daubed, others elegantly and painstakingly embroidered. The ships of the Tsar's navy were given new names like *Citizen*, *Republic* and *Dawn of Freedom*. Even the prostitutes were said to be asking their customers to 'share some fraternity'.[6]

There is a naivety here that is easy to disparage. Many historians do this. All revolutions later fall prey to the conservatism that sees in this 'sense of boundless possibility' only misplaced myth, violence and hollow proclamations. Historians who reflect the conventional wisdom rarely do themselves any harm. Pessimism about the possibilities of change is usually seen as realism. Utopian energy, it is argued, is the most dangerous of all. If the historian then clothes the sneer of disdain in the high-flown language of a fashionable theory, acclaim can be the reward. Such has been the fate of the French Revolution, and such is also the fate of the Russian Revolution.[7]

But the irony is that it was the sober realists on each side who stood behind the outbreak of war in 1914 and a world which by 1917 was dripping in blood. The realism of the time had led to global conflict. It would lead there again and again in the years that followed. An earlier politics limited by 'conventional wisdom', by accommodation to what existed, had helped to lay the basis for a system based upon the most grotesque inequalities, and one which was itself quite prepared to resort to what has been called 'the mass manufacture of death' to resolve its differences. Winston Churchill would later write how in the First World War 'torture and cannibalism were the only two expedients that the civilised, scientific, Christian states had been able to deny themselves, and these were of doubtful utility'.[8] In 1917, in contrast, the men and women who took to the streets in Russia were reaching out to a different and better world by challenging this system.

THE ROOTS OF REVOLUTION

Russia in 1917 was trapped in the third year of this terrible war. But the war was no accident, or perhaps it was rather an accident waiting to happen. The immediate cause lay in the different responses to the assassination of the Austrian Archduke Franz Ferdinand in Sarajevo on June 1914. These were conditioned by the way in which tension had been building up in European capitalism in the previous decades.

As industrialisation had spread outwards from its base in north western Europe, it had knitted the world more closely together. Millions of people moved freely between countries in search of work. Investment flowed in huge quantities. In Russia in 1915 41 percent of capital in joint stock companies was foreign owned. The share of trade in world output rose from a puny 3 percent around 1800 to some 33 percent in 1914, and Russia became linked into it as an exporter of grain, raw materials and semi-manufactured goods.[9] Within a century the world had become integrated to a degree never known before. But this did not bring harmony. The process of growth was a competitive one. One reflection of this was the division of the globe into colonial empires. But behind this there was an ongoing struggle for position and power to ensure control of raw materials, markets, investment outlets, and so on. This competition had come to involve more and more state elements and growing militarism. On the left there were growing fears before 1914 that the result would be catastrophe. Theorists struggled to make sense of the developments. International conferences were held to oppose any moves to war. The Socialist (Second) International, which had been created in 1889 to bring socialist parties together, passed resolutions calling on the international socialist movement to be at the forefront of challenging the way that capitalism was laying the basis for global conflict.

But when war broke out in August 1914 most of the international socialist movement was overwhelmed by it, and most socialists loyally supported their respective governments. Each proclaimed that theirs was a sacred defensive fight, that the enemy was the incarnation of evil. In Russia the Tsar said to his people: 'God is our witness that, not for vain and worldly glory, not for violence and oppression have we taken up arms, but only to defend the Russian state.' Others argued that their government should be supported in 'the war to end war'. But their naive faith that 'their' side was different was belied by the cynical secret treaties and deals that each side did as they sought to maximise their gains from this global conflict.

To those who were not taken in by the argument that the struggle for international class unity had now to give way to a bloody fight in defence of national self-interest, the reaction of the majority of socialists seemed to be the great betrayal. Nowhere was that betrayal greater than in Germany, where the Social Democratic Party (SPD) was the biggest political party in the world, the trade union movement well organised and the co-operative movement a major force. Rosa Luxemburg called the German SPD the 'great shining jewel of the Second International'.[10] Shocked by the events of August 1914, she even contemplated suicide. Opposition to the war seemed to be completely marginalised. Representatives of the weak anti-war tendencies met in neutral Switzerland at

Zimmerwald in September 1915 and Kienthal in April 1916. Trotsky would later tell of how the delegates tried to relax on a trip into the mountains: 'The delegates themselves joked about the fact that half a century after the founding of the First International it was still possible to get all the internationalists in four coaches'.[11]

But the patriotic wave was shortlived. By 1917 there was a growing tension in all countries. War had involved the mobilisation of society in a battle of attrition of men, equipment and economies. Slaughter on this scale had never been seen before. Many of the battles of the Western Front remain etched in popular consciousness even though their survivors are no longer with us. The battles of Ypres, Verdun, the Somme, and so on, stand as a condemnation of a system that sacrificed the youth of Europe in a struggle for world power. The war memorials record the names of hundreds of thousands whose bodies, blown apart, had 'no known resting place'. But the battles of the Eastern Front were no less bloody. The pattern was settled in August 1914 at the Battle of Tannenberg, where the Russians lost perhaps 30,000 dead (the German side said 45,000) and 90,000 prisoners. General Aleksandr Samsonov committed suicide when he realised the scale of the defeat, but the commander in chief said: 'We are happy to have made such sacrifices for our allies'.[12] The strain built up everywhere, and by 1917 a number of countries were close to breaking point. Thus the revolution that broke first in Russia was a product of a Europe-wide crisis, and its development could not help but be conditioned by it.

This linkage is also apparent if we look more closely at conditions in Russia. Industrial capitalism had been developing unevenly in Europe. In Russia, despite some earlier antecedents, it only really took off in the 1890s. Then and since many hoped that a backward country 'taking off' would quickly move forward to the same levels as the more advanced. But follower countries had to fit in with the opportunities available. Russia's backward agriculture became a major supplier of grain on world markets. Its mines supplied coal and ores. Manufactured goods were imported. So too was machinery to help build the small but modern industrial sector. Supported by tariffs and state subsidies, it could help supply (along with craft industry) some of the needs of the domestic market, and products such as textiles could hope to find markets abroad in countries less developed than Russia itself. Modern forms came to exist alongside more backward ones. Trotsky described this as a process of *combined and uneven development*. Development brought together the modern alongside the traditional, but it also combined them, creating new linkages and hybrid forms that came to have a life of their own. There was no guarantee that the backward would catch up – rather inequality in the level of development between and within countries seemed to be inbuilt into the nature of the global economy.[13]

These hybrid forms could be seen throughout Russian society. They were there too in the political structures. In 1914 Russia's population of 160 million was ruled over by the Romanov Tsar, whose autocratic power rested on the court and the wider group of landowners, the church and the state. Social change had partly undermined their power by creating a bourgeoisie, professional classes and an urban working class, as well as radically affecting the lives of the mass of the population – the peasants. Had change been able to follow earlier patterns then 'the rising middle class', supported by discontented workers and peasants, might have challenged the power of the Tsar and created a liberal constitutional regime. However, no such repetition was possible. The process of economic change had begun to tie together interests at the top and helped moderate the degree of political antagonism. A gap between the regime and the bourgeoisie still existed, but it was much reduced. Bourgeois radicalism was also reduced by suspicion of the Russian working class. Their numbers were small compared with the 120-130 million strong peasantry. But their militancy was high and growing, inducing a degree of caution among the bourgeoisie for fear of unleashing an uncontrollable force.

Something of an early 19th century style polarisation did occur in Russia in 1905, when revolution erupted in the wake of Russia's disastrous involvement in the Russo-Japanese War. In the end the Tsar managed to head off revolt by concessions, with some of the more radical liberals disconcerted by the fact that, as well as the Tsar and the old order, they too faced hostility from below. But the reforms that were introduced were partial, and the Tsar and his supporters still held liberals and the bourgeoisie at arm's length. This did not change when war broke out, and this further undermined liberal support for the regime as their patriotic offers of participation in running the official war effort were spurned. The problem was to know how far to push opposition. For Pavel Miliukov, historian, theorist of Russian liberalism and politician, the last years of the regime had been based on a 'pseudo-constitutionalism'. The Tsar had granted a parliament with one hand and used the other to constrain and limit it in all directions. Miliukov ridiculed those who joined the newly formed Octobrist Party to defend the 'ambiguity' of the Tsar's 'insincere concessions', which the Tsar himself said had been made 'in a fever'.

But Miliukov's radicalism, and so much of Russian liberalism too, could not recognise what he called 'the complete and unlimited sovereignty of the people'. This was partly because he believed that the people had been 'deliberately held in darkness and ignorance by the adherents of [the Tsarist] regime'. But it was also because in principle he thought this a dangerous concept. The correct position was one of 'trust...limited by common sense'. What he meant was the right of the liberals to mould a liberal constitutional regime from above in order to create a modernised capitalist Russia. In this he expressed the best and worst of liberalism. He had sympathy with popular discontent – he was prepared to act as a voice for it. But it had to remain within moderate channels. And he remained implacably opposed to really radical change. To the contrary, before the war and during it, he, like many liberals, began to combine the argument for change in Russia with the idea that if it came it would better enable a new government to achieve Russia's Great Power interests. Russia would become more unified within. It would help win the war, and it would realise long coveted gains like strategic control of Constantinople.[14]

At one level February seemed to open up just such possibilities. 'The Russian Revolution is the most patriotic, the most national, the most popular of all time,' said the philosopher N A Berdiaev.[15] But February already contained within it the elements that would push most Russians in a much more radical direction during 1917.

POPULAR RADICALISM AND CLASS CONSCIOUSNESS

At the heart of the process of revolution in 1917 were the actions of ordinary Russians who, for a time, became the freest people in the world. Russia was alive with politics because politics mattered. It mattered because the radicalisation promised more than just the occasional vote for a distant government. It opened up the possibility of democratic control of society from the bottom up. Initially the glimpse of this was only partial. People first found a dignity and pride in engagement. They would often go in their best clothes to be photographed on demonstrations. Even the waiters and waitresses of Petrograd went on strike. A photograph shows them gathered beneath a banner which reads: 'We demand the human being in the waiter be recognised'. Behind them are union banners saying: 'Down with tipping'. There was a new yearning for knowledge. 'There are no words to explain the shame and the pain that engulf a man when he realises that even what has been given to him is too hard to understand, and is like a stone instead of bread,' said one peasant.[16]

Of course not everyone gained a wider vision. In the feverish days of February criminals as well as political prisoners were released from the jails, and some went straight back to crime. Crime rates rose as 1917 progressed. Some saw the chance of quick gains – others grew desperate. There was also political violence. Some of it was symbolic – as when workers humiliated hated foremen and 'carted them out' of the plants in wheelbarrows. Some of it was very real. The mood of the crowd could be volatile. But its scale was limited. People were throwing off the old society that had visibly scarred them, and some of this rebounded on their old masters – even the more liberal ones.[17] They would have been less surprised had they remembered that Leo Tolstoy had rebuked the limits of their earlier concern: 'I sit on a man's back, choking him and making him carry me, and yet assure myself and others that I am very sorry for him and wish to ease his lot by all possible means – except by getting off his back'.[18]

But it is the signs of the growing political consciousness that are the more remarkable. Every walk of life was affected. Women, school students and children

🎋 2.1. THE RUSSIAN WORKING CLASS

In January 1914 the Russian Empire had a population of 167.5 million (139.9 on the pre-1939 borders). Most people were peasants. Some 17.5 percent of the population lived in towns. But a complex class structure was emerging, with a small but strong working class employed in industry, crafts, building, transport etc. To these must then be added the non-working dependants of these workers. The working class in its widest sense was 15-20 percent of the population.

Dimensions of the working class and wage labour force in Tsarist Russia[i]

	1861 (millions)	1913 (millions)
1. Mining and manufacturing	1.60	6.10
(a) Factories and mines	0.80	3.10
(b) Rural and urban domestic industries	0.80	3.00
2. Construction	0.35	1.50
3. Transport and communication	0.51	1.41
(a) Railways (including clerical staff)	0.01	0.82
(b) Waterways	0.50	0.50
(c) Post, telegraph and telephone	–	0.09
4. Other non-agricultural employments	0.80	4.07
(a) Unskilled day labourers	na	1.10
(b) White collar staff	na	0.55
(c) Trade and tourism	na	0.87
(d) Domestic servants	na	1.55
5. Agricultural labourers	0.70	4.50
TOTAL	3.96	17.58

The core were the factory workers. In 1914 two fifths worked in large plants of more than 1,000. This figure is somewhat exaggerated by the exclusion of the smallest works from the statistics, but it was still remarkable. Many workers still had ties with their villages. The extent varied by trade and town. In the most advanced areas a hereditary working class had emerged. Women made up 18 percent of industrial workers in 1900 and 27 percent in 1914. Some 40 percent of the population was literate, but 64 percent of industrial workers were (men more than women). A higher share of young people had some literacy in society at large because of the recent rapid expansion of schools.

War further increased the numbers of workers — especially in sectors producing for the army. In 1917 3.6 million workers now laboured in the modern factory and mining sector. Most skilled workers were exempt from call-up because they were more valuable in the factories. They provided a continuing radical core which could lead the new young workers who came into the factories.

all demanded rights. There were attempts to organise prisoners still in jail. Groups formed spontaneously to try to deal with local problems. Even the Orthodox church was swept up. 'Bolshevism has captured a significant number of clergymen,' said a special church commission. The priest A A Vvedensky was elected to the Petrograd soviet, preaching that Christianity was anti-capitalist. It was merging with 'Bolshevism in the struggle on behalf of the poor'.[19]

This was a time of talk on the streets, in the queues, on the trams. John Reed describes how the Putilov armaments factory in Petrograd would 'pour out its 40,000 to listen to Social Democrats, Socialist Revolutionaries, anarchists, anybody, whatever they had to say, as long as they would talk'.[20] It was also a time of marching on countless demonstrations (and some counter-demonstrations). Petrograd had some of the biggest. On 23 March perhaps 1 million came out to commemorate the 'February Martyrs'. Other peaks were 18 April (1 May in Western Europe), June and the July Days. But there were many more. Historians have counted many features of 1917, but they seem to have forgotten the humble demonstration.

It was also a time of reading. Newspapers, pamphlets and leaflets poured from the presses despite the growing economic difficulties. In the decade before 1917 something of an educational revolution led to higher literacy rates among the young. The mainstream press, minus right wing titles that were banned, continued to be published. Alongside it daily socialist papers grew up. Print runs varied. The Menshevik *Rabochaia gazeta* fluctuated from 25,000 to 96,000 copies, the Bolshevik *Pravda* from 42,000 to 100,000, and the SR *Delo naroda* from 58,000 to 78,000. Most parties had several other titles. By October the Bolsheviks were printing four dailies. There were peasant papers, soldiers' papers and national papers. *Izvestiya* was the paper of the Soviet movement itself. Hundreds of pamphlets were published. Their print runs ran into many tens of millions. The leaflets remain too many to be counted.[21]

But most of all it was a time of joining, participating and organising. Political parties sprang into life. More than 100 were formed. Most were small or operated in parts of the empire. The major part of the Russian left was divided into three main parties which had formed at the turn of the century. The Socialist Revolutionaries looked to the countryside and a huge peasant base. The Mensheviks and Bolsheviks, on the other hand, looked to the towns and the working class. They had divided in the 1900s over a number of issues whose significance at the time often seemed obscure, but which would become clearer during 1917. The biggest party was the Socialist Revolutionary Party. 'The motley, many-headed street poured resistlessly into its ranks,' said Victor Chernov, one of its most popular leaders.[22] But no party's membership was stable. Some joined only nominally, while others changed parties as radicalisation increased. Some had no choice. So militant was the mood in parts of the SR party in September that the Voronezh, Tashkent and Petrograd organisations were expelled for being too left wing.

Trade unions had enjoyed a first period of growth in 1905-07, but their role was then cut back by repression. In 1917 they grew explosively. When the Third All-Russian Congress of Trade Unions met on 21-28 June 1917 there were nearly 1,000 unions with 1.4 million members. By October membership was more than 2 million in 2,000 unions. Moderate socialist politics dominated the railway workers. The Mensheviks were strong among the printers. But bigger unions, such as the textile workers (175,000) and the metal workers (400,000), pulled further to the left towards the Bolsheviks. The congress elected a council of 13 Mensheviks, 13 Bolsheviks and three SRs, but in the congress itself there were 73 Bolshevik delegates, 36 Menshevik, 35 SR and 31 non-aligned.

Within the factories, committees of workers spontaneously formed from February. In large factories each section would elect a committee, from which would then come a committee for the whole factory. Some 2,151 factory committees have been counted in 1917. Some 687 were in plants employing more than 200, suggesting that the bigger the plant the more common they were. The most advanced were in Petrograd, where there were over 120. In June they came together in their first congress. Others followed, and then on 17-22 October, on the eve of the October seizure of power, the First All-Russian Conference of Factory Committees met in Petrograd.

Alongside the factory committees a 'Red Guard' developed. In February the Tsarist police had collapsed, and in its place had come various militias. The Provisional Government wanted to create a citizens' militia as the basis of a new police. But in many factories workers had already formed groups of Red Guards to police order. These Red Guard units had an erratic history, but they mobilised prominently in late August when Kornilov attempted his coup, and by October there were perhaps 150,000 Red Guards across Russia.[23]

In the countryside too peasants took action. Their focus was the land that they believed to be rightfully theirs. Some in the villages remembered being born into serfdom before 1861. Many more remembered the decades of payments required as part of the price of ending it. Rural militancy also reflected current grievances. Food prices fell behind those of manufactured goods, which were in increasingly short supply. Rural revolt was most intense where poverty was greatest. Its form was affected by the agricultural year. Only as the harvest was gathered did the level really rise and point in the most radical direction of seizing the land.

The army itself, the core of the state, was beginning to disintegrate. Nikolai Golovine, a Tsarist general who became a historian, said there was a law that armies collapse at the rear and not the front. This was an officer's way of dealing with the enormity of what happened. At the front the threat of death at the hands of the enemy could crush the space for independent thought. In the rear there was air to breathe and time to reflect on the front and its wider politics. Front and rear were therefore closely connected. Even at the front, Golovine recognised, soldiers subconsciously began to vote with their feet. In 1917 the number of the sick rose rapidly, and so did requests for home leave. Sabotage began to take place on a wider scale. At Easter 1917 on parts of the front there was fraternisation across the lines, similar to that seen on parts of the European Western Front at Christmas 1914. Attempts to rally the spirit of the army had only a short term effect. In June 1917 a major offensive was launched with the best units of the army. Around 40,000 were lost, and after an initial advance the collapse intensified. Golovine talked of his prize units becoming 'tumultuous crowds'. 'Authority and obedience exist no longer,' said a report on the Eleventh Army, 'for hundreds of miles one can see lines of deserters, armed and unarmed, in good health and on high spirits, certain they will not be punished'.[24]

Committees also appeared in the armed forces. The High Command tried at first to regularise them in the hope that they would help restore order. But they still became vehicles for discontent and conflict. The most radical were on the Western and Northern fronts, where the Bolsheviks would later win 60 and 50 percent of the vote in the elections for the Constituent Assembly. On the South Western, Romanian and Caucasian fronts it was the SRs who were the more influential (with roughly 40 percent of the later Constituent Assembly vote to the Bolsheviks' 30 percent and the Ukrainian parties' 25 percent). The fleet, especially the 100,000-strong Baltic fleet, were more radical still. This has been explained by their smaller peasant intake and the factory-like conditions of the ship. Based at Kronstadt, Revel (Tallinn) and Helsingfors (Helsinki), rank and file sailors challenged authority, sometimes violently, from February onwards. In April 1917 they elected the Tsentrobalt – the Central Committee of the Baltic Fleet, chaired by the sailor Pavel Dybenko.

The highest form of all this activity were the 'soviets', or councils, that spread across Russia, bringing together delegates from the workplaces and various committees. The creation of this widening structure of soviets shows that we are not simply dealing with a destructive movement. The old order was collapsing, its state disintegrating, but something new was emerging chaotically from below to replace it. By May there were perhaps 400 soviets in Russia, by August 600 and by October 900. The most developed was the Petrograd soviet, which emerged first and had moral authority in Russia at large. When it met in full there were almost 3,000 delegates. On a day to day basis it was run by an elected executive committee, and it had a dozen or more 'commissions' overseeing its different and widening areas of activity. In June the First All-Russian Congress of Soviets of Workers' and Soldiers' Deputies met (there was a separate congress for peasant soviets). A Central Executive Committee dominated by Mensheviks and SRs was elected. But the democratic

✸ 2.2. THE DEMOCRACY OF THE SOVIETS IN 1917

Soviets — or elected councils of workers, soldiers and peasants — arose everywhere in 1917. The biggest cities had district-wide and city-wide soviets. Soviets were more than talking shops. They began to organise society from below. By October there were some 900 soviets in existence. Nationally they came together in an All-Russian Congress. Between the first and second congresses its composition changed, giving the Bolsheviks a majority.

The composition of the first three congresses of soviets[ii]

	Soviets represented	Number of delegates	Percentage of delegates				
			Bolshevik	Left SR	SR	Menshevik	Rest
First (3 June 1917)	305	1,090	13	–	34.5	37	14.5
Second (25 October 1917)	402	1,012	52	15	13	14	5
Third (10 January 1918)	619	1,800	53	21	5	4	16

Probably as many people voted in soviet elections as voted for the Constituent Assembly. Parties were elected on a proportional basis, usually for six months. But delegates were liable to recall at any time. John Reed said:

'No political body more sensitive and responsive to the popular will was ever invented. For example, during the first week of December 1917 there were parades and demonstrations in favour of the Constituent Assembly — that is to say, against soviet power. One of these parades was fired on by some irresponsible Red Guards, and several people were killed. The reaction to this stupid violence was immediate. Within 12 hours the complexion of the Petrograd soviet changed. More than a dozen Bolshevik deputies were withdrawn and replaced by Mensheviks. And it was three weeks before this sentiment subsided — before the Mensheviks were retired one by one and the Bolsheviks sent back'.[iii]

Lenin spoke for the Bolsheviks, the Left SRs, anarchists and the wider supporters of the revolution when he rejected any place for the Constituent Assembly after October:

'To relinquish the sovereign power of the soviets, to relinquish the soviet republic won by the people for the sake of the bourgeois parliamentary system and the Constituent Assembly, would now be a step backwards and would cause the collapse of the October workers' and peasants' revolution'.[iv]

nature of the soviets meant that they quickly reflected shifts in the popular mood. When the Second Congress met in October it would be with a majority of many more revolutionary delegates.

DUAL POWER AND THE TRIALS OF THE PROVISIONAL GOVERNMENT

Russian liberalism fell at the first hurdle in February 1917. With tension rising the Tsar ordered the Duma to disperse. Weak and inadequate though the Duma was as a parliament elected on a corrupt franchise, its leaders might have seized the moment. A radical like the socialist Alexander Kerensky wanted them to. Before them was the image of France in 1789, when the Third Estate had defied the king to form the embryo of the National Assembly. But the Duma leaders meekly submitted to the Tsar. Then, as tension continued to grow, on 27 February members of the liberal Progressive Bloc met to form a Provisional Committee of the Duma from which the Provisional Government emerged on 1-2 March. The earlier failure of nerve meant that it could claim no mandate from the old Duma. The Provisional Government had no elected members. Indeed, no member of the Provisional Government could ever claim an elected mandate, save some of the socialists who later joined it. Miliukov inadvertently gave the game away when, responding to a heckler who asked: 'Who elected you?' he said: 'We were elected by the Russian Revolution... We will not retain this power a single moment after representatives freely elected by the people tell us that they want to see in our places people more deserving of their trust'.[25]

Things were quite different for a group that also met on 27 February. Ironically, they too were in the Tauride Palace, where the Provisional Government was being formed. These were socialists released from prison who immediately called for the creation of a soviet along the lines of those that had appeared in the failed revolution of 1905 in Russia. From the garrison and factories of Petrograd came elected delegates, and the new soviet immediately acquired an enormous authority as both a political focus for the popular movement and an institution that could meet their needs. Tellingly, in the first hours it was the soviet, not the Provisional Government, that took up the practical issue of how the crowds were to be fed. Later Aleksandr Guchkov, the first minister of war in the Provisional Government, would say that 'the Provisional Government has no real power at its disposal... It is possible to say flatly that the Provisional Government exists only so long as it is allowed by the Soviet of Workers' and Soldiers' Deputies'.[26] This was the basis of what was called 'dual power' in 1917 – two potential governments existing side by side. Describing the role of the Petrograd soviet in 1905, Trotsky captured its essence in a way that applies even more to 1917:

> *The soviet was a workers' government in embryo… Prior to the soviet we find among the industrial workers a multitude of revolutionary organisations… But these were organisations* **within the proletariat**, *and their immediate aim was to achieve influence over the masses. The soviet was, from the start, the organisation* **of the proletariat**, *and its aim was the struggle for revolutionary power.*[27]

Why then did the Provisional Government rule and the soviet (and those formed elsewhere) follow? Partly it was because the leaders of the Provisional Government also had an aura of authority as liberal oppositionists of the old regime. Partly it was because in the honeymoon days of March there was an outpouring of trust. It was partly also because the leaders of the soviet and the political parties behind them saw the revolution as essentially a bourgeois one in which the popular movement would play an ancillary role.

The leaders of the soviet came from the Mensheviks and the SRs, and other smaller parties. They argued that capitalism still had a role to play in Russia, and the task of the revolution was therefore to get the most radical concessions while still recognising and supporting the bourgeois nature of the revolution. This meant not doing anything that would frighten off the liberals in the bourgeoisie, as had happened in 1905. Some Bolsheviks, including the then obscure Joseph Stalin, had sympathy with this position. But already in March a significant part of the rank and file did not. When Lenin returned to Russia in April 1917 and challenged this argument the Menshevik *Rabochaia gazeta* responded that the revolution would work:

> *…only so long as it is able to remain within the limits which are predetermined by objective necessity (the state of the productive forces, the level of mentality of the masses of people corresponding to it, etc). One cannot render a better service to reaction than by disregarding those limits and by making attempts at breaking them.*

To liberals like Miliukov such views were welcome. What they could not achieve themselves the socialists might hand them. Patronisingly he welcomed the learning process of socialists who defended this view:

> *The socialist parties now see the immediate tasks of the Russian Revolution in a much more reasonable light. They seem to have learned much from what has happened and regard it as axiomatic that the Russian Revolution cannot, any more than any other revolution in our time and in the past, be a victory for the socialists and the socialist order — that this revolution is predominantly political, a revolution which is, in their terminology, bourgeois in character, and not at all directed toward the immediate victory of socialism.*[28]

But the trust displayed in the Provisional Government was nevertheless made conditional even if the significance of this was not immediately appreciated. The Russian phrase used was *postolku-poskolku* – 'insofar as'. Time and again resolutions and speeches said: 'We will support you…insofar as.' There was no immediate sense that the Provisional Government and the soviets would not continue to work together but, when a gap began to open up, the conditional nature of the support became more apparent, as did the Provisional Government's lack of a base.

The Provisional Government was soon in difficulties, and in the months of its existence it proved unequal to the task of consolidating a degree of order in society and stabilising the legitimacy it had in March. It talked of ending the war but could not break with the Allies. It remained trapped from within by its links to Russia's traditional interest groups, and trapped from without by pressures from Britain and France. It proved no more able to inspire the workers with confidence than it could supply them with food and respect, and develop workplace democracy. Promising land to the peasants, it continually prevaricated and lost support too with the biggest group in Russian society. Different policies might have produced different results, and there are plenty of historians keen to rewrite the history of the Provisional Government in terms of 'might have beens'. But the more serious historical task is to trace how the limits in its thinking and policies were produced by the real contradictions of its position that could not be escaped.[29] The consequence was that when the slogan 'Bread, peace and land' was raised it came to symbolise the things that the Provisional Government could not deliver. Even the calling of the Constituent Assembly was delayed in large part for fear that its composition would prove far too radical, and members of the existing government would not find a place in the new one.

The Provisional Government struggled through a succession of crises. Its first prime minister was Prince Lvov. On 1-2 March he formed a cabinet made up of liberals, industrialists and Alexander Kerensky, nominally an SR and member of the Petrograd soviet, but in reality playing to his then role as 'the idol of the street'. So, far from being a normal politician, Kerensky claimed he was 'a hostage of democracy in the first Provisional Government'.[30] The first Provisional Government only lasted a month. At the start of May Miliukov, then foreign minister, sent a note to Russia's allies that effectively meant the Provisional Government had taken on the foreign policy of the Tsarist regime, war aims and all. Demonstrations and protests led to his resignation and that of Guchkov. On 5 May Lvov formed a new cabinet that now included five other socialists as well as Kerensky and 10 'capitalist' ministers, ie liberals and industrialists. It survived until the 'July Days', when militancy in Petrograd, rushing ahead of the rest of the country, drew tens of thousands of protesters onto the streets. The flavour of those days is given by the workman who told Chernov, now an SR minister: 'Take power when it is given to you, you son of a bitch'.[31] As order was restored Lvov resigned as prime minister on 7 July in favour of Kerensky, who for some time had been trying to play the role of 'statesman of the revolution'. After prolonged negotiations a third Provisional Government (and second coalition) was formed, with six 'capitalist' and nine 'socialist' ministers. But by this time Russia was rapidly polarising. Right wing forces encouraged the new commander in chief, General Kornilov, to attempt a coup, and there were even suggestions that Kerensky was implicated. Who did what is still disputed. But popular mobilisation defeated Kornilov. The cabinet resigned on 27 August, leaving Kerensky in command, and it took him until 22 September to form the fourth Provisional Government and third coalition. It is symptomatic that by this point the Provisional Government had lasted nearly 200 days but spent over a quarter of them without a functioning cabinet. It is no less symptomatic that its socialist members were continually under pressure to moderate their policies to keep liberals and industrialists on board. No one suffered more in this respect than the leading SR, Chernov. As minister of agriculture he was committed to land reform, but he made concession after concession to the 'moderates'. He had, he later said, 'sacrificed to the fetish of unachievable party unity the energetic defence of the very programme which the party had formally adopted at my initiative'.[32] It would not be Chernov who would implement his programme for the peasants but the Bolsheviks with the Decree on Land, one of the first acts of the new government that replaced the discredited Provisional Government after it was driven from power.

BOLSHEVISM AND OCTOBER

The one party to see a clear way forward was the Bolsheviks. Their perspectives began to be crystallised in April 1917, when Lenin returned from exile and argued that the party should not support the Provisional Government. It should stand on the most radical wing of soviet democracy under the slogan 'All power to the soviets'. The leaders of the other socialist parties were horrified. So too were some Bolsheviks. But these arguments struck a chord with many existing members and attracted new ones, and initial hesitations were soon put aside. The precise numbers who joined the Bolsheviks are uncertain. An element of guesswork is involved in the figures for all parties at this time. But it seems likely that from 10,000-20,000 members in February the party grew to some 200,000-350,000 in October. Much depends on where the line is drawn between party member and active party supporter.

The arguments that were forged within the Bolshevik Party helped them to orient to the popular movement, and they increasingly pulled much of that movement to them. This was not, as many historians would later suggest, because the leadership manipulated the party, and the party the movement. We must guard especially strongly against simplistically linking 1917 to Stalin's later top-down view of the history of the revolution. On the contrary, Bolshevik organisation in 1917 was the *most* democratic internally and the *most* insistent externally on democracy from below. Some readers will be taken by surprise by this argument. But even the most cursory survey of the other parties shows leaderships over which members had limited influence, and which invoked support for policies that many members felt lukewarm about at best. It is this that led both the Mensheviks and the SRs to experience a haemorrhage of support in the late summer and autumn of 1917, much of which shifted to the Bolsheviks.

The arguments that became associated with Bolshevism were not born of some immaculate conception. They grew and changed throughout 1917, bringing together the insights of theorists and activists like the young Nikolai Bukharin and Leon Trotsky. After years of independent activity Trotsky, like a number of other figures of the left, joined in 1917 and became a leading member of the party – indeed, its public face in 1917. Their welcome and speedy acceptance was another sign of the flexibility of the party. But Bolshevik arguments also picked up elements from debates and arguments within the popular movement. Lenin added his own elements, but it was he above all who saw the links, brought the arguments together, and gave them a clearer and sharper political edge than anyone else. In 1917 no one codified these, and emphases differed, but the thrust was and is quite clear.

The foundation was internationalism. The Russian crisis, the Bolsheviks argued, was part of an international crisis – self-evident in one sense, since it was taking place in the midst of world war. Capitalism, now in its imperialist phase, had brought the world together only to rip it apart in destruction and barbarism, something it would do again and again if it was not overcome. But opposition to this system was growing in Europe. Where the mainstream socialist parties had failed in 1914, the revolutionary tendencies and parties had to succeed, and they had been given a new chance to succeed by the growing breadth of the disillusionment with the war and the system that had led to it.

The Russian dimension was that there was no real possibility of capitalism solving the country's basic problems. It could not develop it in a Western European fashion, it could not answer the peasants' demands for land, and it could not meet the grievances of the workers. The popular radicalism that continually pushed against the bourgeois limits of the revolution therefore reflected the fact that these limits were too narrow. Instead an alternative base of power had to be built on the new institutions of the committees and the soviets. It was a vision that Lenin captured in his *State and Revolution*, the most important work of 1917 in the way that it outlined the possibility of a higher form of soviet democracy. It was these ideas that stood behind the slogans of soviet power – the demands for immediate peace, that land should be given to the peasants, and that workers should take control of their factories. In a new society built from below, people would no longer be controlled from above, whether by employers or the state. But 'so long as the state exists there can be no freedom. When freedom exists there will be no state,' wrote Lenin in August 1917.[33]

In September and October these arguments gained a sharper edge. Lenin now argued that the Provisional Government had lost all credibility – it could no longer offer the prospect of stability to the bourgeois forces. The support for the Kornilov coup was a sign of this. Its defeat had been a setback to the right but had not removed the threat. The longer that the popular movement delayed action, the more hesitant the soviets were, the more likely that they would provide an opportunity for a renewed assault from the right. The moment had to be seized before it was too late. Critics then and later saw this logic as a gamble. But in the years since there have been many revolutionary crises when the moment was not seized, only for the right to reassert itself and sweep away not only the left, but also the revolution and any form of democracy.

This fate, Lenin, Trotsky and others insisted, could be avoided if a decisive move forward could be made in Russia. But it could not be a break for socialism. Given Russia's backwardness, it lacked the basis to build society anew. What could happen was that revolution in Russia could act as beacon to workers across Europe to call on them to end the war, and the system that had created it. Once begun, the revolution could spread, end Russia's isolation and in the process, in Trotsky's phrase, become *permanent*. Its base would widen and, as cooperation was built from the bottom up between workers in Russia and, say, Germany and Italy, so the revolution would deepen.

The composition of the soviets began to swing to the Bolsheviks and the left of the SR party. Their arguments too echoed many of these themes. Chernov, the leader of the party's centre, would later write of the party's 'swollen left wing, which showed a strong psychological descent into Bolshevism'.[34] In municipal elections in Petrograd the Bolsheviks had got 20.4 percent of the vote in May. It rose to 33.4 percent in September, and in November it would be 45 percent. In Moscow their vote share jumped even more spectacularly from 11.9 percent in June to 50.9 percent in September.[35] The Petrograd soviet, representing the workers and soldiers, swung to them, and so did the Moscow one. Meanwhile Kerensky as prime minister struggled to form a new coalition government, trying to create some new basis of legitimacy by calling a Democratic Conference. When it met it merely exposed the polarisation between right and left. It also exposed the paralysis of the leaderships of the Menshevik and SR parties. They could not support a new coalition, but they hesitated to dispense with the Provisional Government altogether.

It was exactly this that the Bolsheviks, their supporters and the Left SRs argued for. They began to plan an uprising that would give power to the soviets and land to the peasants (the SR programme). When, on 24 October, Kerensky tried to use force to stop the slide, the Bolsheviks and their supporters were able to brush aside the authorities and seize control of Petrograd. It was virtually bloodless compared with February – perhaps 15 died. Support had simply drained from the Provisional Government. The next day, when the Second All-Russian Congress of Soviets met, 505 of the 670 delegates voted for the resolution on 'All power to the soviets'. Some 300 of them were Bolsheviks and 193 from the SRs, but more than half were from the left of that party. The hesitant socialists to the right of that party and the Mensheviks were in a clear minority. With the future unknown, and fearing that their Petrograd base might not last long, the Bolsheviks issued a stream of decrees and proclamations to Russia and the world. In the city, said John Reed, snow came, covering the mud. With 'Russia plunging dizzily into the unknown and terrible future...the life of the city grew gay, and the very revolution ran swifter'.[36]

CONSOLIDATING THE REVOLUTION

The spread of the revolution took some three months. In Moscow and some other places there was bitter fighting. But more often the weakness of the established order led to a peaceful transition. Lenin spoke of the 'triumphal march of soviet power'. It was not quite that easy, but local radicals, sometimes on their own, sometimes inspired by news and proclamations from Petrograd, sometimes assisted by agitators brought by the railway network, did take power.[37]

One reason for the ease of the transfer was that Lenin was right in sensing that those who might lead a counter-revolution were still divided and disoriented. October demoralised them even more. Kerensky tried to rally troops outside of Petrograd but failed to sustain an attack, and fled. More serious in the short term were strikes from middle class groups and the sullen non-cooperation of some professions and the old bureaucracy. But, cut off from effective leadership, this opposition led nowhere. With a makeshift army of Red Guards and soldiers from the disbanding army the Bolsheviks were able to defeat military resistance in the northern Caucasus, southern Urals and the Ukraine, where opponents of the revolution were briefly reinforced by generals and bourgeois politicians fleeing from central Russia. By the end of January 1918 it appeared that the 'civil war' had been won relatively painlessly and, had it not been for later foreign intervention, it might have been.

The government that won these early victories was a coalition of Bolsheviks and Left SRs. The Mensheviks and SR leaders recoiled from the Bolshevik seizure of power in October and, despite misgivings, Iulii Martov, the leader of the left Mensheviks and in other respects close to the Bolsheviks, left the Second Congress of Soviets with the Menshevik delegation to go, as Trotsky said, 'to the dustbin of history'. Despite latter-day attempts to portray the Mensheviks as realists, Trotsky's rebuke remains valid. Before October the Mensheviks and SRs were paralysed by the question of power. Now they rejected the Bolsheviks' action without having any alternative of their own. Martov's position was especially problematic. 'Understand please,' he said, 'what we have before us after all is a victorious uprising of the proletariat – almost the entire proletariat supports Lenin and expects its social liberation from the uprising'.[38] Yet he abandoned the very group that he had pinned his hopes on. For all the talk of

Bolshevik tendencies to one-party rule, it was this action that narrowed the political base of the new regime. When Martov left the Congress of Soviets, Nikolai Sukhanov, the Menshevik chronicler of the revolution, went with him. All historians of 1917 depend on Sukhanov's account, which in its Russian version runs to several volumes. But Sukhanov's assessment of the significance of the Menshevik action and his own feelings about it are rarely quoted. It was, said Sukhanov, the greatest crime of 1917, which he never ceased to regret.

> I was thunderstruck. Nothing like this had ever entered my head...
>
> First of all, no one contested the legality of the congress. Secondly, it represented the most authentic worker-peasant democracy...
>
> [The Menshevik actions] meant a formal break with the masses and with the revolution.
>
> And why? Because the congress had proclaimed a soviet regime in which the minute Menshevik–SR minority would not be given a place!... The Bolsheviks, not long ago...themselves constituted the same impotent minority as the Mensheviks and SRs now, but they did not and could not draw the conclusion that they had to leave the soviet.[39]

Attempts were still made to create a broad left coalition based on the soviets. Lenin and Trotsky were sceptical, and this is often used to explain the failure of the negotiations. But the Bolsheviks made serious efforts to compromise – no equivalent gesture came from the leaders who had walked out to the frustration of the 'neutrals' sponsoring the negotiations. Thus when a coalition did come into being it was formed between the Bolsheviks and the Left Socialist Revolutionary Party. In mid-November Left SRs were appointed as newly named People's Commissars in charge of agriculture, justice, posts and telegraphs, local government, and state property. Two more were made Commissar without portfolios.

Together the Bolsheviks and Left SRs faced the next hurdle – the Constituent Assembly. In a revolutionary situation the ground shifts rapidly. Before October it had been radical democracy that had called for the Constituent Assembly, and the centre and right who hesitated. In one sense their hesitations were validated by the results which, as we have seen, hardly endorsed a bourgeois Russia. But opponents of the revolution now began to sing the praises of the forthcoming Constituent Assembly because they saw in it a chance to regain the initiative. Firstly, they hoped that the assembly would be an alternative centre of power to the soviets. Secondly, within it the old party leaders could construct an anti-Bolshevik coalition. Given the huge vote for the SRs the role that their leaders would play was crucial. The Bolsheviks and Left SRs confronted both arguments. The future of democracy, they argued, lay in broadening the base of soviet power, not overturning it or subordinating it to a discredited parliamentary form. The claim that the SR vote was a mandate for the old leadership was also challenged, not least by the Left SRs. In November the Left SR break with the old party had been completed, and they carried with them the bigger part of the membership. The peasants too were overwhelmingly supporting the decree on land. It was only because a joint list had been presented at the time of the election, which had been manipulated to reduce the influence of the Left SRs, that the old leaders were able to gather so many delegates – 370 to the Left SRs' 40 and the Bolsheviks' 175. Thus when the Constituent Assembly met on 5-6 January 1918 and its key figures refused to make any move towards the new regime, the Bolsheviks and Left SRs united in agreeing to disband it.

This left the most contentious issue – that of peace. Following October, calls for peace poured out to the governments of the day, with other appeals urging workers to challenge them and stop the war. As was expected, the appeals were ignored or met with ridicule from governments committed to the bloodshed. In the next year, before the war ended, a further 1-2 million would die and a greater number would be maimed.

The bigger issue for the revolutionaries was how the workers would respond. The hope was that anti-war radicals and socialists could build an opposition in Europe that sooner rather than later could use the opportunities available to bring change in their countries. In the meantime the revolution in Russia had to keep the beacon alight. Accordingly in December 1917 a 28-day ceasefire was agreed with Germany. Fighting ceased and negotiations began. Trotsky's attempt to conduct a revolutionary diplomacy and expose the nature of German militarism bemused the German delegation. But by late January the German High Command was preparing to move if it did not get its own way. The scale of the concessions demanded provoked consternation on all sides in Russia. Many believed, with Bukharin and the left of the Bolshevik Party, that the revolution had now to fight a revolutionary war against imperialism: 'We always said...that sooner or later the Russian Revolution would have to clash with international capital. That moment has now come'.[40]

Lenin, no less internationalist in his arguments, insisted that throwing away the revolution in Russia would set back the whole of Europe. It was better to retreat temporarily and keep the flame alight. He could not carry the argument. As a compromise Trotsky made one last gesture and simply broke off negotiations, saying that Russia was withdrawing from the war. Once the German High Command had recovered from the shock, Trotsky's bluff was called. The German army rapidly advanced, facing no serious opposition. With defeat facing them, the debate raged on the revolutionary left. But in the Bolshevik Party Central Committee Lenin was just able to carry the day that peace had to be signed at any cost. On 28 February 1918 the treaty of Brest-Litovsk was signed by a makeshift delegation that no one wanted to be a part of, and it was ratified at the Fourth Extraordinary Congress of Soviets on 15 March.

Brest-Litovsk secured the revolution and enabled the Bolsheviks to keep alight the beacon of international revolution as Lenin had hoped. Indeed, if anything it redoubled efforts in this direction. But it also vastly complicated the immediate situation. The price that German imperialism demanded was money, supplies and territory in the south. Puppet regimes were set up which attracted the revolution's opponents. Miliukov, Chernov later said, 'went quite calmly to the zone of German occupation to seek salvation in friendship with the enemy of yesterday'.[41]

The dislocation of the territorial losses and supplies encouraged further turmoil in the economy as the core of Russia was cut off from food, fuel and raw materials. Politically the Bolshevik Party was divided, with the left now pulling against Lenin. The Left SRs also rejected the treaty and, against the advice of some of their most prominent leaders, resigned from the government, leaving the Bolsheviks alone. Worse, part of the party would try to break the peace by assassinating the German ambassador in June 1918 and leading an uprising against the Bolsheviks. It would be this act that broke the broader front of the revolution and left the Bolsheviks alone. The one-party state was not a principle. It was something that the Bolsheviks had forced on them, firstly by the other socialists walking out in October and then by the Left SR actions in the early summer of 1918.

DEEPENING THE REVOLUTION

Despite the difficulties in the months after October the revolution deepened. The period from February to October had been characterised by growing disintegration. Lenin now argued that the best defence against this was self-organisation: 'Comrades, working people! Remember *you yourselves* are at the helm of the state. No one will help you if you yourselves do not unite and take into *your* hands *all affairs* of the state... Get on with the job yourselves, begin right at the bottom, do not wait for anyone'.[42] Since there were no blueprints available, the actions that were taken were often groping, uncertain and sometimes contradictory. But a new structure of power did begin to emerge with some semblance of order as institutions were knitted together and competencies defined. Conflicts inevitably occurred, and critics have mined these for the first signs of the separation of the leadership from the base. But a new order was as much demanded from below, and the context remained a vast confidence that though socialism could not be built in Russia some constructive steps could be made. The new Russia would be that of the commune state, a vast 'commune from sea to sea', said some Left SRs.

In the countryside the post-October period saw the really big transfer of land. It was the continuing combination of urban and rural revolt that made the revolution so powerful. It was this combination too that lay at the basis of the idea of a worker-peasant alliance and turned it into reality. Villages, acting through the traditional peasant commune, confiscated the land of the aristocracy, institutions and rich peasants. Their action was often symbolically legitimised with some ceremony, and the land was then redistributed broadly on the basis of the size of family. The extent and timing of this reflected the pattern of revolution and counter-revolution. In the civil war that broke out later, counter-revolutionaries tried to halt redistribution and even threatened to return land to the old landowners. By 1920 in the 39 provinces of European Russia 96 per cent of peasant households were in the commune.[43] But the wider 'rural revolution' was only really completed in the early 1920s. It created a vast movement of equalisation as land, livestock and equipment were shared. The numbers of both rich and very poor peasants declined. Table 2.1 shows the situation after the distribution for land and animals (1 desiatin equals 2.7 acres, or just over a hectare).

TABLE 2.1. DISTRIBUTION OF PEASANT HOLDINGS BY SIZE OF LAND AREA AND HEAD OF CATTLE AND PIGS ON BASIS OF 1922 SAMPLE CENSUS[44]

	LAND IN DESIATIN	HEAD OF CATTLE	NUMBER OF PIGS
None	6.7	37.5	23.6
Up to 1	24.0	49.0	59.3
2	27.7	10.1	14.2
3	17.8	2.1	2.2
4-6	8.8	–	–
6-10	4.0	1.3	0.7
11 plus	0.8	–	–

From the perspective of the urban population the crucial issue was the food supply. This had been failing before October, less because of shortages than the unwillingness of the peasants to sell when there were few manufactured goods available at prices they could afford. Some elements of rationing had been introduced by the Tsarist government in 1916. To ensure a continuing flow of food the Provisional Government quickly established a state grain monopoly in March 1917 and then widened rationing more. But the daily bread ration in Petrograd continued to fall. By the autumn it was 370 grams per head. It fell to 205 on the eve of the revolution, 152 in December, 102 in January, and a mere 49 grams per head in May 1918.[45] There was grain in the countryside, but the peasantry were reluctant to sell because there was little coming to them from the towns to buy. With the December ceasefire there were attempts to convert arms factories to production for the countryside. But there was no easy solution to breaking out of the vicious circle of decline that existed. In the spring therefore the Bolsheviks, borrowing the idea from wartime Germany, formed a 'food supply dictatorship'. 'Food supply detachments' went from the town to try to get food and to encourage 'class war' in the village led by committees of poor peasants or *kombedy*. Some 120,000 *kombedy* were created but the policy was not a success. This was in part because of the equalising tendencies which unified villagers against potentially disruptive outsiders. These policies were soon moderated, but as the economic situation worsened and the civil war began to develop in the summer an even more blunt method of solving the food problem had to be found.

In the towns the reconstruction from the bottom up involved building on the factory committees, trade unions and soviets, and resolving the differences between them. Initially the factory committees that were formed after February were concerned more with supervising and checking employers than taking over the plants themselves. But crisis, the actions of the employers and the changing views of the workers themselves pushed them in a more radical direction. Already in May 1917 it was said that 'the factory committees do not hesitate to engage in economic activities...they are forced to do so, otherwise many a factory would have had to shut down'.[46] In this way the more limited idea that the committees would oversee employers could give way to the idea that they might replace them. By October this process had gone furthest in Petrograd. Even there workers were groping towards a clearer conception of factory power. But where this began to emerge it helped to concentrate minds on the wider issue of state power. This helps to explain the otherwise strange contrast between Petrograd and the rest of Russia in the autumn of 1917. In the country at large September and October saw some 2 million workers striking – the high point of the year. But in Petrograd itself, as one historian describes it:

> The workers' realisation that there was no salvation from economic collapse without the seizure of power, along with the preoccupation with keeping the factories open, explains in large part the surprising calm that reigned in the capital...when the rest of Russia was experiencing an economic strike wave of unprecedented proportions.

The September conference of factory committees in the city insisted that 'it is necessary to concentrate all the workers' energies on organisational work for the forthcoming solution of the question of constructing state power and a swift end to the three-year slaughter'.[47] Workers' control was therefore a developing process that reflected workers' attempts to deal with economic disruption and employer-manager hostility.

The Decree on Workers' Control on 14 November 1917 tried to encourage the factory committees but also give order and legitimacy to the new structures developing from below. After October most industry still remained in employers' hands. Firms even published their balance sheets and profits until they were nationalised in June 1918. In December 1917 the All-Russian Council of the National Economy (VSNKh) was created to oversee economic activity. The issue that now arose was how the factory committees and the trade unions could relate to one another and the centre. The intense concern of the factory committees with their own plants led to accusations of parochialism, and at the First All-Russian Congress of Trade Unions on 7-14 January 1918 it was argued that they should become the work-based cells of the wider structure of the trade unions. 'The parallel existence of two forms of economic organisation in the working class with overlapping functions can only complicate the process of concentrating the forces of production,' said David Riazanov.[48] Despite opposition this view prevailed, but the continuing dislocation led Lenin to support a further shift in the spring. Now he argued that 'state capitalism' even in the form of one-man management would be an advance if it helped to secure production. To the left, who were already opposing Brest-Litovsk, this seemed a further dangerous retreat that they opposed.

New initiatives were also forthcoming in the wider social and cultural sphere. This was a time of enormous hope, albeit tempered by a realistic understanding that many aspects of life remained desperate. 'Surely you must understand that there is a great deal of moral satisfaction in deciding whether you want thick cabbage soup or thin cabbage soup,' joked Alexandra Kollontai to Louise Bryant when they discussed the choices possible for social welfare.[49] Yet alongside this 'the sense of boundless possibilities' remained. Some suggested that the past should be rejected and the slate wiped clean. Others argued that it had to be built on, cleansed of oppression. When Anatoly Lunacharsky and others heard, wrongly, that much of Moscow's finest architecture was being destroyed in street fighting they resigned in horror. But they came back, and Lunarcharsky became People's Commissar of Education to oversee experiments there. Schools were taken over. Councils of staff (of all kinds) and students met. Adult schools were created, the doors of universities opened and special 'workers' faculties' established. At the most basic level many needed to be taught to read and write, especially in the countryside. 'We know that across the vast expanse of the Russian land there are those corners where people have not yet heard the voice of a person who can read and write. That's where we want to go,' two nurses wrote to Lunacharsky at the end of 1917.[50] Those who believed that education had to be moulded by authority were appalled by the new freedom. But the spirit of enthusiasm swept some of them up, and it won grudging admiration even if in the chaotic circumstances of the time hopes outran achievements.

Creating a revolutionary order involved a continuing struggle for the soul of the popular movement. In the first days drunkenness presented a major problem. As conditions worsened angry crowds and groups continued to lash out. But this was challenged. The very first case heard by a revolutionary tribunal, set up to replace the old court system, was against a member of the militia who was dismissed for firing his rifle while drunk. When revolutionary sailors murdered two former government ministers, agitators were sent out to confront the uglier side of the popular mood. But for some hostile intellectuals it seemed as if 'dark forces' had been unleashed from below. They were rebuked by the poet Valery Briusov:

> O you fantastics, you aesthetic throng,
> Must all your dreams have faint and far away wings?
> Was it in books alone, made safe in song,
> You lived remarkable and shattering things.

Alexander Blok in his poem *The Twelve* captured the contradictions better than anyone as he described a Petrograd night in January 1918. A blizzard is blowing and a Red Guard unit is patrolling, and bringing together the worst and the best: 'Refusing to show pity, prepared for any strain/onwards they march with sovereign tread/in the rear, the hungry cur/up in front Jesus Christ'.[51]

The growing difficulties, especially in Petrograd, did not make any of these tasks easy. The Bolsheviks (and often the Left SRs too) now had to argue for order. 'Each lost hour of labour intensifies hunger and tightens the noose around the working class,' they said.[52] Intense debate continued. Hostile papers were suppressed only to reappear under new names. The popular mood fluctuated, and in the spring there was resurgence of support for the Mensheviks and the Right Socialist Revolutionaries in some places, in others a swing to the Left SRs. They were able to capitalise on the difficulties that the revolution faced. But they remained incapable of deciding whether they were a loyal or disloyal opposition in a state whose overall form was now set out in the constitution adopted at the Fifth Congress of Soviets on 4-10 July 1918. By this time, however, the emerging civil war and the Left SR revolt had begun to change the whole complexion of the revolution.

Then and since there has been much debate over which was the definitive socialist policy. Was it that of winter 1917-18 or the partial retreats of spring 1918? Perhaps it was that of War Communism in the civil war that followed, or the New Economic Policy that came in 1921? The simple answer is that it was none of them. 'The term "Socialist Soviet Republic" expresses only the determination of the Soviet Republic to forward the passage to Socialism. It in no way constitutes a claim that the new economic order in Russia is a socialist one,' said Lenin in 1918.[53] The revolutionaries were attempting something that had not been done before. They recognised that the backwardness of Russia limited what could be done. It was a constant theme that real socialism could only be built in an international context, which was why spreading the revolution remained central. In the meantime they were stuck with what they had, and the sharp, sometimes bitter, debates should not obscure the way in which they were moulded by circumstances. The problem was less the sacrifice of principles to 'realism' than later attempts to elevate the realism of the moment to a principle, to legitimise or delegitimise alternatives for all time.

These debates, doubts and arguments were cut short by the eruption of the real civil war. For the next three years turmoil deepened. The counter-revolution would eventually be defeated, but only at a catastrophic price for the ideals and hopes of these first days, and ultimately for the future of the revolution.

Both working and middle class women queue to see Lenin's body in the early days of the cult. The banner reads: 'Lenin — sun of the future. Lenin has gone but the party remains. Let us draw closer to it'

3 DEGENERATION

Most accounts of revolutions take the view that they are bound to end in failure. 'All power corrupts', and perhaps 'all revolutions corrupt'. This is a neat theory to bolster the status quo. In the discussion of revolution it concentrates responsibility for any problems on the revolutionaries themselves, and in particular it points the finger at their minds, at the 'totalitarian impulse'. Looked at from the perspective of revolution from below the theory is no less neat. Of course, it says, ordinary people lose out, but they were foolish to think it could be otherwise. Power inevitably gravitates upwards. Lenin's idea that 'every cook should govern' was simply demagoguery for the street. Far better that every cook should cook rather than get ideas above their station. The sociologist Alvin Gouldner once said that such theories expressed a 'metaphysical pathos'. It is a grand phrase. By pathos he meant that these were theories of sadness and pity. 'We like your world,' say those who espouse them, 'but it cannot be.' By 'metaphysical' he meant that these were theories that derived not from an analysis of actual social processes but abstract, general reasoning. This is the way it is, this is the way it has to be. Such 'metaphysical pathos' is everywhere in discussions of the fate of the Russian Revolution.

Against it we want to insist that the degeneration of the revolution was not inevitable. The revolution was a revolt against the barbarism of the First World War and its 10 million deaths. It was a revolt against the system that produced the war. But it needed an echoing voice from the West. Instead the warring powers turned on the fledgling state and tried to crush it by supporting a devastating civil war. Daily life was wrecked, and with it much of the revolution. The popular base of the revolution that was established in 1917 was undercut, and this led to a degree of separation of party and class. In the 1920s external and internal pressures continued to mould the new regime. An important layer of the Bolshevik Party and the state bureaucracy began to move away from the central message of 1917 – the need to reconstruct society from the bottom up. In the 1920s the power of this layer was far from absolute. Its policies were challenged by various opposition groups within the party, led most notably by Trotsky. It was forced to tolerate and even encourage certain material gains for the workers. But as the separation developed, the contradiction between the material interests of those who made up this social grouping and those of the rest of society became sharper. At the head of this group was Stalin. Under his leadership the layer began to turn on those who resisted it. But Stalin too was a product of these social pressures. The man of 1928 was not the man of 1917 or even 1922, whatever his deficiencies at these earlier dates might have been. As the layer he was part of developed, so he developed into the person who would become infamous. Eventually, at the end of the 1920s, under the pressure of world events, the separation would be completed, and the regime would be turned to forced accumulation in diametrical opposition to the working class and peasantry. No longer a detached layer, this group would become a class for itself, and Russia would cease to be 'soviet' in any meaningful sense.

THE FAILURE OF INTERNATIONAL REVOLUTION

To make sense of this process we need first to understand the problems created by the failure of the revolution to spread in the years 1917-21. Arguments that link what happened within Russia after 1917 to international revolution and foreign intervention are not popular today. It is much easier to write the history of the revolution as a monstrous aberration, to condemn the revolutionaries for their temerity in challenging the brutalities of capitalism. Those outside who lacked the capacity or courage to make the same break can then be excused.

But Europe came close to revolution on several occasions. The end of the war led to a massive social crisis which lasted until 1921. Further opportunities arose in 1923. The crisis stretched from Spain to Scandinavia, and across the Atlantic to the US and Canada. It can be traced on the graphs of strikes. It can be found in the rapid growth of trade unions and the political shift to the left. It can be seen in the fears of Europe's rulers. 'The whole of Europe is filled with the spirit of revolution. There is a deep sense not only of discontent but of anger and revolt amongst the workers against pre-war conditions. The whole existing order in its political, social and economic aspects is questioned by the masses from one end of Europe to the other,' said British prime minister David Lloyd George.[1]

Broadly three levels of crisis can be distinguished. Few countries with an industrial workforce escaped some radicalisation, even if they had not been directly involved in the war. In other countries a second level of crisis emerged. Here state power perhaps wobbled, but it remained more or less secure in the face of levels of deeper radicalisation that had not been seen since the first half of the 19th century. Britain and France are examples. The third and deepest level saw state power under challenge, especially in Germany between 1918 and 1921, and again in 1923, in Austria in 1918-19, and in Italy in the 'Two Red Years' of 1919-20. A Soviet regime was also established in Hungary in March 1919, but it was soon crushed by an invasion from Romania that the Allies encouraged.[2] The German events were the most significant.

Why were revolutionary situations like that in Germany not capitalised on by the left? Germany was the linchpin of Europe. As the war ended a naval mutiny broke out in Kiel. Workers' councils were set up across the country. 'The revolution is on the march,' said one German paper. Radicalism surged from below. 'The characteristic feature of this rising lay in the elemental force with which it broke out,' said one Berlin shop steward.[3] The combination of war, collapse and revolt weakened and disoriented the old order, and the giant German Socialist Party. On at least five occasions between 1918 and 1923 the whole edifice of German capitalism was at risk, and though the challenge from the left then weakened, it was only finally removed after the victory of Hitler in 1933.[4] As the level of class conflict moved up and down in the years 1918-23 in Germany, so the mood of the ruling class swung from confidence to despair. In late 1918 for example, General Groener, perhaps the key military figure of the time, reported that 'the influence of the workers' and soldiers' councils prevails amongst whole sectors of the army'. In the factories another report said that 'the employers are as powerless as the managerial staff. All power is in the hands of the workers' committees'.[5]

Why did revolution fail? When something does not happen it is easy to say that the objective circumstances were against it. The dominant histories take exactly this position, claiming that Western European regimes had reserves of strength that Russia's rulers lacked.[6] But the subjective element – the element of political leadership and organisation – is most important at such times of crisis. Rosa Luxemburg had seen this when she heard of news of the Russian Revolution in her prison cell in Germany in 1917. She wrote to Luise Kautsky, the wife of the great German Marxist theorist Karl Kautsky, asking:

> *Are you glad about the Russians? Of course, they won't be able to maintain themselves in this witches' Sabbath*
> *— not because statistics show that their economic development is too backward, as your clever husband has*
> *worked out, but because Social Democracy in the highly developed West consists of a pack of piteous cowards*
> *who are prepared to look on quietly and let the Russians bleed to death. But such an end is better than 'living*
> *for the fatherland' — it is an act of world historical significance whose traces will not be extinguished for aeons.*[7]

To encourage and lead the shift to the left, the Third International or Communist International (Comintern) was formed in Moscow in March 1919. It was little more than a token gesture to begin with, a signal born of optimism and hope. The optimism remained there until 1921. Zinoviev told the 200 delegates at the Second Congress in July 1920: 'I am deeply convinced that the Second World Congress is the precursor of another congress, the World Congress of Soviet Republics.' The parties attached to the Comintern and its periphery quickly began to attract a real membership. By the Third Congress in 1921 the 605 delegates included representatives from 48 new Communist parties in 52 countries.[8]

But Luxemburg's fears were well founded. Luxemburg and her fellow socialist Karl Liebknecht were murdered along with other revolutionaries in early 1919 by members of the right wing volunteer Freikorps. The socialist government had unleashed them to try to contain the challenge from below. 'Social revolution... I do not want it – in fact, I hate it like the plague,' said Ebert, the moderate socialist leader.[9] The Freikorps would be used again a few months later in the suppression of the Bavarian soviet. 'It's better to kill a few innocent people than let one guilty escape... You know how to handle it... Shoot them and report they attacked you or tried to escape,' said one Freikorps officer.[10] Everywhere it seemed that Social Democratic and trade union leaders worked to contain the radicalisation. They believed that they could both preserve the system and reform it while receiving gratitude for their work from the wider ruling class. 'It is our glory and our pride that we prevented the outbreak of revolution which the extremists desired,' said Ludovico D'Aragona, secretary of the leading Italian trade union organisation.[11] But the gratitude was limited. In Italy in 1922 the ruling class swung behind Mussolini's Fascism, and dispensed with the Social Democratic leaders as easily as it did with those to the left of them. In Germany in 1933 Hitler seized power with the complicity of broad sections of the ruling class. The Social Democrats suffered as much as the Communists. The Freikorps, the volunteer forces that their ministers had encouraged in 1919 and who had killed Luxemburg and others, became lauded as prototypes of the Nazis.

The more left wing leaders between 1917 and 1921 oscillated between revolutionary and Social Democratic politics. Karl Kautsky described the strains in late 1918 on the left wing German Independent Socialists who had broken from the old German Socialist Party (SPD): 'Our party presented a grotesque appearance, as perhaps no other party has done in the history of the world. Its right wing was in government and its left wing worked for the downfall of that same government'.[12] But in Germany and elsewhere the leaders of these tendencies, groups and parties would not come down in support of Bolshevism. For them the old Second International was discredited. But the new Third International was a step too far. So they moved between right wing socialism and Bolshevism, forming for a time their own international, mischievously nicknamed the Second and A Half International. They were, said their revolutionary critics, playing the game of centrism, which could only exist so long as the popular mood remained high. But these critics on the revolutionary left, the smallest group, partly through weakness and partly through inexperience, themselves allowed opportunities to slip. Communist parties began to emerge, but only as the crisis began to decline did they come to have a real political life. This was the great difference with Russia. There a revolutionary party had been in existence at the start that could have mass influence.

The result was not simply that the Russian Revolution remained isolated. Worse, the leading powers turned on it to help to crush the revolution. 'Everything that happens in Russia is comprehensible, and represents an inevitable chain of causes and effects,' said Rosa Luxemburg in 1918. 'The starting point and end term...are the failure of the German proletariat and the occupation of Russia by German imperialism'.[13] Had she lived longer she could have added the Allied intervention that peaked in the year after her murder. In April 1918 Trotsky told the Bolshevik Central Committee: 'Our internal enemies are pitiful.' The problem was 'the all-powerful external enemies who utilise a huge centralised machine for their mass murder and extermination'.[14]

FOREIGN INTERVENTION AND CIVIL WAR

It is also now commonplace to disparage the role of foreign intervention. Many historians see the civil war as a mass of confused fighting in which the differences between the sides were dissolved. But this is quite false.

We have already seen the impact that Brest-Litovsk had on the revolution. When the First World War ended in November 1918 the treaty became void. But by that time Allied intervention was already well under way. The initial aim was said to be to get Russia back into the war. After November 1918 the anti-Bolshevik thrust became more evident. The motive was to halt the general threat of revolution, but there were also specific fears about the impact of the loss of Russian markets, the fate of foreign investment, and the danger that Tsarist state debts would not be repaid. Anti-Bolshevik propaganda tried to discredit the revolution, and to undermine radicals at home: Lenin and Trotsky were fighting each other; the revolution was only surviving because it was using Chinese troops; it had nationalised women. The tales were legion. Reactionary forces rallied in opposition to 'Bolshevism'. In Britain the secret service held 'Bolo Liquidation Lunches' at the Cafe Royal.[15] But the degree of enthusiasm for intervention varied between states and within governments. When it became obvious that the chances of success were limited, support for the counter-revolution was wound down in 1920 and new tactics developed. But without foreign intervention the civil war could not have been carried on to the extent that it was, or with the devastating effect that it had.

An enormous imbalance of power existed between the revolutionary state and the 14 states which eventually joined against it. For them intervention was 'low cost' – reminiscent of colonial and post-colonial wars. For the victim the impact was quite different. Blockade in the war had cut off many of Russia's outside links – now the isolation became more or less complete. Large numbers of foreign troops were landed on Russian soil. These troops saw little direct fighting – some none at all. But this did not alter the force of the gesture. Aid flowed to the counter-revolution. No proper account has been made of its total cost but it was considerable, especially in relation to the poverty-stricken state of revolutionary Russia. Large quantities of weapons and equipment flowed to the Whites, as the counter-revolutionary forces became known. The Red Army could draw on Tsarist stocks and repairs, but little could be produced in the civil war itself. Only 1 million new rifles were produced, for example, whereas Britain alone supplied nearly 1 million to White forces.[16] With equipment also came skilled advisers. But another contribution should not be ignored. This was the confidence supplied to the counter-revolution. Now it seemed that behind the defeated rulers of the old Russia stood the West, and so long as it was there a degree of composure returned.

There were five main areas of action: White forces, backed by intervention, advanced under Kolchak from Siberia; there was smaller action in Transcaucasia; major fighting took place in the south with the Whites under Denikin and Wrangel; in the north east the Whites advanced under Yudenich; and in the far north there was conflict spreading south from Archangel, where foreign forces had also landed. Fortunately these actions were not coordinated. Even so, revolutionary Russia was quickly reduced in 1918-19 to the central Russian lands, with a population of 60 million. Worse, it was now even more cut off from food, fuel and raw material supplies. Yet by early 1920 most of the White forces had been defeated. Then in April, encouraged by the Allies, Poland (with an army of 740,000) invaded the Ukraine, and war continued until October 1920. The civil war pattern was also confused by 'third forces'. Attempts by socialist opponents of the revolution to create independent governments failed or were swept aside by the Whites. More important were 'green forces', large peasant bands under leaders like Nestor Makhno. These had no interest in the Whites, and on occasion played an important role in helping defeat them in the south. But their politics were erratic. Their actions too were brutal, belying the romantic aura with which they have been invested by some.[17]

Why did the counter-revolution lose? There were military reasons – lack of coordination, the control of the centre by the revolutionaries, and so on. But the main reasons were political. The White armies forged a unity around a vision of a return to the past, a 'Russia – one and indivisible'. This smacked too much of Tsarism. So too did their support for returning land to the land-lords. The White forces suffered from endemic corruption. They displayed enormous systematic and obscene brutality. The Whites emerged from the old order, which had sacrificed nearly 2 million soldiers in a senseless war, to say nothing of those killed on the other side. They linked groups now used to killing with embittered members of the old ruling class, and local leaders who had to be given their head if their support was to be retained. The British General Knox reported to London that Kolchak in Siberia was 'honest, patriotic and capable'. Graves, the American general in Siberia, was more squeamish, recording much of the brutality and the narrow base of the Whites: 'The Kolchak government has failed to command the confidence of anybody in Siberia, except a small discredited group of reactionaries, monarchists and former military officials.' The US government withheld recognition from Kolchak but still sent him guns, ammunition and loans.[18] White pogroms killed 60,000-100,000 Jews. They were worst in the Ukraine. Proud of their handiwork, White forces took photographs. Some still survive. One, dated August 1919, shows Cossacks posing over a row of dead Jews wrapped in their prayer shawls. It evokes an instant association with later Nazi atrocities. Tens of thousands fled within Russia and beyond to other parts of Europe, the United States and Palestine.[19]

But the defeat of the counter-revolution was no easy matter. The Red Army had to be built up from scratch using volunteers and then conscription. At the end of 1918 it had a paper strength of 500,000, by July 1919 2.3 million, and by July 1920 4 million. Initial hopes of a new form of army organisation proved unrealistic. But the Red Army still remained one of the most democratic armies yet known. Debates ranged over the use of ex-Tsarist officers. The army often lacked weapons and equipment. Discipline was a problem. Trotsky was as prepared as any First World War general to see weakness in the face of the enemy punished harshly: 'An army cannot be built without repression. Masses of men cannot be led to death unless the army command has the death penalty in its arsenal'.[20] But there was another side too. Unlike in the White armies, a constant campaign was kept up to reduce atrocities, and to raise the moral and political standard. It did not always work.[21] But the aim was to make the Red Army an army of liberation, not conquest, and exemplary punishment was used to dissuade others from rape, murder and pillage.

BEHIND THE LINES – CRUCIFYING THE REVOLUTION

Behind the rapidly changing fronts revolutionary Russia struggled to survive a growing social catastrophe as hunger and cold grew. Life was trapped in a vicious circle of decline that changed both the priorities and the form of the regime. Denied fuel, food and raw materials, factories closed and workers starved. By 1920 industrial output was 31 percent of the 1913 level, and total output 38 percent. Supplying the army from the diminishing resources became the first priority. In areas that were short of food the towns emptied. Petrograd's population fell from 2.3 million in 1917 to 1.5 million in 1918, and 740,000 in 1920 – only 32 percent of the 1917 level.[22] To the novelist Alexei Tolstoy, Petrograd in the winter of 1918 was 'starving...bitten through by polar winds, a town without coal and bread, its factory chimneys extinguished, a town like a raw human nerve'.[23] In areas where food was available refugees flowed to fill out the countryside and the provincial towns.

Petrograd suffered especially badly because of its isolation from its main sources of supply. The city had, remember, 400,000 factory workers in 1917. Many were badly affected by the problems of the initial months. Then things got even worse. One historian has calculated that from the summer of 1918 40,000 Petrograd factory workers joined the Red Army. A further 20,000 were involved in food and fuel requisitioning. Perhaps 10,000-15,000 were sent to work in other areas of Russia. Looking at the total decline from October 1917, it seems that by 1921 only 50,000 of the original 1917 factory workforce remained.[24] But there was a qualitative aspect too. It was the best militants who left to extend and defend the revolution.

An idea of the wider experience of the working class can be gained from table 3.1. The first column shows the overall decline, which is understated because towards the end many non-workers were being dragged into factories to keep them going. Column two shows the working class in the core areas that remained under Bolshevik control. Column three is a crude attempt to estimate the size of the working class in areas under Bolshevik control as the civil war fluctuated.

TABLE 3.1. ESTIMATES OF THE SIZE OF THE INDUSTRIAL WORKING CLASS IN RUSSIA, 1913-22[25]

	RUSSIA	INDEX (1917=100)	24 PROVINCES OF EUROPEAN RUSSIA	AREA UNDER BOLSHEVIK CONTROL	INDEX (1917=100)
1913	3,100,000	86	–	–	–
1917	3,600,000	100	1,850,000	3,600,000	100
1918	2,500,000	69	1,071,000	1,150,000	32
1919	1,400,000	39			
1919 AVERAGE FIRST HALF	–	–	910,000	910,000	25
1919 AVERAGE SECOND HALF	–	–	760,000	760,000	21
1920	1,500,000	42	735,000	1,500,000	42
1921	1,200,000	33	–	1,200,000	33
1922	1,100,000	31	–	1,100,000	31

The most difficult thing was to get food from the peasants when, with industry collapsed, there was nothing to buy in return. Towns were stripped of goods to offer for food, but these were soon exhausted. The solution adopted in the summer of 1918 was grain requisitioning. Provinces, areas and villages were assessed and then required, by force if necessary, to hand over surplus grain. Peasant resentment was enormous, and conflicts were common. But desperate times required desperate measures. Grain requisitioning had been used elsewhere, and no one has offered an effective alternative in the midst of hunger and shortage. Moreover peasant hostility was ultimately contained by the knowledge that if the Communists came for the grain, the Whites threatened to take both the grain and the land.

State control was widened and centralisation imposed across the economy. Formal market relations were marginalised, although the black market boomed. The overall system of control that developed was given the name 'War Communism'. It was really a form of 'Barrack Room Communism' in response to military necessity. This was how most Bolsheviks saw it. Of course the idea of a primitive egalitarianism had attractive elements. But claims that significant illusions about a leap into communism were widespread either misread or ignore the contemporary evidence. One official of the Food Commissariat summed things up when he said: 'What do you think, the People's Commissariat of Food does this for its own satisfaction? No, we do it because there is not enough food.' Dire necessity was the biggest determinant of policy.[26] No war economy in the 20th century has avoided major state control. Few war economies have had to cope with the scale of collapse in Russia in these years.

The statistics tell of increasingly appalling social conditions. The working class, said Preobrazhensky later, became 'a commune of beggars which waged war under terribly severe conditions'.[27] Workers were increasingly paid in kind, until by 1920 they got over four fifths of their wages this way. By that time the value of their wages in both goods and kind had fallen to only one tenth of the 1913 level. No family could survive on this. To make do the workers had to rely on selling what property they had, stealing or making goods to sell to the peasants for food. By April 1921 wages in goods and kind made up only two fifths of family income. One of the few social conditions to improve was housing – at least in theory. As people fled, once overcrowded families had the choice of more accommodation. But this was little comfort when water pipes froze, sewers froze and burst, and people shivered in their rooms. Then a small overcrowded room might be an advantage.

Only disease and death could flourish in this environment. Typhus, typhoid, malaria, cholera and tuberculosis carried off huge numbers. Yet people still tried to maintain an element of dignity amid the horror. In Petrograd the price of coffins soared. Only the more wealthy could afford them. The rest had to hire them. With the body emptied into the grave, they were then taken away to the next funeral.

An estimate of one part of the human cost of all of this is set out in table 3.2. This shows the different types of losses from which it can be seen that the military losses were only a very small part of the bigger losses from epidemic and endemic disease.

TABLE 3.2. ESTIMATES OF TYPE OF POPULATION LOSSES IN RUSSIA, 1914-22 (MILLIONS)[28]

	1914-17	1918-20	1921-22
Military losses	1.8	0.8	–
Excess civilian deaths	1.5	7.0	c5.0
Birth deficit	5.0	5.0	4.0
Emigration			c2.0

The Bolsheviks could not escape the political consequences of this social collapse. Bukharin, writing in the civil war, said that in any revolution when 'the productive forces are going down and the great masses are materially insecure there will inevitably be a tendency to "degeneration", ie the excretion of a leading stratum in the form of a class germ'. But he argued that this could be counteracted by the growth of the productive forces, which would improve the material situation of the workers, and 'the abolition of the educational monopoly', which would broaden political and cultural horizons.[29] But the scale of the dislocation in the Russian civil war was so great that this process of degeneration was hugely intensified. As the working class dissolved, so power shifted to the party. But the party itself was also continually in movement. Members were drained to meet needs elsewhere, and local ranks filled with new and perhaps less reliable replacements. Lenin hoped that the threat of 'death on defeat' would act to deter new careerist members. It is not so clear that it did. But the more important point is the dilution of the generation who carried within them the self-confidence of victory in 1917. In Petrograd, for example, by March 1919, with the party three fifths of its peak level just over a year before, only 46 percent of members had joined before October. Two thirds of those who had been Bolsheviks in the city in 1917 had gone elsewhere. By 1922 the figure of pre-October recruits in the city party was only 15 percent. Power shifted upwards. But there were problems there too. In the fifth Petrograd soviet (January-June 1920) less than 23 percent of Bolshevik deputies had joined before October. It was only in the Petrograd soviet executive that the pre-1917 and 1917 generations dominated, forming nearly 90 percent of the committee. There was therefore a gap between party and class, but also between party and leaders. Elsewhere it was even worse. By 1921 only 45 percent of Communist members

❧ 3.1 ON CAVEMEN, HARES AND TROUSERS

The dire circumstances of the civil war years continually pressed against the hope for a better world. Conditions were worst in Petrograd, where a daily struggle to survive sapped much of the élan of the revolution. The writer Yevgenii Zamiatin described Petrograd as 'an ice kingdom' — its population were 'cavemen, wrapped in hides, blankets, rags' retreating 'from cave to cave' and moving 'deeper and deeper…here they must last out the siege or die'.[v]

The memoirs of another writer, Ilia Ehrenburg, capture some of the tensions and horrors produced by the civil war. Ehrenburg initially fled the revolution, but late in the civil war he came back. Already of some prominence, he was set to work in the Moscow Children's Theatre where Durov, the great clown and animal trainer of the age, wanted to show children how things could change. One of the shows was **Hares of All Lands, Unite!** Hares were the traditional cowards of Russian folklore, but in this play they became heroes, leading their own revolution, firing guns and storming the palace to victory. The children, 'pale and thin' from hunger, could glimpse for a moment a different and better world. They could also learn through the changed roles of the animals that even the weak could become strong.

But poverty, cold and hunger were never far away. Durov's baby elephant died of cold. The bear cub outgrew his clothes, for there were not even enough for humans. When Ehrenburg arrived in Moscow he recalled that his trousers had disintegrated at the knees. But now with his new job he could get a clothing coupon. 'Comrade Ehrenburg must be clothed,' said the note. But a note was one thing — finding clothing was another. Eventually he pushed his way to the head of a queue at one clothing depot. Because of the depth of the economic collapse in the civil war he had to choose between a winter coat and a suit: 'The choice was very hard. Frozen as I felt, I was ready to ask for a winter coat, but suddenly I remembered the humiliations of the past months and shouted: "Trousers! A suit".'[vi]

The revolution had been about the assertion of human dignity as well as political change. Now at the lowest point of the civil war everyone — poet, writer and worker — was forced to focus on 'bare necessities'.

of provincial soviet executive committees had joined the party in 1917 or before, and in the smaller district committees the figure was a mere 20.3 percent.[30]

This was a bitter world of privation and hunger. Those who had were privileged against those who had nothing. There was no sharper critic of this than the anarchist Emma Goldman. But when she feared illness would carry away her friends, she too found herself using her connections to get what she could.[31] The dangers were obvious. Yet in the longer run it was the political displacement of power that was the more serious. With no base to argue with, no base to push, cajole and, if necessary, defeat them, the capacity of the old guard to maintain the perspectives of 1917 was limited.

With the challenge of intervention and counter-revolution in the summer of 1918, revolutionary Russia became an armed camp, effectively under martial law. The Bolsheviks did not flinch from talking of 'terror' in a conscious echo of the emergency defence of the French Revolution. With enemies who showed no mercy there was little secretiveness about the 'Red Terror'. Its aim was to deter by example, and it was believed the measures were justified. However, there is much confusion about the elements involved. At the front civilians might get caught up in Red Army actions. Behind the lines grain requisitioning units came into conflict with the peasants. Revolutionary courts dealt with crime. 'Counter-revolution', whether in terms of risings, strikes, sabotage, speculation or whatever, came under the control of the Cheka, whose powers extended as the civil war progressed.[32]

The Cheka was formed on 7 December 1917, under Bolshevik and Left SR control. But with the Left SR uprising it became a Bolshevik organisation. Initially small armed detachments were added, and from late 1918 to 1921 it had 40,000-50,000 members. The numbers shot by the several different types of tribunal, including the Cheka, in these years as they tried to maintain order is disputed, but it appears to have been in the range of 50,000.[33] Certainly the terror was very real, though the rhetoric of threat did not always mean action, as some historians assume. Nevertheless, this aspect of the defence of the revolution has been always been used to attack the Bolsheviks. Their defence was open.[34] While excesses were real, so too was the counter-revolution, and its excesses were the greater. And behind them stood 'Western civilisation', happy to turn a blind eye to what the forces it sponsored did, and happy to practise its own carnage in the war. It is salutary to note, for example, that some 100,000 British troops died in fighting *after* Germany had asked for an armistice and while its terms were negotiated. But the crucial defence was that the terror was a product of the crisis the revolution faced.

Despite difficulties in the big towns, the revolutionary order held until the summer of 1918, and there were few deaths at the hands of the new regime. Forces opposed to the revolution were less discerning. The Bolsheviks were horrified by the killing of 20,000 or more revolutionaries in Finland in early

1918. The formal liberation of Finland from Russia was one of the achievements of 1917. But the country, with a population of 3.4 million, was then precipitated into civil war. The figures for the dead remain uncertain – 30,000 is commonly quoted, 10,000 Whites and 20,000 Reds. At least 10,000 of the Red deaths were those of prisoners in camps after the White victory.[35] Similarly in parts of the Russian countryside the number of soviet, party and poor peasant activists killed numbered possibly several thousand by the summer of 1918.[36] Foreign intervention and the Left SR rising compounded the pressures, and led to the decree of 16 June 1918 reintroducing the death penalty. As the civil war worsened in July and August there were assassinations, including an attempt on Lenin, which led to the September 1918 decree introducing the Red Terror. The general pattern then varied with the fortunes of the civil war. In January 1920 an attempt was made to relax repression and abolish the death penalty. But with the war with Poland it was reintroduced again. Sections of the Cheka did get out of hand, and there were openly expressed fears in the party about this. Membership of the Cheka was initially seen as a job for experienced and reliable socialists, exemplified by its leader, Felix Dzerzhinsky. But in the civil war there was a desperate shortage of such people everywhere. 'The party had few men of his stamp,' said Victor Serge, and many Chekas 'gradually came to select their personnel by virtue of their psychological inclinations. The only temperaments that devoted themselves willingly and tenaciously to this task of "internal defence" were those characterised by suspicion, embitterment, harshness and sadism'.[37] Sometimes too the Cheka acted under panic as the threat of defeat came nearer. Serge has left a vivid description of how this could happen.[38] This was why it was believed that at the end of the civil war there was no place for the Cheka. Lenin led the call for a return to revolutionary legality, and in February 1922 the Cheka was abolished. The aim was now to have a new and more limited organisation in the form of the GPU (State Political Administration). And in the first years of the NEP this is exactly what happened.[39]

But the shift away from the policies of the civil war began almost a year before in the midst of the biggest crisis so far for the revolution. In the spring of 1920 there had been hope of relaxation, but the attack by Poland prevented this and even deepened the internal difficulties. The fighting on the Polish front consumed relatively enormous resources given the poverty-stricken state of the revolution. Yet in the first instance the Red Army astonished Europe with the way it pushed the Polish forces back. As they retreated, the opportunity opened up of driving into Poland in the hope of igniting revolution. The option looked attractive to the some of the left. It also looked attractive to some of the old officer class who had joined the Red Army.[40] Lenin too was caught up, whereas Trotsky saw the dangers of the whole adventure. He was proved right. Far from igniting revolution, Polish nationalism was able to use the Russian threat as a rallying cause, and things were made worse by disagreements in the Red Army command over tactics. Brilliant victories in Russia gave way to defeat in Poland before peace was agreed.

When the war ended in the late autumn the regime remained trapped both mentally and practically in the cycle of crisis measures. The patience of the peasants snapped in some regions. There was a huge revolt in Tambov. Urban conditions worsened over the winter of 1920-21. In February strikes broke out in Petrograd, and then discontent spread to the naval base of Kronstadt. Ever since the legacy of Kronstadt and its suppression has been shrouded in controversy.

Several arguments are involved. Attempts have been made, notably by Trotsky, to explain the revolt by the dissolution of the class consciousness of the sailors, whose political commitment had been weakened by new recruits. But it is not clear how true this was, and in any case the grievances that inspired the revolt were born of real frustration. In a material sense they could not have been relieved by an earlier abandonment of war policies, as some have claimed. Even after policies were changed, it was not until the harvest of 1922 came in that a real recovery began. But an earlier response to peasant discontent might well have had a positive psychological effect. Certainly there seems no doubt that the local Petrograd leadership (especially Zinoviev and Kalinin) inflamed grievances by their responses. The difficulty was that, whatever the intentions of the sailors, their revolt did threaten to reopen opportunities for the counter-revolution and intervention. This was why someone like Victor Serge, who never ceased to have doubts, nevertheless saw no alternative but suppression of the revolt once it was under way. 'They wanted to release a pacifying tempest,' he said, 'but all they could actually have done was to open the way to counter-revolution... Insurgent Kronstadt was not counter-revolution, but its victory would have led – without any shadow of a doubt – to the counter-revolution.' Against this possibility the Bolsheviks, for all their faults, still represented the best of the revolution. But those faults were real, and included the inability to resist executions after the rebels were defeated (though these were partly provoked by the enormously greater loss of Communists than Kronstadters in the fighting). Even as the rank and file fought on, said Serge, 'the crack of the timbers in the whole building' could unmistakably be heard.[41]

At the Tenth Congress of the party in March 1921, therefore, civil war policies were abandoned in favour of what was called the New Economic Policy (NEP). 'We know that so long as there is no revolution in other countries,' said Lenin, 'only agreement with the peasantry can save the socialist revolution in Russia'.[42] The aim was to try to use the market to assist recovery. Market relations were legalised, most importantly the sale of grain. Peasants were to be subject to a tax in kind in place of requisitioning. They would be able to buy what little was being produced even if prices rose. Recovery might then get under way. However, as we shall see, NEP created a new set of difficulties and the longer term question was how the collapse in the social and political base of the revolution could be dealt with.

NEP – WHERE WAS THE REVOLUTION GOING?

The paradox of the civil war was that the Bolsheviks emerged victorious but isolated. They were isolated abroad because the international revolution that they had looked to had suffered a succession of setbacks. They were isolated at home because the terrible social and economic dislocation had destroyed the working class that had made the revolution. The party had become a party of organisers, of administrators, of Red Army members, and so on. Very few of its worker members remained 'at the bench'. Power had gravitated upwards under the pressure of trying to hold everything together. This was the first stage of degeneration, and it created the base for later developments. The extent of the emergence of a separate layer arose not from 1917 itself but the intensity of what came after it. The real 'pathos' of the revolution lies here, in the extent to which the old order rose, almost casually, to help to crush it.

The inauguration of the New Economic Policy was an attempt to find a way out of the dilemmas that this external and internal isolation created. But the years between 1921 and 1928 were contradictory. This was a time of relative social peace and experiment. Most of the repression of the civil war disappeared. Some of the elan of 1917 began to re-emerge. It inspired new movements in science, education, social policy, art and culture. 'More and more poets – good ones and various,' cried Mayakovsky, the revolutionary poet. For a period it seemed that the revolution would live up to part of the dream of creating the most progressive society in the world. It could only be part of that dream because culture of all kinds remained trapped by clear limits. These were partly material. NEP Russia remained a world of endemic poverty, so much so that pawn shops had to be reintroduced. The limits were also partly social. Trotsky sharply criticised the idea that improving standards of everyday life and personal behaviour was in itself a socialist achievement. To encourage the use of handkerchiefs was a step forward in a backward country, but this did not make the handkerchief socialist. But the limits to the possibility of cultural revolution were also political. One of the most symbolic ideas of the time was the conductorless orchestra – Persimfans, made up of some of Russia's finest musicians, 'a community of players, democratic, socialist, egalitarian'.[43] The image fitted the noble aspirations of a revolution that would lay the foundations for human emancipation. But to generalise this it needed an active and vibrant society, and much of this is what had been crushed by the civil war.

Behind these limits, however, were deeper tensions that were never resolved. The result was that the degeneration evident in the civil war continued and intensified as the 1920s progressed. To understand the social base of this process, we need to see how several elements interacted. The revolution had only begun a process of potential change. It now faced external and internal contradictions rooted in the old order that had not yet been overcome. Externally, as an isolated state, the question arose of how the longer term economic and military pressures of global capitalism would be dealt with. Internally, too, much of the underlying structure of the old order remained. Both created pressures pulling the crippled revolution backwards. Within the party and state the question arose of whether the elements of bureaucratic degeneration created by the civil war could be overcome. There was tension here too. The base of the revolution had been severely weakened, but elements of workers' power survived, partially institutionalised at the base. In the party too, buoyed by ultimate victory in the civil war, many members remained loyal to the original vision, and their pressures acted to restrain the layer that had begun to emerge out of the civil war. The vision of this layer too was initially tied to the early goals and aspirations. But the extreme weakness of the working class in the NEP years, especially early on, meant that the regime had to be run bureaucratically, and the position of this layer gradually strengthened. It became more and more detached. Many of its members now began to reflect the social and ideological pressures created by their own situation, seeing their own role as central and needing to be more fully rewarded. They responded too to the wider external and internal pressures acting on Russia at this time. This was not a simple two-sided conflict. Sections of the party and bureaucracy, typified perhaps by Zinoviev, vacillated between the different perspectives that emerged – supporting the more bureaucratic trends at one moment and then opposing them at another. There were personal factors too. The death of Lenin removed a significant constraint. Had he not been so incapacitated by illness from 1922, his immense prestige might have tipped the balance against further degeneration long enough to buy more time for the revolution to break out of its isolation. Stalin's personal characteristics worked in the other direction, pushing the process forward. But the essential point was that his rise and the eventual complete break with 1917 are much more than the story of individuals. They are rooted in social processes, as we can see if we explore how these different elements interacted.

THE EXTERNAL CONTRADICTIONS OF NEP

In the first years of NEP recovery often involved no more than the basic task of the restoration of industry. This was difficult enough. When the gates of one Petrograd factory that had been put 'on ice' were opened, workers saw 'heaps of rubbish, a building collapsing from lack of repair, broken lathes. The machinery and rooms were dirty, there was no water, it was carried from a distance... But the worst thing was the cold... We feared that we had already forgotten how to work'.[44]

But the bigger context of any future development was set by the outside world. Under the pressure of global competition, the world economy was continually moving forward. By the mid-1920s most economies had regained their 1913-14 levels of production. By 1929 some of them, most notably America, had greatly exceeded them. Soviet rates of recovery were also impressive, but so great had been the collapse that 1913-14 levels were only regained in 1927-28. Thus the gap with advanced capitalism was greater in 1929 than 1913. As long as the Soviet Union remained relatively weak, as any isolated state had to be, then the pattern of development had to emulate that in the wider world economy and be conditioned by it. The Soviet state was developing, Trotsky said in 1927, 'directly or indirectly, under the relative control of the world market. Herein lies the root of the question. The rate of development is not an arbitrary one – it is determined by the whole of world development, because in the last analysis world industry controls every one of its parts, even if that part is under the proletarian dictatorship and is building up socialist industry'.

This global pressure had specific forms. One was military. NEP brought agreements with a number of countries to reopen trade. The first was the Anglo-Soviet agreement of 1921. In the short run it was hoped that Soviet diplomacy could provide some sort of *modus vivendi* with Western states. The need for economic recovery would lead them to see Russia as a valuable market, and tensions between them would prevent another hostile coalition forming quickly. But these were seen as temporary gains that might be lost if circumstances changed. The Soviet Union needed therefore to have a degree of defensive preparation. But how much?

One solution was to combine military readiness with continued support for and reliance on the spread of the revolution. This was effectively the policy of the early NEP period, though the military readiness was not that great, as the Red Army was demobilised after the civil war. In 1924 the Central Committee heard that the Red Army was 'unfit for military action'. It numbered 562,000 from 1924-27, and overall defence spending fell as a share of the state budget. By 1926-27 it was perhaps only 40 percent of the 1913 level.[45] The opposition continued to support the centrality of international revolution. 'The development of the [international] revolutionary movement...is the primary fundamental guarantee of the inviolability of the USSR and the possibility of peaceful socialist development,' said Zinoviev.[46] But if international revolution was abandoned as the primary guarantee then the whole weight of survival would begin to fall onto military defence. The Soviet Union would have to begin to act more like a conventional state, responding in a conventional way to a conventional military threat. In January 1925 Red Army commander Mikhail Frunze warned that in the future 'we shall have to deal with splendid armies, armed with all the latest technological advances, and if we do not have these advances then the prospects for us may prove very, very unfavourable'. The implication, which in 1925 was barely understood, was a strategy of modernised military defence supported by the mobilisation of the economy. The Soviet state would be sucked into the military competition that was coming to be a central part of the way that capitalism had developed since the time of Marx and Engels.

There is less excuse today for blindness to these developments. War and military action have been present over most of human history. But modern war does not hang in the air. It is moulded by the system of which it is a part. 'Nothing is more dependent on economic conditions,' said Engels, 'than the army and navy. Armament, military structure and organisation, tactics and strategy, depend primarily on the existing level of production and on communications'.[47] This relationship works two ways – from capitalism to military competition and, once in place, military competition feeds back into the cycle of capitalist development. In the most extreme case, as happened between 1914 and 1918, and again between 1939 and 1945, this competitive struggle could take the form of total war. Many of the normal features of 'peaceful' competition were suppressed, the better to maximise other features that would allow the enemy to be defeated on the field of battle. The extent of these pressures in the 1920s can be seen in the record of global arms spending. Peace ended the military mobilisation of 1914-18. But by 1929, with the exception of Weimar Germany and Soviet Russia, most states had returned to or exceeded their pre-war levels of arms spending.[48]

But pressure from the world economy also arose from a more narrowly economic direction. Russia badly needed trade and investment. Its isolation meant that the terms on which these were available were set by the wider interests of Western capitalism. Little investment was in fact forthcoming in the 1920s despite the efforts to attract it through various concessions. Trade relations were re-established, but the threat was that more competitive goods from abroad would flood into the economy in exchange for foodstuffs and raw materials. 'We are connected with the external market from which we cannot tear ourselves away,' Grigorii Sokolnikov, a leading Bolshevik and one-time commissar of finance, told the Fourteenth Congress in December 1925. Cheap commodities, said Zinoviev, were the 'heavy artillery' that would break the revolution's defences.[49] The state monopoly of foreign trade was an attempt to reduce this threat. By having trade flow through a controlled channel, it was hoped to limit the direct pressure of the world market. But this insulation was relative rather than absolute. What it in effect meant was subsidised protection to domestic producers. And the greater the gap between the price and quality of domestic products, the greater the costs.

THE INTERNAL CONTRADICTIONS OF NEP

If the external problems of NEP were enormous, so too were the internal ones. The central question appeared to be the balance of power between the different social groups, which in turn was seen to rest on economic relations. There was little real threat from the old bourgeoisie. Their position had been undermined by revolution, civil war and emigration. But in the towns a new class of traders or 'Nep Men' arose, some with wealth that they were happy to flaunt. However, the bigger problem appeared to be in the countryside. In 1917 the peasants had been allies of the revolution. During the civil war the majority had oscillated between support and neutrality. Now a longer term relationship had to be established with the mass of the population. This involved cooperation, an alliance or *smychka*. 'A proletarian dictatorship which is in a state of war with the peasantry can in no way be strong,' said Bukharin. But two factors complicated this. One was the problem of social differentiation in the countryside. We have seen how there had been a considerable levelling effect, but as the countryside began to recover so too did a degree of social differentiation. There were widespread fears that a richer peasant class of kulaks, owning more land and animals, and employing hired labour, might form the basis of a new rural bourgeoisie. This sense that the countryside was both ally and threat was widely taken up in the 1920s. 'The kulak in the countryside is far more dangerous than the Nep Man in the towns,' said Zinoviev.[50]

The second problem was economic. In a peasant country it appeared that the greater part of the surplus for the development of urban industry had to come from the countryside. Yevgenii Preobrazhensky, a leading left wing economist, borrowed a term from Marx's discussion of early capitalism and talked of 'primitive socialist accumulation'.

> *The more economically backward, petty bourgeois and peasant in character is the country making the transition to a socialist organisation of production, the smaller is the legacy which the proletariat of the country receives at the moment of socialist revolution to build up its own socialist accumulation, and the more in proportion this socialist accumulation will be obliged to rely on the expropriation of the surplus of production of pre-socialist forms of the economy.*

In the light of what happened later it was an unfortunate choice of terms. Many have since interpreted 'primitive' to mean 'crude' and 'exploitative'. But Preobrazhensky wanted 'accumulation by way of an appropriate price policy' which would transfer more of the rural surplus to the process of rebuilding industry. In 1922 he had written that a return to 'non-economic suppression would be a terrible mistake'.[51] But squeezing the peasants too much might create serious political problems for the *smychka*. It could also backfire economically, for the countryside was also a major market. 'The greater the buying power of the peasantry, the faster our industry develops,' said Nikolai Bukharin in opposition to Preobrazhensky. It was this view that came to define the policy of the centre in the 1920s. It meant that development had to be conditioned by the need to keep the support of the mass of peasants even if, as Bukharin said, this meant development at 'a snail's pace'. He went further. Rural prosperity would consolidate the *smychka* and the economic recovery, and thus 'to the peasants, to all the peasants, we must say: "Enrich yourselves, develop your farms, and do not fear that constraints will be put upon you".'

To critics of Bukharin and the centre these arguments seemed to play into the hands of the wealthier peasants, the kulaks. They made the revolution a prisoner of the countryside. The argument therefore polarised between those who wanted to strengthen the revolution by a bigger transfer of resources, and those who feared that it was just such a policy that would weaken it, and that more balanced growth had to be preserved.[52]

This whole discussion was based on the assumption that NEP would continue into the indefinite future. It was an argument about the emphasis within it. It was also an argument that shifted as development took place in the 1920s. Although there was sustained recovery, its speed varied, especially in relation to rural conditions. When a balance existed between town and country, things went well. When it did not, political controversy sharpened.

Hindsight enables us to pose these issues of the external and internal contradictions of NEP more clearly than was done at the time, but it also disables us if we become blasé in the face of the originality of these dilemmas. The eventual solution that the group around Stalin would find was a policy of state-directed industrialisation. Resources would be squeezed from *both* peasants and workers to help build up a heavy industrial base to support a strong military defence of Russia. But nothing like this had ever been attempted before. It is true that elements can be found before 1914, as weak states, including Tsarist Russia, responded to the economic and military challenges of backwardness. But these were only elements. War had involved massive controls, but in the 1920s peacetime levels of state action were still low in every country compared with what would develop subsequently. Originality also arose from the way that these problems were being discussed by revolutionaries who had never intended or wanted to be in this situation. They were groping in the dark. Sometimes their dilemmas and possible outcomes could be illuminated by sharp insights, but no one was able to pull these together in a consistent way until much later. Most importantly, the originality arose from the way that the ability to solve these problems was limited by the nature of the degenerating revolution. This created both theoretical and practical limits to these debates. The crucial theoretical limitation was that no one thought in terms of massive exploitation of the working class or peasantry. Everyone recognised that progress depended on the reinvestment of a surplus, but they assumed that this was limited politically and socially by the non-capitalist nature of the regime. Both Bukharin and Preobrazhensky shared the view that there were limits to the extent that the standard of living of the working class could be held down. Their differences on the peasantry did not extend to Preobrazhensky imagining anything on the scale that eventually happened. It is true that in 1928-29 he and others did see in the beginning of Stalin's new policies a move in the direction of their arguments, but they were quickly disabused. Preobrazhensky, deprived of the right to speak openly in the 1930s, still denied the idea that Stalin's policies were in any sense his:

> *Collectivisation, that is the essential point. Did I foresee collectivisation? I did not... Neither Marx nor Engels...visualised just how village life would be revolutionised... What was needed was Stalin's remarkable farsightedness, his great courage in facing the problems, the great hardness in applying policies.*[53]

But, as we have suggested, these limits rested on more than ideas. Basic forms of capitalist relations began to reassert themselves in the 1920s. But their complete sway was limited both by elements of continuing dislocation and the remnants of the heritage of 1917, even though these were progressively weakening over time. Generating the surplus necessary to drive the economy forward therefore required the destruction of these elements. The ambiguities in the role of the state had to be removed. Workers and peasants had to be firmly subordinated to the goal of competitive accumulation. This required leaders at the top to push these policies. But it also needed a group beneath them on whom they could base their policies, and whose interests they would themselves reflect. This process of bureaucratic degeneration towards a new class marked the whole of the 1920s, and it stood behind the great political debates of the time.

BUREAUCRATIC DEGENERATION

In 1921 no one could be happy with the extent to which power rested on 'state' and 'party'. Within the party the Workers' Opposition argued that power should be shifted to the trade unions as representatives of the working class. But this too was an illusion. Trade unions were also victims of the collapsed working class base. 'The industrial proletariat is *déclassé*,' said Lenin in October 1921. 'It has ceased to exist as a proletariat. Since the great capitalist industry is ruined and the factories immobilised, the proletariat has disappeared'.[54] The aspirations of the Workers' Opposition were admirable, but the workers whose name they evoked were as ghostly a presence as those in whose name the leadership spoke. When Lenin invoked the leading role of the party at the Eleventh Party Congress in the spring of 1922 Shliapnikov, one of the Workers' Opposition leaders, said: 'Permit me to congratulate you on being the vanguard of a non-existent class.' It was a bitter reproach. It was an accurate reproach. But it pointed to the difficulty of everyone's position, including Shliapnikov's himself. No one could find a quick solution to this dilemma.

The immediate response was for the party to try to buy time to help heal the wounds, by drawing closer together and finding new ways of resisting bureaucratic pressures while society recovered. In March 1921, at the Tenth Party Congress, it was agreed to ban factions. In this desperate situation the party could not afford organised internal opposition. With hindsight it is easy to see this as a disastrous mistake, especially as attempts to deal with the issue of bureaucratisation failed. But what the ban on factions became was not what it began as. It was not intended as a permanent policy. It was not intended to stifle debate. The aim was to avoid the party being pulled apart. Ironically debate was perhaps more intense after it. The 1920s saw a mass of de facto factions supporting different positions. But the weakness of the party was reflected in the way that the ban became semi-permanent and then permanent. It did help to legitimise the power of the centre, and to delegitimise those who tried to fight against it.

Measures were also taken to try to reduce the build-up of bureaucratic layers in state and party. Again there were contradictions. In April 1922 Stalin was made general secretary of the party to help introduce some order to its internal workings. Attempts were also made to strengthen inspection of the party and state to reduce corruption. But these were essentially a bureaucratic response to a problem of bureaucracy.

Lenin saw much of this clearly. 'The proletarian policy of the party is not determined by the character of the membership, but by the undivided prestige enjoyed by the small group that might be called the old guard of the party,' he said. But this group did not have an infinite capacity to float above circumstances. It had already been affected, and would quickly be affected more by the pressure of the situation. This was only in part a question of material privileges. The real issue was more the way that people reacted to the wider situation. The affectation of self-discipline and morality might be made, it might even be there in reality, but behind it ideas and policies would shift in ways not anticipated when the leadership had to engage with a genuine party based on a vibrant working class.

Lenin's struggle with these developing tendencies – it has been called his 'last struggle' – is important, because it helps to give the lie to simple claims of continuity from Lenin to Stalin. Indeed, the struggle came to focus on his fears about Stalin. This partly reflected Lenin's acute political sense. But there was another dimension. In May 1922 he had his first stroke, a second in mid-December and a third in March 1923. In the intervening months he was forced to detach himself from day to day politics. This perhaps gave him a sharper sense of the scale of the problems.

Lenin's first inkling of the extent to which a different politics, culture and behaviour was developing at the top of the party came in late 1922. He learned that Stalin and Sergo Ordzhonikidze had been bullying Georgian

Communists over the nature of Georgia's relationship with the plans for a federal union. Ordzhonikidze was even reported to have assaulted one of the Georgians. Lenin immediately dictated a memorandum attacking 'this 100 percent Russian phenomenon, Great Russian chauvinism, which is characteristic of the Russian bureaucracy.' Then, fearing what his death would bring, he dictated his testament in December 1922. This warned against splits but also set out the strengths and weaknesses of his comrades. 'Comrade Stalin,' he said, 'since he became general secretary, has concentrated enormous power in his hands.' With more information coming through on 4 January he added a postscript suggesting that 'Stalin is too rude, and this defect, though quite tolerable in our midst and in dealings among us Communists, becomes intolerable in a general secretary. This is why I suggest that the comrades think about a way to remove Stalin from that post.' In the next weeks, despite his failing health, he worked on more proposals to reorganise the supervisory agencies that Stalin led. Then he learned that his wife had been on the receiving end of Stalin's abuse and bullying. Gathering his strength, he dictated a personal rebuke to Stalin, with copies to Kamenev and Zinoviev, a letter of support to the Georgians, with copies to Trotsky and Kamenev, and a note to Trotsky asking him to take up the Georgian question. This was followed by a verbal message that he was preparing to come out against Stalin. But three days later his failing body suffered its third catastrophic stroke.

Paralysed and speechless, drained of his earlier looks, Lenin's image was captured on photographs. They were images of a ghost. His political life had been cut down in May 1922, and it ended completely in March 1923. What happened next was fatal for the revolution. Fearing division, the leadership pulled together, and agreed to ignore Lenin's warnings and proposals. They would bitterly regret this, because such was the speed with which Stalin was accumulating power that he was able quickly to consolidate his position. When the Twelfth Party Congress took place in April 1923 the delegates from Georgia were the centre's supporters, not its victims.

This was only possible because of the underestimation of the speed and extent of the degeneration. And the situation would quickly worsen further. The state apparatus partly incorporated structures from the old regime. Much of it also reflected the restructuring of activity after 1917, the takeover of previously 'private' functions and the development of new ones. This makes it almost impossible to compare the numbers of the Tsarist and early Soviet bureaucracy. Their structures were quite different. Lenin, however, feared that there was too much continuity: 'With the exception of the People's Commissariat of Foreign Affairs, our state apparatus is very largely a survival of the old one, and has least of all undergone serious change. It has only been slightly repainted on the surface, but in all other things it is a typical relic of our old state apparatus.' In fact the quantitative continuity varied, but this was perhaps less significant than the qualitative pull of the old groups and the old ways: 'The culture [of the bureaucrats] is wretched and contemptible, but it is still higher than ours.' Together the administrative layers of the state and the party represented an enormous vested interest. 'If we take the huge bureaucratic machine [the state], that huge pile...we must ask: who is leading whom? To tell the truth, it is not they [the Communists] who are leading, they are being led,' said Lenin. And again: 'The machine refused to obey the hand that guided it. It was like a car that was not going in the direction the driver desired, but in a direction someone else desired, as if it were being driven by a mysterious, lawless hand, god knows where'.[55]

As general secretary of the party, Stalin – 'Comrade Card Index' – was the person who was able to capitalise on much of this. Into the secretariat and working closely with it came lesser names who would later help Stalin run Soviet Russia – men like Viacheslav Molotov, Valerian Kuibyshev and Lazar Kaganovich. Those who were oppositionists or suspect were moved to the periphery. Sometimes, as in the case of Nikolai Krestinsky or Christian Rakovsky, they were sent abroad as ambassadors with the approval of the Politburo. But this was only the tip of the iceberg. Within a year of Stalin taking up his position 37 provincial secretaries were removed in 50 provinces of European Russia, around 10,000 assignments were made, and all this before Lenin's third stroke. By the time of his death things were beginning to be unrecognisable. 'The present regime...is much further from any workers' democracy than was the regime of the fiercest period of War Communism,' said Trotsky in autumn of 1923.[56] In *Pravda* another party member complained:

> During the last year the conservatism of the committees has increased. In some committees the idea of elections has been entirely given up, and the constitution of the party is flouted... The minutes of the committees consist of nothing but orders... The way in which the committees are being transformed into bureaucratic departments controlled by a lot of unnecessary officials is simply deplorable... A Communist must now regard his local committee no longer as the centre of his political life, but an institution which, on the one hand, may supply him with a position and help him in his career, or, on the other, may punish him, or expel him from the party.[57]

The numbers on the Central Committee were increased from 27 full members in 1922 to 63 in 1925 and 71 in 1927. The idea was to broaden its composition. The reality was that Stalin was able to fill it with loyal and efficient administrators, like the provincial secretary Anastas Mikoyan. In 1921 only 20 percent of CC members had been party officials. By 1924 the figure was 38 percent and in 1927 it was 45 percent. In that year another 20 percent of members came from the economic administration. The domination of officialdom could also be seen in the party congresses. At the Tenth Party Congress in 1921 24.8 percent of delegates were party officials. At the Twelfth Congress in April 1923 the figure was already 55.1 percent. This, said Trotsky later, was the last real congress of the party. A year later, in May 1924, at the Thirteenth Congress the share of party officials was 65.3 percent, and not a single member of the opposition was elected as a voting delegate.[58]

By the mid-1920s there were 25,000 party officials over whom the membership had little influence. At the turn of 1924 Bukharin described the balance of power in party life in terms no less damning than the opposition:

> To judge by the Moscow organisation, the secretaries of the party cells are usually appointed by the district committee... Normally the putting of the question to a vote takes place in a set pattern. They come and ask the meeting 'Who is against?' and since people more or less fear to speak out against, the individual in question finds himself elected secretary of the bureau of the cell... The same thing can be observed in a somewhat modified form in all other stages of the party hierarchy as well.[59]

Both in the party and the state, the administrative layers were prey to external and internal pressures. Compared with the Tsarist period they were hardly privileged. But they did have privileges and a different lifestyle.[60] There was a natural tendency to want to preserve and develop this. No less these layers also had confidence in their own abilities, their contribution to the regime and the regime's reliance on them. Stalin flattered exactly these tendencies. The party secretaries, he said, were 'an order of Teutonic knights at the centre of the Soviet state'.[61]

When the developing oppositions attacked the leadership, the leaders often responded by an ever stronger denunciation of bureaucracy. But there was a ritual character to this. The centre had no solution. A part of a 1927 CC resolution reflected this impasse:

> The group of Communist employees, numbering hundreds of thousands in recent years, constitutes a barrier, because of its relative weight, to the altogether natural desire of the party to retain the dominant influence of those workers who are directly engaged in industry. On the other hand there are too few party members in the directing force and employee personnel of the government apparatus. To strengthen Communist influence, it would be necessary to expand the membership in the party of government employees.[62]

Did the growing weight of this bureaucratic group suggest a more basic threat? Bukharin, for example, speculated that 'the embryo of a new ruling class might emerge through the control of the state'. But he drew back at the implications of this, expressing a naive faith in the party to deal with this prospect. The opposition had fewer illusions, but they too were reluctant to face the implications that a new class might be emerging. But in 1930 Christian Rakovsky and a group of the opposition more broadly broached this possibility: 'Before our very eyes there has been and is being formed a large *class of rulers* with their own subdivisions, growing though controlled co-option... What unites this peculiar sort of class is the peculiar sort of property, namely state power.' The bureaucracy, he said, was not yet a class, 'but it is the nucleus of a class, which will not be the bureaucracy but another hitherto unknown one. Its appearance will mean that the working class will become another oppressed class. The bureaucracy is the nucleus of some kind of capitalist class, controlling the state and collectively owning the means of production'.[63]

The problem was not simply social. The emergence of this layer helped to shift the ideological perspectives of the regime. At the time of the war with Poland sections of the party had began to bend towards a more nationalist position, but so long as international revolution was felt to be a more immediate possibility movements in this direction were restrained. After 1921 the space for these widened. It widened more after 1923, when a revolutionary crisis arose first in Bulgaria and then, more importantly, in Germany. In both cases inexperienced leaders threw away possibilities that might have led to success, and the depressive significance of this in the Soviet Union was enormous. Capitalism appeared to be stabilising, and isolation was now at least a medium term scenario. The doctrine of socialism in one country was a response to this. It was first suggested by Bukharin and then taken up by Stalin. Russia, they argued, did have the capacity to develop on its own. International revolution would be a help but it was not a precondition for major advance. The doctrine appeared in a full blooded form in April 1924 at the Fourteenth Party Congress. Stalin now said, overturning the argument that he had supported as much as anyone else, that 'in general the victory of socialism (not in the sense of final victory) is unconditionally possible in one country'. The full implications of this were not understood, though ironically some on the right who had been opposed to the revolution (and even fought against it) were now attracted to what they saw as new Great Power possibilities. Russia, they said, was becoming a 'radish' – red on the outside, white on the inside.[64]

When Trotsky and others insisted that the original goals of international revolution remained a precondition for a real deepening of the revolution (rather than some economic progress), many no doubt did feel that socialism in one country was practical politics compared with revolutionary romanticism. This argument had a special appeal to the controlling layers that we have been examining. It was they who would lead the Soviet Union forward, their skills, their abilities that it was being suggested that progress depended on. The opposite view risked what they had achieved and cast doubt on their role. Of course, if international revolution came, then at this stage no one would have objected, but in its absence the balance had to be tipped to put the new regime first.

ᵈ⅊ 3.2 SOCIALISM IN ONE COUNTRY

The replacement of the internationalism of the early revolution by the idea of socialism in one country is often seen as a victory for 'political realism' over 'revolutionary romanticism'. But the idea that there was an indissoluble link between revolution in Russia and its progress abroad was based on realism about the internal and external difficulties an isolated state would face. 'Socialism in one country' quickly backfired. It was an accommodation to nationalist perspectives. Externally, faced with enemies, Soviet Russia was forced into a more conventional diplomatic and military policy. Internally the weight of resolving backwardness was thrown onto the Russian people. Moreover this was now to be done in separation from the wider achievement of global capitalism. In the long run none of this proved 'realistic'.

As the doctrine of 'socialism in one country' began to affect policy, it created new contradictions within the international Communist movement. If 'socialism in one country' was 'political realism', then perhaps there was a contradiction between the immediate interests of Russia and those of the wider socialist movement? In 1923 the failure of Communists in Bulgaria and Germany to seize revolutionary opportunities was due as much to incompetence as the malign influence from Moscow. By 1926-27, however, the international movement was clearly being manipulated from there. By 1928-29 it was completely subordinate. Moscow used the Communist movement as a foreign policy tool. The chances of radical change were lost. 'Realism' was now loyalty to Stalin and his great power goals. 'A socialist state [sic], I believe, in that position can do no wrong, and is doing no wrong…so these are the reasons why personally I commenced to turn political somersaults, because this is what it means,' said the British Communist philosopher Maurice Cornforth in 1939.[vii] *His 'realism' simply earned him the ridicule of history. Others paid the ultimate price for putting their belief in loyalty to Stalin and a great power above international socialism. Some 1,400 Communists who fled to Stalin's Russia expecting sanctuary ware shot in the purges.*[viii] *Many others died in the camps. It would be left to others on the margins of the international socialist movement to keep alive the vision of a genuine socialist internationalism as an alternative to global capitalism.*

AN INERT PARTY, AN INERT CLASS?

To understand the muteness of so much of the party the extent of the rot therein needs to be appreciated. As NEP began to get under way in August-December 1921 a party cleansing or purge – the word had a quite different meaning then, simply meaning the withdrawal of cards – took place. Around 175,000 members were expelled as unworthy. But the rot went deeper. Many of those considering the fate of others may have been no more immune from the disease that they were trying to cure. Before his death Lenin argued for 'fewer but better' members to limit the problem. But after his death, ironically in his name, the leadership agreed to a massive expansion of the party. The result was to create a huge base of more pliable members. Table 3.3 shows the basic data.

TABLE 3.3. MEMBERSHIP OF THE COMMUNIST PARTY, 1917-29[65]

October 1917	200,000-350,000
March 1920	611,978
March 1921	730,000
1922	514,800
1923	485,600
1924	472,000
1925	798,804
1926	1,078,185
1927	1,147,074
1928	1,304,471
1929	1,532,362

The huge expansion is clear. But so too is the qualitative impact. By 1927-28 the majority of members were tools of the centre. The generation of 1917 or before had been reduced to 5 percent of the membership, that of the years 1918-20 to 29 percent. Around 66 percent of members by the end of the 1920s had joined in the NEP years, most after the death of Lenin.[66] They lacked confidence in their own abilities. The cult of Lenin became a crutch for them and the party more generally. In 1925 alone 6,296 titles of 'Leninania' were published.[67] Radek called it 'political priestcraft', and condemned 'the hysterical estimate of Lenin's historical role'.[68] 'Leninism' became a catechism to be learned. From Stalin's *Foundations of Leninism* they learned that, instead

of unity coming from vibrant debate, what was important was voluntary sub-
mission to iron discipline. Internal opposition was 'pollution', a product of
'opportunism', and 'the party becomes strong by purging itself of opportunist
elements'. Lenin's ideas became as much a corpse as the body in the tomb.
And just as that sterile body occasionally needed a new nose or ear to preserve
the illusion, so new elements of 'Leninism' were grafted onto the catechism as
they were needed.

But there is a no less dramatic indicator of the changed nature of the party
which few commentators have noticed. This is the disappearance of the
'revolutionary generation', much of which had died or melted away. In 1924
Preobrazhensky regretted the way that death was carrying off the old
Bolsheviks – they were 'becoming extinct faster than the cherry orchards in
Turgenev's nests of gentlefolk were being cleared'.[69] As we saw in the previous chapter, the mass growth of the Bolshevik Party in 1917 left a confusing
pattern of evidence in terms of numbers. If the party did indeed have
350,000 members, then by 1927 only 11 percent were still in the party. If the
1917 figure was nearer 200,000, then 20 percent remained. Either figure
was catastrophic in terms of continuity with 1917. Around 80-90 percent of
the revolutionary generation who had known the exhilaration of its heights
and aspirations had gone.[70]

Workers, too, were a prisoner of the situation. The numerical recovery of the
industrial core of the working class is set out in table 3.4.

TABLE 3.4. NUMBER OF WORKERS IN LARGE-SCALE INDUSTRY[71]

1917	2,596,400
1921	1,185,500
1922	1,096,200
1923	1,434,600
1924	1,548,700
1925	1,781,900
1926	2,261,700
1927	2,365,800
1928	2,531,900
1929	2,788,700

This social recovery did not automatically mean political recovery, but it was a precondition for it. As can be seen, by 1928-29 numbers were back to levels similar to those a decade earlier. But this had been a slow process. Many of the formal and informal workplace and community structures that had been so important in supporting confidence in 1917 had been wrecked or transformed. Many workers had gone through hell to survive, and were different from what they had been in 1917. Indeed, many of those who had been in the workplace in 1917 were no longer to be found there during NEP. The evidence for this lies in data (which has not always been properly interpreted) from surveys at the end of the 1920s. In the cotton industry, for example, by 1929 just over half the workers had an employment length of 12 years or more, in engineering and oil it was only 35-40 percent, and in coal it was less than 30 percent.[72]

Conditions remained poor in the towns. Unemployment was widespread and everyday life remained difficult. It is perhaps not surprising that when Eisenstein's film mythologisation of October was shown in 1927 some Russian audiences preferred the even more mythological vision of the silent Hollywood classic *Robin Hood*.[73] But the positive side of NEP did pull a wider section of the working class into activities of various kinds that reflected a spiritual and political growth. Inside the workplace too there were conflicts and difficulties. In 1921-22 184,000 workers struck, and 154,000 in 1922-23. Thereafter the number of strikers declined to 50,000 in 1924 and 20,000 in 1927.[74] The difficulty was that effective leadership of the working class did not develop. This was partly because enthusiastic workers were swept up into administrative positions. One estimate is that as many as 20,000 Communists a year left the workbench for white collar jobs in the 1920s.[75] It was also because 'protesting' and 'striking' against the 'workers' state' created tensions for everyone. Then, when protests became associated with the opposition, they became even more difficult.

Recovery did improve the material condition of the workers, but it remained limited by the contradictions of NEP that we have analysed. These worsened in 1927-28. Trotsky and the left insisted that 'a socialist advance ceases to be such if it does not uninterruptedly, openly and tangibly improve the material position of the working class in its daily life'.[76] But Communists in the factory were expected to help pacify the workers in the interests of the policy of the centre. Their difficulties can easily be imagined. Tellingly, in April 1929 at one Moscow factory meeting a woman said: 'Although I am a Communist I am still for the working class'.[77]

THE POLITICAL RISE OF STALIN

It was Stalin and the people who loyally supported him who eventually emerged as the beneficiaries of these processes. The battle to resist them and keep alive the revolution went through three stages. Each of these involved four main issues: bureaucratisation; the balance between town and country, worker and peasant; the related questions of the rate of development; and the problem of international revolution or socialism in one country. Positions changed and to an extent clarified over time, and none of the participants, including Stalin, initially had a clear idea of where things were heading. But building on his band of supporters he began to develop, especially from 1927, a clearer vision of a way forward that no one had anticipated before.

With Lenin incapacitated, the party leaders made a strong show of collective unity. 'To lead the party otherwise than collectively is impossible. Now Ilyich [Lenin] is not with us it is silly to dream of such a thing, it is silly to talk about it,' said Stalin.[78] But tensions emerged between the dominant figures of Zinoviev, Kamenev and Stalin (the 'Troika'), and the left, with Trotsky at the head. In this first phase between 1922 and 1925 the left rallied around a policy of a return to earlier democratic traditions, support for international revolution, and a faster rate of internal development, if necessary by putting more pressure on the peasants, in order to ease the economic difficulties, and strengthen the political and social base of the revolution. It is symptomatic of how difficult things had become that at the January 1924 conference, held just before Lenin died, the leadership so manipulated things that on a key resolution they had 125 votes to the opposition's three. Following Lenin's death, therefore, an audience was already in place to respond to Stalin's quasi-religious vows to fulfil Lenin's 'behest with honour'. When word began to get out of Lenin's doubts about Stalin, Zinoviev assured the party that 'the fears of Lenin have not been confirmed'.

The conflict now moved to a second phase. The troika quickly began to break up under the pressure of events in 1924-25. Zinoviev and Kamenev now realised how much power Stalin was accumulating. Zinoviev also sensed the extent to which Stalin's arguments for socialism in one country marked a serious break. Indeed, he was at first more publicly identified with opposition to Stalin on this issue than Trotsky. The two also feared what they saw as the excessively pro-peasant orientation pushed by Bukharin with Stalin's support. However, at this stage the tension between Zinoviev, Kamenev, and Trotsky and the left was too great for an alliance to be made. Zinoviev and Kamenev presented strong indictments of the policies of Stalin and those around him, which culminated at the Fourteenth Party Congress in December 1925. But the system that they had used to defeat the left was now turned against them. Mikoyan taunted Zinoviev that 'when there is a majority for Zinoviev he is for iron discipline, for subordination. When he has no majority...he is against it.' Kamenev was met with jeers when he told the congress: 'I have come to the conviction that Comrade Stalin cannot fulfil the role of unifier of the Bolshevik general staff. We are against the doctrine of one-man rule. We are against the creation of a "chief".' But it was Stalin who was able to present himself as the unifier and the moderate, and to appeal to his placemen. On the key resolution Zinoviev and Kamenev were defeated by 559 votes to 65, with all the 65 coming from Zinoviev's Leningrad base.[79]

Their defeat saw their marginalisation. At the centre policy was now under the influence of Stalin, with Nikolai Bukharin as chief theorist, Aleksei Rykov as prime minister and economic leader, and Mikhail Tomsky heading the trade unions. Together they pushed further down the road of socialism in one country, seeing the New Economic Policy as a longer term basis for internal development, and further weakening the commitment to international revolution. Trotsky, Zinoviev, Kamenev and their supporters now made common cause, and the middle phase of opposition moved into its second moment. But the United Opposition was subject to renewed ideological onslaughts, and their supporters continued to be bureaucratically pushed aside. In October and November 1926 Zinoviev, Kamenev and Trotsky were removed from the Politburo. Zinoviev and Kamenev would soon make their peace, but Trotsky refused to yield personally and politically. From September to November 1927 he was successively removed from the Comintern, the Central Committee and the party. Trying to defend himself in October he was verbally abused by Central Committee members. Inkwells, glasses and books were thrown at him, and one CC member tried to pull him off the platform. Later other leading oppositionists were beaten up when the flat of Trotsky's supporter Smilga was raided. In this poisonous atmosphere Adolf Joffe, a leading oppositionist, committed suicide, driven to despair by what was becoming of the revolution he had fought for.[80]

The battle at the top now turned to its third and final stage. The ascendancy of Bukharin, Rykov and Tomsky alongside Stalin was shortlived. From mid-1927 onwards the Stalin group, at first only gingerly, began to push a harder line in the countryside, and pushed for a more sustained industrialisation. This shift is often portrayed as arising from internal factors. The economy was reaching the limits of recovery and needed new investment. The peasants were more reluctant to yield grain to the towns, trying to force concessions and higher prices. The truth of both arguments is contested. But the more serious problem is that this focus misses the key issue, which was the perception that Russia's external situation was worsening.[81]

The failure of the general strike in Britain in 1926 seemed another wasted opportunity. More seriously perhaps, in May 1926 a military coup in Poland gave effective control to Pilsudski, the invader in 1920. Consciousness of the war threat was stimulated throughout the country by the founding of a mass organisation, the Society of Friends of Defence, Aviation and Chemical Construction, in January 1927, with over 2 million members.[82] In the spring problems worsened when revolution in China was defeated. As in the early

❧ 3.3 THE LEFT OPPOSITION

At the end of the 1920s Stalin was pragmatically groping for a solution that suited the social layer around him. His opponents were groping too, trying to understand what was happening to the revolution. It was the Left Opposition which made the clearest defence of the revolutionary heritage. But their difficulty was to know where the real challenge was coming from and what form it was taking. We have the advantage of hindsight. They did not. They knew the power of Stalin and the bureaucracy was growing. They knew the party was failing the workers. But who or what was the greater enemy? What was the nature of the party-state bureaucracy? Was it still possible to rescue the party?

They called Stalin's group 'centrist', believing that it swung between left and right. In this way they underestimated Stalin himself. They also underestimated the capacity of the layer he represented to lash out against both the workers and the peasants. They retained some faith in the party's capacity to heal itself.

In 1927 and 1928 a groundswell of workers' discontent grew as problems mounted for the regime. 'Opposition activity was spreading like a river in flood. The opposition organised mass meetings of industrial workers. At a chemical plant in Moscow shouts were heard: "Down with Stalin's dictatorship! Down with the Politburo!"[ix] But should the opposition use their limited room for manoeuvre inside the party for reform or mobilise without? Their dilemmas intensified in 1928-29 when Stalin led the harder line in the countryside. Was this the 'centre' zigzagging again and responding to calls for more emphasis on industry to help improve the position of the workers, or was it something new? Misconceiving it as a temporary turn in their direction many of the Left Opposition went along with it at first. 'In its own barbaric and sometimes stupid way, the Central Committee is building for the future,' they said. It was a fatal mistake.

The objective situation of the left worked against success. But their faulty and incomplete analysis also contributed to their problems. It would only be possible to go beyond this when the more permanent form of the new system became clear. But the left would struggle to understand this from their prison cells — victims of the counter-revolution from above.[x]

cases of Bulgaria and Germany, the weaknesses of local Communists and mis-guided, even stupid, policies from Moscow were the cause. But this was still a major setback. In May the British government, followed by Canada, appeared to invent a pretext to break off diplomatic relations. The threat this implied was the greater given that Britain was still the leading global power, and a number of other states had not re-established relations with Soviet Russia. Then in June the Soviet ambassador in Poland was assassinated. A nationwide 'defence week' was held in July, and over the summer a war scare developed in Russia and especially Moscow.

It is now commonplace to disparage the threat of war in 1927, which, given the prevalence of war in modern foreign policy, seems rather naive. The threat was certainly manipulated by the party leadership. But they were reacting to genuine sabre-rattling. It was this that brought home the hole at the centre of the doctrine of socialism in one country. How could Russia defend itself if its development could only take place 'at a snail's pace'? But if more rapid development was attempted this would come up against the limits of NEP. From late 1927 these limits began to be stretched. This underpinned the idea of faster industrialisation. It underpinned the harsher line in the countryside. 'In addition to the usual taxes...the peasantry also pays a certain super-tax in the form of overpayment for manufactured goods, and in the form of an under-payment received for agricultural produce... We need this super-tax to stimulate the development of our industry and to do away with backwardness,' argued Stalin in April 1929.[83] Discussion about peasant resistance and the challenge of richer peasants or kulaks complicated matters, but they should not be allowed to obscure the basis of the shift.

The stronger policy of the centre created confusion in the ranks of the opposition, because at first it seemed as if the Stalin group was bending to their arguments. Those who bent would quickly be disabused of any illusions. Trotsky insisted that there could be no compromise with Stalin, because there was no change in the political ascendancy of the bureaucracy. Then, as 1928 became 1929, pressure was increased to drive the economy forward. Bukharin and others began to oppose Stalin too. But, even more than the earlier oppositionists, they were prisoners of the system, and much of their protest was carried out behind closed doors. Nevertheless in their panic there were more flashes of insight into the scale of what might happen and their eventual fates. But they were now powerless to resist effectively.

CONCLUSIONS

Ever since, the scale and speed of Stalin's victory have created a degree of bafflement. We have tried to show that it is explicable in terms of several elements. The first and most important was the enormous pressure created first by the civil war, and then by internal and external isolation at the start of NEP. The 'old guard' was left with authority but no base to resist the wider pressures that Lenin had sensed. Stalin certainly played a clever game, but we need to beware here. Stalin did use the situation, but he was also a product of it. He manipulated the party and to an extent the workers, but the weaknesses he used were products of bigger factors. His victory was a personal victory, but it was also a social and a political one. Less principled than Trotsky and the left, or even Zinoviev, Kamenev, Bukharin, Rykov, Tomsky and many others, he was prepared to bend the regime, to be able to drive it forward in a new direction. Whatever the political deficiencies of his opponents – whether Trotsky, the strongest, or Bukharin, one of the weakest – it is to their credit that they held as long as they could to a different vision that was still marked by the ideas of emancipation that characterised 1917.

In 1928 at the Moscow party conference, Molotov was a handed a note, which he read out:

> Comrade Molotov! You shout about self-criticism, but if someone would criticise the dictatorship of Stalin and his group, then tomorrow he will fly from his post, from his job, to the devil, to prison, and further. Don't think that people follow you and vote for you unanimously. Many are against you, but are afraid to lose a crust of bread and their privileges. Believe me, all the peasantry is against you. Long live Leninism! Down with the Stalinist dictatorship![84]

Captured here was the sense of betrayal and hostility – the idea of degeneration – felt by some members. Here is the frustration with the way in which the leadership was able to use both the stick of fear and the carrot of privilege to defend itself. But above all there is the fact that Molotov felt confident enough to read out the note. Stalin and his supporters were now on the verge of going a step further. Through counter-revolution from above, what was left of the revolution would finally be destroyed and a new regime ruthlessly created. This was a different kind of defeat to that which the socialist movement 'normally' experiences when swings in mass consciousness to the left are followed by swings to the right. Unless the counter-revolution is exceptionally nihilistic, as with Nazism, such swings often leave grounds for hope. Thus in Russia in 1905 revolution had been defeated by brutal counter-revolution, but within 12 years an even bigger and more radical revolution emerged in 1917. But the impact of the counter-revolution that developed at the end of the 1920s was different. Degeneration arose because the material circumstances changed in a way that became fatal for any hopes of the survival of the revolution. Degeneration closed off one road, but it opened up another for a new ruling class to take power.

In 1917 the Putilov works had been at the centre of revolutionary Petrograd. The reconstructed Kirov factory's architecture, like that of other Russian factories, told a story of alienation.

4 ACCUMULATION

In 1931 Stalin crystallised the logic of the new system that developed on the ashes of the Russian Revolution:

No comrades...the tempo must not be reduced! On the contrary we must increase it... To slacken the tempo would mean falling behind. And those who fall behind get beaten. No, we refuse to be beaten! One feature of old Russia was the continual beatings she suffered for falling behind, for her backwardness. She was beaten by the Mongol Khans. She was beaten by the Turkish beys. She was beaten by the Swedish feudal lords. She was beaten by the Polish-Lithuanian gentry. She was beaten by the Anglo-French capitalists. She was beaten by the Japanese barons. All beat her for her backwardness, her military backwardness, for cultural backwardness, for political backwardness, for industrial backwardness, for agricultural backwardness. She was beaten because to do so was profitable and could be done with impunity. Do you remember the words of the pre-revolutionary poet: 'You are poor and abundant, mighty and impotent, Mother Russia'... We are 50 or 100 years behind the advanced countries. We must make good this distance in 10 years. Either we do it or they crush us.[1]

These words evoked the dilemma of any backward state in the world economy, and they unconsciously echoed the dilemma of Tsarist Russia before 1914. In the 1890s the then finance minister Count Witte had tried to concentrate the minds of the Tsar and his circle with an almost identical formulation. What both Witte and Stalin expressed, four decades apart, was the pressure to drive a backward state forward in the search for national security. The aim was not to overturn global capitalism but beat it on its own terms. But it was Stalin who had the greater and more ruthless command of society. Andrew Rothstein, a loyal British follower, hardly exaggerated when he wrote that Stalin's comments, together with a second speech of June 1931, 'made an epoch in Soviet economic development... Stalin's remarks became part and parcel of the national consciousness, and particularly of that of the workers and managers in industry, by being worked over and discussed, at countless meetings and study circles'.[2] The logic of competitive development in one country became ingrained. In 1989 two liberal critics of the Stalinist system could still say of Stalin's vision that 'even today (to say nothing of the 1930s) this seems a conclusion that is impossible to ignore'.[3]

Moreover, since capitalist competition was dynamic the pressure was to keep moving. As one of Stalin's loyal economists pointed out in 1937: 'The task of catching up and surpassing the technical economic level of the advanced capitalist countries does not at all mean the achievement of some kind of immobile target. This target is itself dynamic. Despite the general crisis of capitalism, the economies of the capitalist countries are not at all in a state of total stagnation'.[4]

By the time that Stalin made his speech it had become obvious that the instability in the world economy had grown enormously. The 1927 war scare had brought home the vulnerability of the Soviet Union. The world economic crisis of 1929-33 reconfigured the relationships of the Great Powers in a way that would eventually lead to the second global war of the century. Trade and investment collapsed, partly from the crisis itself and partly from the protectionist measures that the capitalist powers used to defend themselves. Eventually the leaders of both the US and Britain would begin to pull back towards a more open global economy as the best way to maintain their ascendancy. But the challenging 'have not' powers such as Italy, Japan and Germany needed more clearly defined spheres of influence to assert themselves – a policy that was reinforced by the internal dynamics of far right and fascist politics at home. It was these pressures that were the fundamental determinant of policy in Stalin's Russia. The Soviet leadership continued to distrust old enemies like Britain and the United States, but the pressure of global competition increasingly concentrated minds on the nearer threat of Japan in the Far East and Nazi Germany in the West, and on the border states such as Poland, which often had hostile interests of their own, but which might also act as conduits for the pressures of bigger states behind them.

As the 1930s progressed, the pressures of military and economic competition took increasingly dangerous forms. In the Far East Japan moved into Manchuria in 1931 and China from 1937. A quarter of the Russian army was stationed in the Far East. Borders were fortified and railway links strengthened. Serious border clashes erupted with Japan at Lake Khasan in 1938 and

Khalkhin Gol in 1939, which involved 1 million troops.[5] In the West in 1935 Nazi Germany remilitarised, then in March 1938 came the Anschluss with Austria. Months later, after the Munich agreement of September 1938, came the dismemberment of Czechoslovakia and then, in March 1939, the seizure of Memel from nominal Lithuanian protection.

Having abandoned international revolution, the Soviet leadership knew that their security depended on a strengthened military. 'The defensive capacity of the Soviet Union does not depend on international combinations, but is grounded on the unfailing, growing power of the Red Army, Red Navy and Red Air Force,' Litvinov insisted in November 1937. But this 'growing power' required rapid and sustained industrialisation. This issue played a major role in the thinking about the first plan:

> In drawing up our five-year economic plan we must pay great attention to the rapid development of our economic system in general and of our war industries in particular, which will play the main role in consolidating the defensive powers of our country and ensure economic stability in the time of war. Industrialisation also means the development of our war industries.

In the summer of 1930, at the Sixteenth Party Congress, Voroshilov reiterated the point: 'The basis for the arming of our country lies in the accelerated development of our economic system, in the increase of metallurgical production, in the development of our chemical industries, in the production of motor cars and tractors, and in general in the development of our engineering industries'.[6]

This dynamic of military competition operated at several levels. In the first instance competitive pressures encouraged general industrialisation. 'A future war will be a war of factories,' Voroshilov had said in 1927. 'We consider the entire economy to be the basis of defence,' said the head of Gosplan's defence sector. But a priority for military production itself quickly emerged in 1931-32, and thereafter the armaments industry acted as the leading sector of the economy.[7] Direct military competition took a growing share of resources, from 1 percent of output in 1928 to perhaps 6 percent in 1937 and as much as 20 percent on the eve of the war. Soviet expenditures were closely tied to the Nazi threat to such an extent that in 1938 perhaps 70 percent of global arms expenditure was being undertaken by these two countries.[8] Military competition also determined the overall pattern of rapid growth and the strategic priorities within it. Indirectly it affected a whole series of other choices, whether in terms of the location of industry such as the Urals-Kuznetsk Combine and the famous Magnitogorsk development, the design of the Moscow metro or even tractor production. 'The tank is no more than a specially constructed and armoured tractor equipped with weapons, and in 1937 the Soviet Union turned out no less than 176,000 tractors, and the big tractor works have already changed over from the ordinary wheeled tractor to the caterpillar tread variety,' wrote one knowledgeable contemporary. The key was understood to be the capacity to endure defensively in the face of the enemy. 'Suddenness alone will certainly not suffice to determine the result of the preliminary operations,' said Sergiev in the army paper, *Red Star*, in May 1936.[9]

For this to work there had to be a huge increase in competitive accumulation. Depending on the calculations used, the rate of accumulation was either doubled or tripled in the early 1930s to a level that was twice as high as in the West at this time or before 1914 in Tsarist Russia.[10] The pressure was more intense because there was little help from abroad. The original thinking in 1928-29 was that agricultural exports could pay for machinery imports. But the collapse of prices in the world crisis meant that, despite short term attempts to push up exports, the overall export share in output fell from 3.5 percent in 1928 to 0.5 percent in 1938. Stalin's Russia came as close to trade isolation for a short period as it is possible for a modern economy to go.

Investment was driven into heavy industry, into the expansion of coal, iron and steel production, engineering, chemicals and electric power. Stalin had recognised in 1929 that 'the problem of heavy industry is more difficult and more important. It is more difficult because it demands colossal investments of capital...as the history of backward countries has shown... It is more important because, unless we develop heavy industry, we can build no industry whatever, we cannot carry out any industrialisation'.[11] What was disparagingly called 'industrialisation in a cotton dress' could not guarantee the military base of the economy. Heavy industry received over 80 percent of industrial investment in the 1930s. One measure of its new role was the shift in the balance between the production of Sector A goods, means of production (the machinery and equipment that kept the economy going), and Sector B, means of consumption (the production that fed and clothed Russia's rulers and workers). This is set out in table 4.1, from which it can be seen that the new relationship remained a feature of the Soviet economy until the end:

TABLE 4.1. THE SHARE OF HEAVY AND LIGHT INDUSTRY IN OUTPUT[12]

	SECTOR A	SECTOR B
1913	33.3	66.7
1928	39.5	60.5
1940	61.0	39.0
1960	72.5	27.5
1985	74.8	25.2
1989	74.0	26.0

'The weaker the development of industry generally in a country,' said a Russian commentator in 1930, 'then the relatively larger must be the war supply industry in order, in the event of war, to make the country battle-worthy'.[13] He was reviewing the size of the military industry in several countries, but the comment applied with special force to Stalin's Russia. The additional scale of the direct defence burden and the priority given to heavy industry meant it was necessary to squeeze agriculture, to squeeze infrastructure development (railways, for example, were made to carry four times more goods per track mile than in the US) and, above all, to squeeze consumption. It was also necessary to massively increase the labour input by pulling in workers from the countryside and pushing up the numbers of women employed.

Changes like this could only be achieved through using the state to coerce. The share of the state sector leapt from 44 percent of output in 1928 to 96 percent in 1934 and 99 percent by the end of the 1930s. But this process was anything but smooth and planned. The military language of 'battles', 'forced marches' and 'production fronts' dominated. 'We are bound by no laws,' said the economist Strumilin. 'There are no fortresses that Bolsheviks cannot storm.' The slogan was used not only to mobilise but also to overcome every obstacle in the struggle against what has been called 'reaction, drift, spontaneity, and the powerful force of inertia'.[14]

The result was often chaos. This was not planning in any meaningful sense. Throughout its subsequent history the idea that 'Russia had a plan' attracted many on the left. It was believed that the state worked out what was good for people, and then planned the system to achieve it. It might not have been democratic, but it was superior to the anarchy of the market in the West. But there was a double myth here. The first was the idea that real planning could be separated from democracy. If planning is to respond to people's needs it must be democratic at all levels. It cannot therefore be bureaucratic. It cannot be conceived of as a gigantic system of expert balancing to squeeze the last ounce of efficiency out of people. This is the very opposite of human liberation – it is an expression of extreme alienation. But it was this myth that was nurtured by Stalin's propagandists. It seduced a generation or more. It was this that made Stalin's Russia palatable to Fabian or Social Democratic state planners such as Sidney and Beatrice Webb, who wrote, in a book that became notorious for its naivety: 'If we be forgiven an autobiographical note, it is this outstanding discovery in economics, and its application, in unpromising circumstances to the relations between people on one sixth of the earth's land surface, that induced us, despite the disqualifications of old age, to try to understand what is happening in the USSR'.[15]

In a justly famous essay Hal Draper once described socialism as having two souls – that of change from above and change from below. The two involve a difference over both means and ends. The myth of the plan appealed to socialism from above. The Webbs had always been concerned for 'order and efficiency', and the right of what they called those with 'the vocation of leadership' to tell others what to do. At the heart of the fantasy image they built of Stalin's Russia, therefore, was this fantasy of the plan with people as pawns.[16]

But if this was the myth of the model, the second myth was the myth of the practice. It was not that Stalin's Russia did not have some pure socialist planning. It did not have planning at all. At best what we see is clumsy centralised direction. In Russia, said the economist Oscar Lange, 'planning becomes fictitious. What actually is obtained is an elemental development'. Looking back, Moshe Lewin wrote that 'there is no doubt that the whole process was an immense improvisation, guided by the rule of thumb, hunch, and all too often despotic whim'.[17] The First Five-Year Plan ran to over 1,700 pages, but it was never implemented. Subsequent five-year plans were no more than declarations of intent. The second had nearly 1,300 pages, the third 238, and from then on they could be found in an issue of *Pravda* with space to spare. 'A coherent planning system did not exist. What existed was a priorities system of a fairly simple kind,' wrote one visitor to Gosplan, which was supposedly responsible for 'the miracle of the plan'. Indeed, in 1934 planning balances were only calculated for 105 commodities out of the several thousand that were produced. But a logical set of priorities did emerge from behind the myth of the plan. These were determined by the needs of defence and competitive industrialisation. They were embodied in the differing power and status of the various commissariats that grew up to direct development. So powerful were these ministries (as they were renamed in 1946) that they took little notice of each other. Relations between them were characterised by imbalance, waste and contradictions. To resolve these and other difficulties a second economy grew, informal but tolerated, and run by *tolkachi*, or fixers, and the use of influence, or *blat*. *Blat*, the saying went, was more powerful than Stalin. 'All the wheels of the colossal machine are oiled and fouled by it,' wrote Victor Serge. 'Its role is greater than that of planning, because without it the plan would never be reached'.[19] But here too there was a rationale to the use of informal power and influence. Military competition and the needs of competitive industrialisation were again the ultimate arbiters of what happened within the economy. They constituted the barely veiled logic that lay behind the targets of the leaders. They were also the factors that established who had power and influence, and who did not. They thus guided the deployment of formal power and informal *blat*.

This dynamic also determined the systematic pattern of uneven development that can be seen in the different regions of Soviet Russia. The limited capacity to resolve the problem of unequal development across the USSR partly reflected the political centralisation of the system, its nationalism, and the fear that opposing local nationalisms might be rallying points for opposition. But it also reflected an economic logic that required the regime to allocate resources so as to compete and grow effectively. Despite gestures towards peripheral regions, real diversification was limited by this competitive economic imperative. Uzbekistan, for example, became the cotton producer for Russia's factories, and when its leaders drew up a diversification plan, arguing that 'you cannot eat cotton', they were executed in 1938 for 'bourgeois nationalism'.[20] Overlaid on this were other political choices of the leadership. It was politically easier to make the non-Russian population pay more of the costs of Moscow's policies, because the local Russian population in the countryside had had closer links to the workers in Moscow, Leningrad and the Urals. There was therefore the concern that links might be made between urban and rural discontents. Unequal treatment also arose as part of an implicit policy of divide and rule. The positive attempts of the 1920s to overcome national oppression therefore gave way to reinforced patterns of national oppression from the 1930s onwards.

The result was that Stalin had his wish. Between 1928 and 1941 the Soviet Union did leap forward, however chaotically and unevenly. Measuring the scale of the change poses formidable problems. Disputes exist over technical issues of pricing, how to measure waste, what allowances should be made for negative tendencies, and the extent to which the figures were padded. But when all the allowances are made few doubt that progress in the narrow economic sense was considerable. Pig-iron production increased from 3.3 million tons in 1928 to 14.7 million tons in 1938, and steel production from 4.3 to 18.1 million tons. It is equally hard to argue with other indicators of change, such as the figures for urban growth set out in table 4.2. Between 1926 and 1939, for example, the urban population grew from 27.6 to 56.1 million, or 6.5 percent per year (a speed of increase until then unique in world economic history). Russia would not become 50 percent urban until 1961 (more than a century after Britain and half a century after Germany), but this was still major progress.[21]

TABLE 4.2. THE PATTERN OF CITY AND TOWN GROWTH IN SOVIET RUSSIA[22]

	POPULATION (MILLIONS)	PERCENTAGE URBAN	PERCENTAGE OF URBAN POPULATION IN URBAN PLACES BY SIZE				
			Cities over 1 million	500,000 to 1 million	250,000-500,000	100,000-250,000	Less than 100,000
1913	159.2	18	–	–	–	–	–
1926	147.0	17	15.8	15.6	68.6	–	–
1939	190.6	33	–	–	–	–	–
1959	208.8	48	9.1	15.1	10.5	13.9	51.4
1970	241.7	56	14.0	13.4	12.2	15.9	44.5
1979	262.4	62	19.5	10.8	14.0	15.3	40.4
1989	286.7	67	21.8	11.4	14.1	13.1	39.6

But someone had to pay the price for this. To build a society around the goals of competitive industrialisation and accumulation meant that the last vestiges of the revolution had to be destroyed.

THE COUNTER-REVOLUTION FROM ABOVE

In a well known passage in *Capital* Marx describes how investment and reinvestment is the driving force of the capitalist system: 'Accumulate, accumulate! That is Moses and the prophets!... Therefore save, save, ie reconvert the greatest possible portion of surplus value into capital! Accumulation for accumulation's sake, production for production's sake'.[23] We have seen how these pressures to accumulate were present in NEP society but how they met countervailing forces. In the new society that developed from 1928-29 these limits were ripped aside and the full power of competitive accumulation unleashed. For this to occur it needed what Stalin called 'a revolution from above'. In the next chapter we will look at the way in which the secret police and the prison camps were used to assist this process. Here we are interested in the wider issue of the change in social relationships. At the time many were impressed by the growth and chose not to look too closely at its basis. 'By dint of admiring factory chimneys,' said Ante Ciliga, they 'no longer perceived living beings and the social relations between them'.[24]

But it is just these changed relations that were at the centre of the counter-revolution that stripped away the last remnants of the legacy of the revolution. Gorky, writing in 1930 in the context of collectivisation, recognised the violence at the core of the process: 'We are entitled to consider ourselves in a state of civil war. The logical consequence of this is that, if the enemy does not surrender, he is to be exterminated'.[25] This civil war or counter-revolution had both a political and a social aspect. Loyal Stalinists were used to smash any opposition to change at the top. This struggle had three aspects. In the higher ranks of the party, under the guise of an attack on the Right Opposition, Stalin was able to establish his own supremacy. In fact the so-called 'right' merely supported the basic NEP line of the 1920s. Stalin 'manoeuvres in such a way as to make us appear as the schismatics', said Bukharin. In the confusion no one, possibly not even Stalin, was clear about the eventual outcome, but Bukharin half-saw how Stalin and his supporters – second-rank men like Kaganovich, Kalinin, Kuibyshev, Kirov, Mikoyan, Molotov, Ordzhonikidze, Voroshilov and Yagoda – were drawing a line between the old regime and the new. 'Stalin's line is ruinous for the whole revolution,' he told Kamenev in July 1928. 'The differences between us and Stalin are many times more serious than were our former differences with you'.[26] The Stalin group had also to overcome opposition at the top of the trade unions. Ironically the leadership of the unions was attacked for 'trade unionist' tendencies. The trade union leader Tomsky was replaced by the Stalinist Shvernik and eventually committed suicide in 1936. The task of the unions now became to help push up the rate of exploitation. 'The trade unions are called upon to play a decisive role in the task of building socialist industry by stimulating labour productivity, labour discipline, socialist competition and extirpating all remnants of guild isolation and "trade unionism",' said Stalin. Between 1932 and 1949 the Soviet Trade Union Congress did not even meet.

But to drive the political revolution through it was also necessary break resistance at the base, whether in party committees, trade unions or the party in the workplace. This subordination was the necessary accompaniment to the change at the top, and it was extensive. In key industrial areas such as Moscow, Leningrad and the Urals 75-85 percent of the membership of factory committees were replaced as they were turned from being residual organs of workers' representation into state production committees.[27]

By 1934, although there was much still to do, the main change had been effected and Stalin was able to hold the Seventeenth Party Congress as a 'Congress of Victors'. But the victors were the new leaders and their supporters who rode to power on the backs of the mass of the population. 'What sort of workers' power is this which oppresses us?' asked some workers rhetorically in 1930.[28]

But the change went much deeper than the political. For the full logic of competitive accumulation to operate, production relations had to be reconfigured across society, and three groups had to be socially subordinated to the needs of the developing regime. The first were the specialists, engineers, and professionals who might raise questions about the feasibility and rationality of what was happening. 'People who chatter about the necessity of reducing the rate of development of our industry are enemies of socialism, agents of class enemies,' said Stalin.[29] In the spring of 1929 55 specialists were accused from the Shakhty area of the Donbass. This was the first of a series of attacks on specialists which reflected the suspicion of a wider group which had been prepared to work with the regime in the 1920s. In November 1930 another trial followed of the so-called 'Industrial Party'. Then in March 1931 there was a trial of the Menshevik Union Bureau. The secret police also invented a 'Toiling Peasant Party', and swept up a dozen major and more than 1,000 lesser figures into it. The aim of these and lesser actions (which together disposed of several thousand specialists) was also to blame failings on 'wreckers', and to intimidate their colleagues into complicity with the revolution from above.

The second group of victims of Stalin's social revolution were the mass of peasants. Full-scale collectivisation was announced in November 1929. The term 'collectivisation' was a misnomer. The peasants were being dispossessed of their land, and by March 1930 60 percent of peasant households had been forced into collective farms. But with the countryside seething and in chaos the next harvest was threatened, and Stalin called a halt, shifting the blame on comrades who had become 'dizzy with success'. The percentage of farms collectivised promptly fell to 20 percent, but after the 1930 harvest was in the campaign began again and was driven to its conclusion, so that by the end of the 1930s the whole rural population was organised in 240,000 collective farms and 4,000 state farms.

This was portrayed as a revolution 'equivalent in its consequences to the revolution of October 1917'. The comparison was meant positively. Unwittingly it pointed in a different direction – if October was a qualitative change, what sort of qualitative change was this? Some 25 million peasant households had been threatened, coerced and sometimes forced at gunpoint to move as part of the rural revolution. The official *History of the Communist Party of the Soviet Union, Bolsheviks, Short Course*, which became a bible of the regime after its publication in 1938, admitted that 'the distinguishing feature of this revolution is that it was accomplished *from above*, on the initiative of *the state*'. The authors then added that it was 'directly supported from below'.[30] The reality was actually ferocious resistance. Those who resisted were denounced as kulaks and even semi- or sub-kulaks. But opposition came from all sections of the peasantry, and peasant women often played a leading role. The agricultural losses between 1929 and 1936 were equal to 40 percent of the 1928 GNP, and this may be an underestimate.[31]

Collectivisation was so bloodily chaotic that at first sight it seems complete-ly irrational. Stalin himself had argued in 1927 that collectivisation could only be a long term process that required a high level of development and technol-ogy. Yet in 1929 there were only 18,000 tractors and 7,000 trucks available. Much of what subsequently appeared to be improvement was simply the replacement of losses created by the rural revolution. The use of artificial fer-tilisers only replaced the lost manure of the millions of dead livestock. The 265,800 tractors in use in 1938 did not even adequately replace the motive power of the lost draught animals. Indeed, the need to replace lost inputs was so great that some commentators have argued that there was no real shift of a surplus for investment out of agriculture – what was taken with one hand had to be given back with another. The calculations are difficult and disputed, but even if some surplus did shift it was not as great as was once thought, and this means that the bulk of the resources for urban industrial development had to come from the exploitation of the urban working class itself.

Did collectivisation serve any purpose? The answer is yes. Bloody irrational-ities there may have been, but breakneck industrialisation needed the regi-mentation and control of the countryside, and the smashing of potential peasant resistance. Food had to be squeezed out of the villages for the towns and export despite the rural starvation. Between 1928 and 1932, for example, although grain output fell by 10 percent, peasant deliveries doubled as the urban population dependent on state rations grew from 26 million to over 40 million. The requirement was simply to first feed the state and then yourself. A law of August 1932 against petty theft was primarily directed against a starv-ing countryside and peasantry to ensure that the state got its needs met. Peasants had to be pushed out of the villages into the towns to work on the construction sites and in the new factories. Given the low standard of living in the towns, the push-pull process required even lower levels in the villages. Once the peasants had left the village, the appalling conditions there acted as a disincentive to return at a later stage.

The third and decisive group which had to be subordinated by Stalin's social revolution were workers themselves. This was something that was not accept-ed passively either. 'What are people discontented about?' asked one secret summary of letters to *Pravda* in 1930:

> In the first place that the worker is hungry, he has no fats, the bread is ersatz which is impossible to eat... It's a common thing that the wife of a worker stands the whole day in line, her husband comes home from work, and dinner is not prepared and everyone curses Soviet power. In the lines there is noise, shouting and fights, curses at the expense of Soviet power.[32]

We know that strikes, slowdowns, demonstrations and food riots took place in the early 1930s. At one point the town of Ivanovo-Voznesensk was in tur-moil as workers struck. The mood seems to have been more political than in

4.1 COLLECTIVISATION AND STARVATION

The collective farm crisis and Soviet agriculture

	Percentage of households in collective farms	Grain harvest (millions of tons)	Procurement (millions of tons)	Cows (millions)	Sheep (millions)	Horses (millions)
1913–14	–	80.1	–	–	–	–
1928	–	73.3	10.8	66.8	97.3	32.1
Oct 1929	–	71.7	16.1	58.2	97.4	32.6
Jan 1930	21.0	83.5	22.1	50.6	85.5	31.0
Mar 1930	57.6	–	–	–	–	–
Sep 1930	21.0	–	–	–	–	–
1932	61.5	69.6	18.5	38.3	43.8	21.7
1937	93.5	97.4	31.9	47.5	46.6	15.9
1950	99.0	81.2	32.3	58.1	77.6	12.7
1960	99.0	125.5	46.7	74.2	136.1	11.0

Collectivisation was the expropriation of the peasantry. It was a state-led enclosure movement concentrated in a few short years. Peasant families lost control of their land and livestock. They were herded into huge farms so that they could better be exploited. Many resisted. Livestock were slaughtered and lost on a massive scale. In 1932–33 periodic bad weather led to the failure of the grain and potato harvests, especially in the south. This hit a countryside wrecked by collectivisation. The result was catastrophic famine.

Overall in the 1930s there were some 10–11 million 'excess deaths'. The biggest group were peasants. In 1929–31 some 5 million were exiled as 'kulaks', though the name meant little. Perhaps a million died. The famine of 1933 bought perhaps 5 million deaths. The famine was worst in the Ukraine, but hundreds of thousands died in the Caucasus and Volga areas. In 1931–33 in Kazakhstan, where life was still semi-nomadic, 1.5 million may have died as a result of forced collectivisation – 40 percent of the population.[xi]

From 1933 good weather led to a better harvest. But things were bad again in 1936. Another major famine followed after the war in 1946–47. In the long run things did improve but, given the pressure of accumulation and the needs of the urban population, the condition of agriculture and the peasant standard of living remained poor for decades.

other conflicts. 'While they shoot at hungry workers...for demanding bread, here the senior Communists and Red Gendarmes of the GPU fatten themselves, concealed behind curtains,' said one leaflet.[33] But as they were repressed, workers switched to more informal means of subverting labour discipline – moving between jobs (what was called labour turnover in Russia), absenteeism, low quality work – methods familiar to workers the world over. The state reacted to this by more pressure, but it could never stand behind every worker to eliminate the problem.

The subordination of the workers in the workplace was reflected in the clear and unambiguous establishment of managerial control. In September 1929 the Central Committee passed a decree establishing *edinonachalie* – what is often called 'one-man management'. What the term really meant was 'unified control', ie making the workplace party and trade union groups subordinate instruments of management. In practice there was much 'mismanagement', but the constant reiteration of the term for unified control shows its role as a new ideal and a model. Kaganovich simply said: 'The earth should tremble when the director walks around the plant.' And in the 'best' managed plants it did. John Scott, an American engineer in Magnitogorsk, described the plant director there as a 'supreme commander...a virtual dictator'.[34]

Managerial power was reinforced by the increasingly draconian labour legislation, which is set out separately. Labour shortages meant that these laws were not always fully enforced, but all workers felt their pressure. 'To hell with wage rates, wage scales, the seven-hour day, labour protection. We're working as in wartime, and yet there's no war!' said one worker in 1931.[35] But the link to managerial power was explicit – the decree of December 1932, for example, which gave managers control over part of the food supply, aimed 'to strengthen the powers of directors of enterprises'. And in these circumstances workers hardly needed the protection of the Commissariat of Labour, and this was abolished in 1933. 'The law oppresses the workers, as in a capitalist country,' said a worker who was prosecuted for lateness in 1940. The comment got him a three-year sentence.[36] In fact between 1940 and 1952 10.9 million workers were sentenced to 'corrective labour' in their own workplace under the lateness law.[37]

The subordination of labour had another aspect – atomisation and competition. The traditional capitalist method of piecework, payment by the goods produced, was used both to push up production and to set worker against worker. One of the last genuinely independent letters to appear in the trade union paper *Trud* in July 1929 was from an older workman who complained that workers 'already call current working conditions "sweating", and socialist competition smells directly of capitalist exploitation. As any old worker I share this view, and that is why I don't take part in the competition and don't try to outdo the other fellows' performance'.[38] But the situation in 1929 was to pale

❧ 4.2 THE LEGAL REPRESSION OF THE WORKING CLASS

In the 1920s the letter of Soviet labour legislation was the most progressive in the world. Workers had substantial rights. There were even attempts to give women workers 'menstrual leave'.[xii] The enforcement of labour legislation was uneven. But in the 1920s the state saw improved conditions at work as a matter of pride. And so long as workers had a degree of influence on the state and some power in the workplace they could support improved conditions. This was why the workplace had to be changed in the revolution from above and new relationships enforced by draconian labour laws.

March 1929	*Managers given right to dismiss workers without consulting factory commission.*
February 1930	*Unemployed who refuse jobs denied benefits.*
September 1930	*Job quitting defined as disciplinary offence in RSFSR and put in pay books.*
October 1930	*Unemployment benefits ended.*
December 1930	*September decree extended to USSR. Workers who quit are only to be hired via labour exchange.*
January 1931	*Dismissal for absenteeism and violations of labour discipline.*
August 1932	*Sentences for theft of state or collective farm property raised to death.*
November 1932	*One day's unjustified absence defined as truancy. Discharge with loss of plant rations and housing.*
December 1932	*Introduction of internal passport.*
June 1933	*November 1932 penalties extended to loss of housing in housing associations.*
December 1938	*Labour book introduced. Lateness defined as 20 minutes.*
June 1940	*Decree criminalising labour offences.*
	(1) Forbidden to leave without permission on threat of two to four months imprisonment.
	(2) Absenteeism of 20 minutes, or less than 20 minutes if it occurs three times in a month or four times in two months, a crime punished by corrective labour at work and 25 percent wage reduction.
	(3) Work day extended with no extra pay.
April 1956	*Decree 'On Abolishing Court Liability and Wage Earners for Leaving... and for Absence...', preceded by major relaxation of use of law from 1951 on, finally removes criminal sanctions.*

in comparison to what followed. The figure of workers paid by the piece rose from 57.5 percent in 1928 to 76.1 percent in 1936, and it was still at 77 percent in 1953.[39] More notorious still was the Stakhanovite movement. Workers were encouraged to emulate the achievements of Alexei Stakhanov, who in 1935 mined 102 tons of coal against the norm of seven tons. It was a set up. Stakhanovism was used as another way of intensifying competition and exploitation. The hatred it created was captured in a joke of the time. A group of women Stakhanovites are awarded various consumer goods, but the best gets the top prize of Stalin's *Collected Works*. 'Just what the bitch deserves,' says a voice at the back of the hall. Some Stakhanovites were ostracised, some attacked and some killed. Victor Serge said that he knew a hospital director who thought up 'favourable treatment' for Stakhanovite patients. Overall the movement quickly broke down, but this was partially disguised by claiming that almost everyone had become a Stakhanovite worker.[40]

What was the extent of the rate of exploitation? We know how dramatically the consumption share was cut in the 1930s. We also know that ever greater numbers of workers were pulled into production. Money wages rose because of inflation but real wages were slashed – possibly by as much as a half by 1932-33. The year '1933 was the culmination of the most precipitous peacetime decline in living standards known in recorded history,' said one historian half a century later. There was some recovery to 1937, but the value of real wages remained below the 1928 level until the early 1950s. The number of days worked per worker per year was 263 in 1928. Changes at the start of industrialisation pushed this down to 253.8 in 1931, but it was then pushed up to 265.8 in 1933.[41] Labour productivity also fell in the turmoil of the years 1928-32 but it then recovered, and by 1940 was some 70 percent above the 1928 level.[42] But this was no once and for all increase. Soviet workers were now the creators of wealth in a system over which they had no control, and in which they had fewer defences than workers in the bourgeois democratic states where free trade unions existed. But they shared a common fate with workers the world over. The fundamental factor determining their lives was now the logic of exploitation enforced by competitive accumulation.

ECONOMIC AND MILITARY COMPETITION

In the 1930s the link between economic and military competition became closer. On May Day 1938 Voroshilov warned that 'the flames of war are blazing on two continents'. But Stalin's contribution was to extend further the logic of national development and defend Russia's position as a Great Power. The veneer of left rhetoric became wafer thin. 'For Soviet patriots homeland and communism are pressed into an inseparable whole,' said Molotov in November 1939. 'The Bolsheviks come from the bowels of the people, and we prize and love the glorious deeds in the history of our people'. The poet Anna Akhmatova saw it more brutally: 'One cannot live in the Kremlin... Here the microbes of ancient fury still swarm, the wild face of Boris and the malice of all the Ivans, and the arrogance of pretenders instead of the people's laws.' In the long term this meant that 'the Soviet Union must rely first of all on its own forces,' said *Izvestia* in May 1939. But security could also be improved by foreign policy measures.[43] Faced with the challenges both in the West and the East, Stalin sought alliances, and required Western Communist parties to take up Popular Front policies, with the aim of building cross-class alliances to pressure Western governments into more friendly attitudes to the USSR. In 1934 Stalin took Russia into the League of Nations for this reason. In 1936-39 his policy in the Spanish Civil War was to avoid risking the displeasure of potential allies. Moscow encouraged Spanish Communists to throw away a potential revolution in favour of support for a moderate Republicanism that the Western powers themselves had little time for, and which was eventually defeated by Franco. Closer to home Stalin valued the possibility of a series of buffer states on the USSR's western borders. Pressure was therefore brought to bring them into the Russian orbit. 'It does not pay small states to be dragged into great adventures,' Zhdanov warned in December 1936.

But these moves all proved in vain. The leaders of big states such as Britain had their own agendas and remained suspicious of the USSR, with some politicians seeing the advantage of turning Hitler eastwards. The small states remained hostile and, of course, Stalin had far less to offer them than Hitler. When Stalin could not secure Russia's interest by 'collective security', he was quite prepared to throw anti-fascism to the wind and negotiate a deal with Hitler in 1939.

The Nazi-Soviet Pact was signed on 22 August 1939, and with its secret protocols effectively established spheres of interest for Stalin and Hitler. Stalin believed he had made short and long term gains. In the short term, when the Nazis moved into western Poland in September 1939 the Soviet army took the eastern part. Then from 30 November 1939 to 12 March 1940 the Soviet army fought a bloody war with Finland as Stalin tried to extend the Soviet defence line. Finally in June 1940 came the forced takeover of the Baltic states and Bessarabia, then part of Romania. These moves added 20-25 million people to the Soviet population. The longer term gain Stalin got as a result of the deal was supposed to be a stable relationship with the Nazis and security. For this he was also willing to pay with extensive exports and even some Communist refugees from the Nazis who were returned to Hitler.[44]

There seems little doubt that Stalin completely misunderstood Hitler's intentions. It is true that he remained suspicious, and Russia continued to arm itself, but Stalin also believed that he had a deal with a partner he could rely on. The details of the cordial relations between Hitler's and Stalin's diplomats fill out the accounts of 1939-41. Stalin himself drank a toast at the turn of 1941 'to the health of the Führer whom the German people love'. But by that time the planning for Operation Barbarossa, which would eventually unleash an invasion of Russia, was well under way.

On 22 June 1941 the Nazi armies crossed the Soviet frontiers. Victory followed victory amid panic and mass surrender. By the start of 1942 lands had been occupied in which one third of the population lived, and 38 percent of the grain and 60 percent or more of the coal, iron, steel and aluminium was produced. Red Army losses numbered 1.5 million dead and 3 million captured. But Soviet lines eventually held, and the Nazis were defeated at Stalingrad in early 1943. Their weaknesses were confirmed at the great Battle of Kursk in July 1943. At enormous cost the Nazis were pushed back, and on 9 May 1945 they finally surrendered in Berlin. Soviet Russia carried the greatest burden in the Second World War, fighting the bulk of the Nazi army, and losing perhaps 80 percent of all Allied military casualties and some 60 percent of the military casualties on all sides. Victory in the 'Great Patriotic War' now became the legitimating myth of the new Soviet Empire which emerged as part of the division of Europe in 1945-48. The image of a people going into battle crying 'For the motherland, for Stalin' still survives, and for Stalin the war showed that the USSR was 'a society superior to any non-Soviet social order'.[45] But the real story is more complex.

The Nazis dramatically overreached themselves in two senses. Firstly they overestimated their capacity to win a quick victory. Hitler had said in 1940 that an attack would 'make sense only if we can smash the state in one blow'.[46] Although the Soviet economy was still backward it had achieved enough, with some foreign aid, to mobilise for a long term war. 'The war will be won by industrial production,' Stalin said. To save industrial capacity improvised attempts were made to shift plant and 20 million people (including one third of the prison camp population) eastwards. Huge losses of capital and people were sustained, but by diverting two thirds to three quarters of all that was left to military production it was possible to supply a mass army. Wartime employment in consumer and service industries was cut by 60 percent, and women, schoolchildren, pensioners and even prisoners thrown into production. With the Red Army 70 percent peasant, women now dominated the countryside. Between 1940 and 1944 their share in the rural labour force rose from one third to three quarters. In industry it rose from 38 to 53 percent between 1940 and 1942. By this marshalling of resources and the imposition of huge home front sacrifices the Soviet Union, despite its much weaker base, began to outproduce the Nazi regime, building 24,000 tanks and 48,000 big guns in 1943 compared with Germany's 17,000 tanks and 27,000 big guns.[47]

The second mistake that the Nazis made was to allow their racist ideology to alienate the mass of the local population. In the first instance they were often met as liberators, welcomed with banners, bread, salt and flowers in some areas. But Jews were there to be murdered and Slavs to be worked to death, their resources plundered. Himmler expressed the contempt of the Nazi leaders: 'If 10,000 Russian females die of exhaustion digging an anti-tank ditch, that interests me only insofar as the ditch is dug for Germany.' In the ranks the same pleasure in violence could be seen. 'Soon our nostrils were filled with the stench of burning villages. The air trembled with the distant rumble of guns,' said one Waffen SS soldier. 'Our hearts beat faster, seasoned though we were to war – tomorrow's battle never fails to put a clamp round the heart. We wrote our first postcards home'.[48]

A third element that determined the outcome of the war was the Stalinist regime's ability to beat the patriotic drum. This happened from day one of the war. Sholokhov wrote of a local Cossack boasting of the Germans he had killed in 1914-17: 'Now I can talk about it aloud, but in the past I always felt a bit awkward... I won two George Crosses and three medals. They didn't hang them on me for nothing, did they?'[49] The Comintern was disbanded and the Internationale replaced by a national anthem, celebrating 'Great Russia' and the way that it would 'lead the fatherland to glory'. The ghosts of the Russian past were summoned to assist the present – from medieval times came Alexander Nevsky, who had defeated the Teutonic Knights, and Dimitry Donsky, who had triumphed over the Tartars, and from the Tsarist period Suvorov and Kutuzov, who had held out against the Ottoman Empire and Napoleonic France. Peace was also proclaimed formally with 'Holy Russia', and the Orthodox church under Patriarch Sergei grabbed its chance. Russia was 'our divinely protected country' and Stalin 'our God-sent leader...divinely appointed'. Yet such was the hatred Stalin generated that perhaps 1 million Soviet citizens fought against the regime, including hundreds of thousands in General Vlasov's army who hoped to use Hitler as an ally against Stalin.

But in the end, despite the blunders, mistakes and continuing repression, it was enough. In May 1945 Soviet soldiers reached Berlin. Behind them was a devastated land. The physical destruction in Russia left 25 million homeless. The losses of capital were perhaps equal to 10 years production. But it is the population figures that bring home the scale of the tragedy if the mind can comprehend such large numbers. The total number of excess deaths appears to have been 26-27 million, of which 20 million were men, so that in 1945 there were 50 percent more women than men aged 20-29. Some 5.5 million died at the front, 1.1 million in hospitals and 1.2 million in POW camps. A crude estimate suggests that 15 percent of the others who died were victims of slave labour, 35 percent were victims of extermination policies, and 50 percent died of hunger and disease.[50] In addition the birthrate fell by more than 40 percent, creating a wartime shortfall of 11.5 million children. But the birth deficit would accumulate for a generation, as millions of women lived out their lives single and childless in a world with a missing cohort of men.

These sacrifices saved the Soviet people from Hitler, but they did not liberate them from Stalin. One depressed poet wrote:

> And for all our laurels won in war,
> Laying our own country waste,
> We were defeated by ourselves
> — As Rome destroyed itself [51]

In fact in some areas re-establishing control took time. The authorities were faced with considerable guerrilla resistance. But victory did something else. The Second World War shifted the global balance of power. The US emerged dominant, with Britain and France weakened, and Germany and Japan prostrate. And in the East was Stalin and the Soviet Union, militarily strong despite the immiseration of the people. Molotov expressed how things had changed in a speech of February 1946: 'The USSR ranks today among the most authoritative of the world powers. Important relations cannot nowadays be settled without the participation of the Soviet Union, or without heeding the voice of the country'.[52]

COLD WAR PRESSURES AND SOVIET DEVELOPMENT

The years between 1945 and 1989 were dominated by the Cold War. Global tensions were now refracted through the potential for conflict between the United States and Soviet Russia, and their respective blocs – Nato, formed in 1949, and the Warsaw Pact, which came into existence in 1955. The result was the symmetry of the Cold War and the arms race. In the first instance the US had complete nuclear superiority. Stalin put more pressure on the Soviet nuclear programme, and his team of physicists were able to explode the first Soviet nuclear bomb in 1949, although as yet there were no means of delivering it.[53] But the hinge of military competition would now be the nuclear arms race. This was at its most intense between 1947 and 1962. Thereafter the conflict stabilised, and attempts were made to routinise and contain it. Yet the Cold War was always more complex than the clash of two superpowers.

Since 1945 the US has been the centre of gravity of the world economy, with global interests, global power and global reach. Conflict with the Soviet Union was therefore a useful pretext behind which wider ambitions could be realised. US propagandists denounced Soviet expansion and saw America's role as what the liberal historian Arthur Schlesinger Jr called: 'The brave and essential response of free men to Communist aggression'.[54]

But 'Communist aggression' could cover a multitude of sins, allowing intervention against nationalist and other forces that threatened US interests in Latin America, Africa and Asia, as well as Europe. 'Nobody in the military system ever described them as anything other than communism. They didn't give it a race, they didn't give it an age, they didn't give it a sex,' said William Calley, who had led a massacre of 500 Vietnamese villagers.[55] Local regimes could use the threat of communism as a bargaining tool, as in the joke of the Third World leader who set up a Communist party in his country in order to get more American aid. What this meant was that when the Cold War ended the wider pattern of US intervention did not. No area of the world felt the brutality of US power more than Indochina, where American military action killed perhaps 2-3 million people in the 1960s and early 1970s. The conflict was more an attempt to suppress a nationalist movement, and revulsion against the US role there led to a more critical look at US policy by Americans themselves. In the US so-called revisionist historians began to see Soviet policy as essentially cautious and reactive. This is essentially correct, but some went further and treated it in a benign way. What this missed was that both the US and the Soviet Union had 'imperialist' agendas but different capacities to achieve them. Compared with the US, the Soviet Union was a weaker superpower with long vulnerable borders. Beyond the immediate pressure of potential conflict with the US, Soviet leaders could only hope for regional power and regional spheres of interest. This was the basis of the notorious deal that Stalin and Churchill discussed in Moscow in October 1944, and which Churchill describes in his memoirs:

> I wrote on a half a sheet of paper:
> Romania: Russia 90 percent. The others 10 percent.
> Greece: Great Britain 90 percent. Russia 10 percent.
> Yugoslavia: 50–50 percent.
> Bulgaria: Russia 75 percent. The others 25 percent.
> I pushed this across to Stalin, who had by then heard the translation. Then he took his pencil and made a large
> tick upon it, and passed it back to us. It was all sealed in no more time than it takes to set down.[56]

But US leaders were not prepared to see their global ambitions deflected by either Britain or Russia doing such deals. US policy therefore effectively encouraged the incorporation of the UK as a junior partner in its world order, while directing much of the Cold War against the Soviet Union and its local ambitions.

The inability of the USSR to make more than a token projection of Soviet power on a truly global scale remained until the end. The US, for example, had 2,000 foreign bases, whereas the USSR had only 500, and some of these US bases were close to the USSR, whereas Russia's one attempt to locate missiles close to the US, in Cuba in 1962, resulted in a forced retreat. And, unlike the US, Russian and Warsaw Pact troops were only formally deployed in actions suppressing revolts within the Soviet Bloc, and on its borders against China and in Afghanistan. When the Soviet Union wanted to deploy its power more widely it had to act with proxy forces from regimes more or less dependent on it. China played this role in Korea in the early 1950s, and Cuba in Africa in the 1970s. Indeed, while these actions were a sign of Soviet military power, they were also a reflection of its economic weakness. US power made it a natural pole of attraction to other states in a way that the USSR could never be. In terms of crude self-interest the Soviet Union had fewer carrots that it could offer to compensate for the demands it made within its bloc. When leaders with a local base, like Tito in Yugoslavia in 1949 and Mao in China, clashed with 'Soviet imperialism' there was little the Soviet leadership could do to pull them back into line.

In the first instance, after 1945 Stalin's policy seems to have been motivated by security fears and the hope that a series of buffer states could be created in Eastern Europe sympathetic to the Soviet regime. Cold War propaganda claimed that the Soviet intention was to roll their divisions forward wherever they could. But initially Communist parties in the future Eastern Bloc were restrained by Moscow. The Soviet Union was in a desperate plight, and the rapacious exploitation of Eastern Europe in 1945-46 suggested that the intention was to get as much as possible, as quickly as possible, for fear that the opportunity might be lost. Moreover, in other areas the Red Army was withdrawn where Soviet interests were not directly risked, such as Denmark, Norway, Finland, Iran and Austria. The problem was the lands of Eastern Europe. These had been points of entry before for a succession of invaders. As the Cold War began to develop, Soviet policy therefore hardened into one of wanting not merely friendly regimes but regimes under its control.

The result in Eastern Europe was the imposition of more state control and the model of development created in Russia in the 1930s. Communist parties took charge with leaderships loyal to Moscow. For a period much of the brutality of 1930s Russia, from collectivisation to the purges, was recreated in these countries. Industrialisation was encouraged to help rebuild the Soviet economy and create a basis for the defence of the bloc as a whole.[57] The Soviet army was stationed there partly in response to the threat from the West, and partly to give these regimes some backbone. On two occasions when revolt threatened – in Hungary in 1956 and Czechoslovakia in 1968 – the armed forces of the Warsaw Pact were sent in. The suppression of the Hungarian Revolution was the bloodier, but the purposes of 1956 and 1968 were the same. When Czechoslovak leaders were called to Moscow, Brezhnev, according to Zdenek Mlynar, who was present, said that 'the Soviet Union had gained security, and the guarantee of security was the post-war division of Europe and, specifically, the fact that Czechoslovakia was linked with the Soviet Union "forever".'[58]

Similar fears about instability led to the invasion of Afghanistan in 1979. Around 13,500 Soviet troops died there before the Soviet army was recalled in

1989. How many Afghans died is disputed, but it was many times this and, if it was less than the US killed in Indochina, many of the same elements were present. 'Have you ever seen necklaces of dried ears?' said one veteran, 'Yes, trophies of war, rolled up into little leaves and kept in matchboxes! Impossible? You can't believe such things of our glorious Soviet boys? Well, they could and did happen'.[59] When Russian troops eventually left, Afghanistan began to disintegrate, and some fell into the trap of retrospectively seeing the Russian presence as benign. The trophy boxes tell a different story. It was the Russian invasion and repression that paved the way for subsequent developments.[60]

We know from Soviet documents that as the Cold War developed the leadership in the Kremlin grew more confident. But it never ceased to feel beleaguered in the face of long borders with potentially hostile neighbours, superpower competition and constant pressure on its economy. The US and Nato offered the main challenge, though Japan was an additional element of uncertainty in the Far East. For Soviet military and economic planners the US remained 'the main adversary'. The KGB typically reported in early 1983 that 'all American land-based intercontinental missiles, 70 percent of their naval facilities and 30 percent of their strategic airforce are on duty, and in Nato about 70 percent of nuclear facilities are detailed as duty forces'. But the difficulties of the Soviet leadership were intensified by the eruption of conflict with China in 1958-60. The 'eternal friend' became 'the eternal enemy', and a formidable one, with the largest population in the world, the third largest land mass and its own nuclear capacity. In 1969 the tension broke out in open border clashes, and by the mid-1970s the Soviet Union was stationing 40 divisions and an array of missiles in border areas, and devoting 15-20 percent of defence expenditure to the threat from China. The KGB warned in 1977, after Mao's death, that 'the present Chinese leadership remains a serious and dangerous adversary of the Soviet Union'. Racist suspicions about Chinese duplicity and 'the common national psychology of the Chinese' intensified fears not only of China as a direct threat but its capacity to destabilise the Cold War. 'The strategic policy of the People's Republic of China is based on exploiting and, above all, on intensifying the conflict between the two world social systems,' said another KGB report.[61] Russian fears were further accentuated by US-Chinese rapprochement in the early 1970s.

THE FORCE OF MILITARY AND ECONOMIC COMPETITION

The Cold War was a competition of military expenditure and military arsenals, of conventional, biological, chemical and nuclear weapons, of research, of testing, of production, it was a competition of weapons systems stockpiled and systems intended, of missiles, warheads, delivery speeds and so on, a rationally ordered system of monumental irrationality. By 1985 global arms spending had grown to $1,000 billion in contemporary prices, with Nato and the Warsaw Pact accounting for three quarters of this. Between 40,000 and 50,000 nuclear weapons had been accumulated, largely under American and Soviet control. This military race drained both countries and the world of vital resources. The cost of one nuclear submarine alone was estimated to be equal to the amount spent on 160 million school age children in the 23 poorest countries in the world. But the arms race also undercut future potential by not only squeezing investment but distorting knowledge, learning and research, as a fifth of the world's scientists concentrated their efforts on improving the means of mass destruction.

The strain and pressure this put on the leadership in Russia can be seen in the figures for investment and consumption, and the relative weight given to particular industries and sectors.

Russian output per head was at best half that of the US. Military expenditure and investment continued to squeeze consumption, and with it heavy industry squeezed consumer goods production. In Khrushchev's memoirs, for example, he wrote:

> When I was leader of the party and the government, I decided that we had to economise drastically in the building of homes, construction of communal services, and even in the development of agriculture in order to build our defences. I even suspended the construction of subways in Kiev, Baku and Tbilisi so that we could redirect those funds into strengthening our defence and attack forces. We also built fewer athletic stadiums, swimming pools and cultural facilities.[62]

A succession of treaties attempted to stabilise the competition, and these culminated in the 1972 ABM treaty and the policies of detente. Detente implied recognition of Soviet geopolitical power in exchange for economic links and human rights concessions. These were embodied in the 1975 Helsinki agreement. Brezhnev saw this as a triumph and recognition of Russia's Great Power status. But even as it was signed a more hostile atmosphere was emerging. The trouble was partly technical. The different weapons systems and deployments, real and imagined, proved impossible to be satisfactorily traded off against one another. Disarmament did not disarm, and arms limitation did not limit. Rather negotiations and treaties helped to organise, legitimise and mystify arms competition. But the deeper problem was that no state could control the forces of global capitalism that threatened to destabilise relations. It was these that began to unravel the stability that had merged in the early 1970s with the West.

These pressures continued to drive the Soviet economy forward in the decades after 1945. The Polish economist Oscar Lange described the Soviet economy as 'a war economy *sui generis*', and it remained this until its end, as resources continued to be mobilised for defence, and priorities were determined by competitive accumulation built around this. Leonid Polozhaev, who moved from being a Communist manager to governor of Omsk in the 1990s, said bluntly: 'The Soviet economy – let's look the truth in the eye – was created for war and on account of war'.[63] The defence complex remained the linchpin of the economy. Direct defence expenditure remained high and was pushed up more at moments of tension such as the Korean War in 1951-52, the Berlin Wall and Cuban missile crises in the early 1960s, and the second Cold War of the early 1980s. The Soviet dilemma was that from a weaker base it had to match Nato spending and worry about China. Moreover its weak grip on the Warsaw Pact countries meant that, unlike the US in Nato, it could not share much of the burden. The precise levels of military expenditure remain difficult to establish because of technical debates about how to measure and value production. Suffice it to say that all agree levels were in excess of 10 percent of output, and 'at least three times higher (and often more than that) for the group of industrial economies...[and]...the United States'.[64]

This was a formidable development pressure and an area where competition was keenly felt. Of course military production has its own inefficiencies, but in general terms this was an area where the Soviet Union did well. Military research and development was an area where 'performance is far more successful and impressive', wrote a Western observer. Production itself was also of a higher standard. 'Military production is regulated by competition [with Western weapons], advanced technology is introduced without any difficulty. As a result, productivity in such enterprises is much higher,' said Brucan, a Romanian insider.[65]

Western policy during the Cold War, especially early on, blocked the export of high technology goods to the Soviet Union and its satellites. But over time the pressure of military competition was supplemented by more conventional economic forces as the Soviet Union began to re-enter the world market. Trade shares rose to levels not out of line for an economy the size of the Soviet Union. Exports rose to 2 percent of output in 1955 and some 7.5-10 percent in 1980. In 1950 84 percent of trade was within the Soviet bloc, but by 1965 this had declined to 68 percent, and the Eighth Five-Year Plan document talked in 1966 of the USSR taking 'part in a rational division of labour on an internal scale'.[66] However, the structure of the Soviet economy precluded any easy integration. Competitive industrialisation meant that the USSR had an economic structure that was competitive with much of the rest of global capitalism. So long as the goal was building an alternative path of development as an armed superpower, the inefficiencies this created were not a problem. Integration, however, would require complementarities, and here the USSR had little to offer to pay for imports of grain and machinery, save raw material exports, oil and arms sales. By the late 1970s oil sales provided 50 percent of Western currency earnings, and arms sales perhaps around 15 percent.[67]

For a long period the Soviet Union continued to achieve major economic progress to such an extent that 'the main question' in the West in the late 1950s was: 'When would the Soviet Union catch up and overtake the US? Even sober and careful scholars...did not exclude the possibility that this might be imminent'.[68] Khrushchev boasted to the US in 1956: 'Whether you like it or not, history is on our side. We will bury you.' In 1961 the goal of surpassing the US 'within a decade' was put in the party programme.[69] The space race seemed to exemplify this. In 1957 Russia launched the Sputnik – the first artificial satellite. Jubilation in Moscow was matched by panic in Washington. It 'jolted the American psyche' – it was 'another Pearl Harbour', said one contemporary. Looking back at the wave of fear, one historian said that American strategists 'had presumed that their scientific and technical capabilities far exceed those of the Soviet Union, and that supremacy offered a margin of safety in the nuclear area. Sputnik shattered that complaisant assumption.' The balance of terror was now 'delicate' said an article in *Foreign Affairs*, the US foreign policy establishment house journal.[70] When Yuri Gagarin made the first manned space flight in April 1961 the tables seemed to have turned even more. 'Let the capitalists try to catch up with our country, which has blazed the trail into space,' said Khrushchev to Gagarin. Mikhail Sholokhov spoke for the official view at home: 'There's nothing more to say, since one is dumb with admiration and pride at the fantastic success of the science of our native fatherland'.[71]

We now realise that catching up was never likely to happen. Moreover other leaps forward have occurred, such as those in East Asia, which made the Soviet experience look less unusual. But this cannot alter the fact that at this time Soviet achievements were real and substantial, and it was this that gave Western fears, however exaggerated, a real basis. Writing in 1969 Angus Maddison noted that Russia and Japan 'are the only clear cases in the past half century in which the income gap between rich and poor nations has been substantially narrowed'. The Soviet achievement was the more remarkable since Japan had already achieved the 1940 Soviet level of urbanisation in 1910, it experienced less destruction, and it was helped after 1945 by $3 billion of economic aid and $11 billion of military aid, as well as having US military purchases cover one quarter of its imports at the time of the Korean War and still some 5 percent in 1965.[72]

But just as the competition of private capitalist businesses is not a crisis-free process, so the same applies to the competition of state capitals. The illusion that the dynamic of the USSR was no longer capitalist led much of the left, even if they came from an oppositional tradition, to deny this. Ernest Mandel, for example, wrote in 1956:

The Soviet Union maintains a more or less even rhythm of economic growth, plan after plan, decade after decade without the progress of the past weighing on the possibilities of the future... All the laws of development of the capitalist economy which provoke a slowdown in the speed of economic growth are eliminated.[73]

But this whole perspective was falsified as growth rates began to slow in the 1960s. Western growth rates too fell in the 1970s, so the Brezhnev leadership, though concerned, could take comfort in their belief that the Soviet system still retained superiority. The fears of the right in the West seemed to echo the boasts of Russian ideologists. 'The Russians are bent on world dominance, and they are rapidly acquiring the means to become the most powerful imperial nation the world has seen,' said Mrs Thatcher, the future British prime minister, in January 1976. The same day the *Times* wrote of the military balance that 'approximate parity at present exists between East and West, and has done so for several years'.[74] But in the 1980s, even on Russia's own warped statistics, growth rates began to dip below those of the West. It was this that would force Russia's rulers to rethink their strategy, leaving those who had illusions about the supremacy of the Soviet system bemused – not only by the scale of the economic difficulties but the direction change would eventually take.

Moscow State University, one of seven sister skyscrapers from the late Stalin era. Part built by POWs, part financed by reparations, the aim was to overawe the city with monuments of power and strength from which Russia's ruling class could look down.

5 REPRESSION

The regime that came into being after 1928 depended on extreme repression. 'In those days,' said one member of the Left Opposition, 'the Soviet land resembled an enormous concentration camp, surrounded by barbed wire, enclosing millions of Russian people.' Behind this barbed wire stood an inner fence around the prison camp system or Gulag (the Russian acronym for the 'Glavnoe upravlenie lagerei' – the Main Camp Administration), which began to fill up with all those who stood in the way of Stalin and his regime. In the first instance most of the left were taken in. In 1933 D N Pritt, the British lawyer and Stalinist fellow-traveller, with no sense of irony, told his readers that Soviet prisons were so good that it was 'small wonder that a high official of the Ministry of Justice spent three months in one of the "prisons" as an ordinary inmate to see how he liked it'.[1] As accounts accumulated of the real degradation of the system, the myths became harder to sustain. The publication of Khrushchev's 1956 secret speech outside of Russia pulled away another prop from the illusion. Then Alexander Solzhenitsyn's three-volume history of the Soviet prison camps, *The Gulag Archipelago*, secretly compiled from survivors' accounts and his own experience, removed another prop. Any final doubts disappeared with *glasnost* as the archives began to be opened, and victims and their loved ones sought to memorialise and sanctify the sites of repression.

But why was terror so central? The perception of a regime of all-encompassing terror forms the core of totalitarian theory and many looser accounts of the Soviet Union. Similarly the attempt to show that there was an inevitable move from the defensive repression of the civil war years to Stalin's Gulag forms an important part of the continuity argument that seeks to discredit radical change. But such accounts miss the point. Terror was needed to kickstart Stalin's new regime precisely because it involved an usurping of power and a break with the past. It had to be directed *outside* the party against the mass of the population for the reasons we described in the previous chapter. But it also had to be directed *inside* the party to cut it off from the discontent that welled up in society at large. The opponents of Stalin and his supporters first experienced what Bukharin called 'civil execution' – condemnation, ridicule and isolation. Prison and real execution then followed. The fear that this created forced the ruling layers to cut themselves off from any element of the heritage of 1917. It stopped them giving ground to the pressures of workers, peasants and national minorities caught up in the whirlwind of the revolution from above. We know that appeals poured into the centre. In August 1930, for example, workers in an Izhevsk factory signed a mass letter to Rykov: 'We ask you in the name of 50,000 workers from the Izhevsk factory to save us from hunger... Comrade Rykov, we appeal to you. Listen to us, don't be stubborn... We ask you, do not force us into extreme measures, we appeal to you as a comrade... We are many Communists, and we have all come to the same conclusion – the situation is catastrophic. We cannot suffer any more... Save us from hunger.'[2] But Rykov, condemned with Bukharin as part of the Right Opposition, was in no position to respond. Those who did try to organise to confront Stalin in the name of the suffering of the workers and against the revolution from above met with the severest retribution.[3]

If we are to make sense of the terror and repression, it is important first to see that what happened after 1929 was both quantitatively and qualitatively different from the situation before 1929. Once in motion terror then began to take on a life of its own, but its underlying logic was always directed towards reinforcing and consolidating the counter-revolution of 1928-33, and to helping the new regime meet its objectives of competitive accumulation. However, by the time of Stalin's death it was becoming obvious that terror had got out of hand. The regime could not continue to develop on the basis of threat alone. It had to try to establish a more positive commitment from the mass of the population. It was this need that encouraged an eventual shift from a regime based on an abnormally high degree of repression, one of the worst regimes of the 20th century, to lower levels of repression more characteristic of police control in many undemocratic regimes throughout the world in the second half of the 20th century.

HOW DIFFERENT WERE THE YEARS 1917-28?

Victor Serge, who barely managed to escape Stalin's Russia with his life in 1936, said:

> In theory and in practice, the prison state has nothing in common with the measures of public safety of the commune state in the period of battles — it is the work of the triumphant bureaucrats who, in order to impose their usurpation, are forced to break with the essential principles of socialism and refuse the workers any freedom at all.[4]

The idea of extensive state control of people and ideas was anathema in the early 1920s. A strong sense still existed that communism meant the withering away of the state, and that the extent of this was a measure of its success. There was no state monopoly on publishing. Different journals supported different trends. It is true that a censorship system was formalised in 1922, but the system was lax and control of literature was no worse, perhaps less than in the West.

The capacity to develop a really progressive justice and penal system was limited in the 1920s by the same kind of constraints that affected social policy as a whole. The prisons were inherited from Tsarism. Budgets were tight. The broader social conditions accentuated temptations towards crime. But policy had three main directions which set it apart from elsewhere and what came later. Decrees in 1917 and 1918, a set of guiding principles in 1919 and legal codes in 1922 and 1926 tried to remould the legal system and redefine crime. The first aim was to protect the new order. Some offences disappeared altogether, including the 'crime' of homosexuality. For the first time Russians gained freedom of movement. 'The [internal] passport system was a major instrument of police pressure. Soviet law does not recognise a passport system,' said one reference work of the time.[5] The legal codes were an important advance on the initial legal structure set up in 1918 under the influence of the Left SR Steinberg as commissar of justice. A second aim was to give justice a more popular basis by putting it more in the hands of the people. This did not mean that it was to be arbitrary. As the civil war ended, there was a drive to create a more stable basis of legality with independent defence lawyers and procurators. But it did mean that law should no longer appear as an alien or alienating force. A third thrust was to remove the idea of 'punishment'. 'Crime in class society is provoked by the structure of social relationships in which the offender lives,' said the 1919 Guiding Principles. Crime could not be viewed with equanimity. 'For the period of transition to communist organisation,' said the 1922 and 1926 codes, society needed 'measures of social protection'. But it did not need punishment in the sense of retribution. Indeed, the word punishment became frowned on. Society could be protected without excessive suffering to the offender, since both their interests and those of society would best be served by speedy rehabilitation. Exile was eliminated, the use of the death penalty was reduced, and prison terms were shortened. Where possible, prison was to be avoided. In 1923 only 20 percent of people convicted of crimes were imprisoned. The figure rose to 40 percent in 1926 and then fell again. Even the 1926 figure was impressive in contemporary terms. Table 5.1 shows the numbers imprisoned.

TABLE 5.1. NUMBERS OF PEOPLE IN PRISON IN NEP RSFSR[6]

1923	74,019
1924	83,736
1925	94,272
1926	121,018
1927	114,604
1928	111,601

These figures were annual averages. Considerable fluctuations existed over the course of a year, and the peak of imprisonment in the RSFSR was in December 1926, when 145,000 were in jail.[7] Most sentences, however, were short, and there was an attempt to set maximum limits that did not involve the loss of any hope of the return to a normal life.

All prison systems have a great gap between theory and practice. Some of the progressive ideas may also have been naive. But, insofar as can be judged, the approach was having a positive effect, and for its time (and for our time, given the rush to create prison-industrial complexes) it remained a positive step forward. What of the labour camps and the secret police? Camps had been used in the civil war, but they were nothing like those under Stalin. In the 1920s most were abandoned. The system controlled by the GPU, the Cheka's successor, was small. The biggest camp was the Solovki camp in the White Sea, which had several thousand inmates and in which conditions were hard.

But the growing degeneration of the revolution in the mid-1920s began to bring with it increased harshness within the party and society as a whole, which would help pave the way for the shift after 1928. At the height of the civil war party factions had fought out their positions. Even following the ban on factions the Workers' Opposition, despite feeling political pressure, had still been treated as a group of party comrades. This began to change in 1923-24. In 1923, in the midst of strikes, Dzerzhinsky's new GPU had arrested a small dissident party group led by Miasnikov. This saw NEP as 'the New Exploitation of the Proletariat'. But when party members still refused to see some of the longest serving party members as anything other than comrades with different views, Dzerzhinsky asked the Politburo to rule that members had a duty to report activities challenging the party line. These demands helped to crystallise the case of the Left Opposition. If party policy was wrong it had to be fought, and the political space had to exist to do this. Trotsky opposed Dzerzhinsky's call (though perhaps less than he should have done), and 46 oppositionists signed a long letter which argued that 'the inner-party struggle is waged all the more savagely the more it is waged in silence and secrecy'. It called for the relaxation of the ban on factions.[8] But, as we saw in Chapter 3, the centre now united against Trotsky and the left. The centre began to legitimatise a new role for the GPU in supervising the party. No less seriously, the GPU began to change as it became a bastion of the centre. Dzerzhinsky reportedly told one foreign Communist that he had been abandoned by 'the saints' who had supported him in the civil war, and who had some revolutionary honour. He was left with the 'scoundrels'. Subsequently the role of the GPU increased in step with (and helped to further) the degeneration of the revolution. Dzerzhinsky's death in 1925 cleared away an important hurdle to the more cynical deployment of the GPU.

But it was in the increasingly heated atmosphere from 1927 onwards that the real shift could be detected. Now there were no qualms about the suppression of party opposition. The change was also felt in society at large. When Nikolai Krylenko, as commissar of justice, argued at the Fifteenth Party Congress in December 1927 that socialist law should not simply reflect expediency he was sharply attacked. The 1928 grain procurement campaign led to the harsher measures in the countryside. The Shakhty trial encouraged a more hostile atmosphere against intellectuals, and within the party the battle heated up. As the Stalin group came to rely more and more on repression, so the nature of the instruments available had to be changed to make them more repressive. 'The movement for the reform of the criminal code is going on under the sign of a re-evaluation of the significance of the deprivation of freedom in the system of measures of social protection', said one prominent contemporary analyst of the pattern of imprisonment.[9] Krylenko and others bent to this new mood. When the Industrial Party Trial was held he declared that confessions were 'the best clue in all circumstances'. In July 1938 he would be shot on the basis of his own confession, as the whole Stalinist 'legal' system in the 1930s put pride of place in what Bukharin called a 'medieval principle of jurisprudence'.

COUNTER-REVOLUTION AND TERROR

Stalin and his supporters now had to impose themselves on party and society. But to do this they had to both increase the level of repression and transform its character. All restraints had to be removed. In the first instance, while non-custodial sentences continued for many smaller crimes, it was those in the way of the counter-revolution from above who were hit. In early 1930 66 percent of those sentenced for 'counter-revolutionary crimes' – opposing the Stalin revolution – got eight to 10 years. But the harshness gradually affected the whole system, and by 1941 only 33 percent of those found guilty escaped prison. The second element was the new role acquired by the secret police in controlling the rapidly expanding camp system. In the autumn of 1929 more than 60,000 prisoners were transferred to camps. By mid-1930 there were 660,000 there, and by 1932 some 2 million. Thirdly the camps themselves changed. The issue was no longer rehabilitation but punishment, the extraction of forced labour and the creation of an atmosphere of fear. Finally, the definition of crime was widened, and penalties became increasingly harsh. Insofar as Stalin's repression had a 'legal' basis, it derived from modifications to the 1926 code made by a decree on crime issued in February 1927 (the basis of Article 58), a decree on military crimes (July 1927), and decrees of June and December 1934. These widened the idea of state crime, increased sentences and allowed summary proceedings to deal with the accused.

The roots of the intensity of this repression lay in the consolidation of power by a new social group and massive capital accumulation. The fact that the speed and shock led to chaos further reinforced the need to impose top-down control. Opposition had to be atomised, and men and women had to be bullied, cajoled and enthused into storming another fortress. Some commentators have tried to make much of the 'enthusiasm' element. But the military analogy helps put this into perspective. Troops going into battle know the penalty for desertion in the face of the enemy. Their officers know the value of hysteria in whipping men to 'go over the top'. But these officers also know the need to contain it from becoming too unruly. Moreover, given the intensity with which the regime tried to construct and manipulate its 'image', the evidence of real enthusiasm seems small. Nadezhda Mandelstam, whose husband Osip paid with his life for a hostile poem about Stalin, found solace not in the open opposition of workers to the regime – that was too dangerous – but in their gut alienation. Staying with the family of a Kalinin steelworker she found scepticism. 'They're just making fools of us with all that stuff about the working class,' the wife said. 'While the people "up top" fought and murdered each other, they as workers would have nothing to do with it and kept their hands clean.' Working later in a textile factory near Zagorsk, she recorded that there the workers' name for the deity Stalin was 'pock face'.[10]

But this revolution from above required repression and terror for another reason. To consolidate his power Stalin not only needed his ideologists to lie about the past. He had to have the memory of that past destroyed. Success required the death of ideas, and the death of the people who embodied them. Andrei Vyshinsky, Stalin's legal 'expert', who as a Menshevik had opposed the revolution and signed the order for Lenin's arrest in 1917, lauded this transformation: 'Over the road cleared of the last scum and filth of the past, we, our people, with our beloved teacher and leader, the great Stalin, at our head, will march ever onwards towards communism.' The extent to which this led to the destruction of those Bolsheviks who made the revolution, and the continued repression of any attempt from the left to challenge the regime, poses enormous difficulties for those who see the terror as a direct product of 1917. Even in the 1970s one dissident found himself in a psychiatric hospital because, said the medical report, he 'thinks that he must devote his life to the ideal of communism'.[11] As the regime developed it was able to incorporate and reproduce conservative religious, anti-Semitic and other reactionary tendencies. What it could not tolerate was a challenge from the left. Ironically some in the West found Stalin attractive just because his violence had a quite different thrust from that of 'the commune-state'. In Britain, as late as March 1931, Beatrice Webb condemned 'the fanatical brutality of Russian Communism', but she soon changed her tune when she imagined that Stalin was creating the regimented, nationally efficient 'new civilisation' of which she had long dreamed. No less Lloyd George, who had fought real Bolshevism, could say that he was 'jolly glad [Kamenev] was shot'.[12]

This onslaught against an alternative vision was carried on under the guise of the attack on Trotsky, who had been forced into emigration in 1929. The greatest crime in the 1930s was that of 'counter-revolutionary Trotskyist activity'. Trotsky's real influence in Russia by this time was slight, and his own incisive analysis sometimes faltered when trying to make sense of events there. But he stood for the memory of something different, and something that was much bigger than himself or 'Trotskyism'. This was why Trotsky 'the symbol' had to be destroyed. From early 1931 it seems Stalin wanted him dead. Success finally came in August 1940. 'We must strike a blow at the Fourth International [Trotsky's attempt to politically organise an alternative socialist movement],' Stalin reportedly said. 'How? Decapitate it.' As an organisation the Fourth International hardly merited this concern, but its leader could still give the lie to Stalin's usurpation of the ideas of the revolution, and with an icepick an assassin finally brought Trotsky's life to an end in far off Mexico.[13]

But there is also a third element in the explanation of the terror. Although the leaders of the regime were trying to control the processes of social change, they were also inside of them. They were continually buffeted and disoriented by the processes that they believed they controlled and, as with the economy, they were often forced to act in ways and go in directions they had not anticipated. 'At the heart of the darkness' was Stalin, deploying what Bukharin's widow called a 'subtle mastery of the executioner's art'. Extensive archive evidence is now available of Stalin's personal role and knowledge of the scale of repression. But this only confirms what the more insightful sensed at the time. Fedor Raskolnikov, who had played a leading role in the revolution, refused to return from Paris at the height of the purges, and sent Stalin a bitter letter of denunciation in August 1939: 'The list of your crimes is endless. The list of your victims is endless. They cannot be enumerated. Sooner or later the Soviet people will put you in the dock as a traitor to socialism and the revolution. The chief wrecker, a real enemy of the people, the organiser of famine and judicial forgeries'.[14]

The paranoia of the wider leadership, the sense that they were not always in control, had social and political roots. But over time Stalin does seem to have taken pleasure in the elimination of his rivals. Ivan the Terrible, he said, had made the mistake of not decisively eliminating the ruling families beneath him. The implication was clear. 'Every killing is a treat,' said Osip Mandelstam, with a poet's insight, in the verses that led to his death.[15] There was also pleasure too in the discomfort of his closest supporters who found the system deployed against them even as they approved its use against others. Kalinin's wife was arrested in 1938, and Molotov's in 1940. Kaganovich lost a brother to the camps, while another committed suicide. The wife of Stalin's longserving personal secretary Poskrebyshev was arrested, and he was forced to squirm like the others. The wider population sensed the cruelty in its dark humour. Stalin and his wife are sitting in the kitchen. 'Shut the door, Joseph,' she says, 'the baby will catch cold.' 'Leave it open,' says Stalin, 'then he'll die sooner.'

The extent to which the regime was caught up inside the process also helps to explain why it could not always turn terror in the way it wanted. The way that the regime was caught up in the irrationalities of the terror it sponsored is reflected in an appeal from the eastern Siberia area in 1937. One official from there wrote to Zhdanov: 'The party and Soviet leadership was entirely in the hands of enemies. All leaders of regional Soviet departments have been arrested also... Thus there are no officials left to work in either the party or Soviet *apparat*... I ask you urgently – please help by sending us some more cadres from Leningrad'.[16] The problems with forced labour also illustrate the difficulties terror created. As the prison camps expanded, some believed that there was a simple economic explanation – the regime wanted slave labour. But this seems to have been a byproduct rather than a cause of repression. It was a byproduct that was never able to be deployed 'efficiently'. Forced labour armies built the White Sea/Baltic canal between 1931 and 1933, and 60,000 of those who survived the ordeal got (at least formally) reduced prison sentences. Other forced labour armies built railways and roads, laboured on construction sites, dug coal in Vorkuta, and mined gold in the huge Kolyma region in the far north east of Siberia. This was the most notorious of the camps. 'Transfer to Kolyma was in Soviet labour camps the equivalent of the German "selection for the gas chamber",' wrote one ex-prisoner.[17] This was an exaggeration, but reality was sufficiently horrific for between a quarter and a third of inmates to die there in the 1930s and 1940s. Prisoners sent to the Kolyma region arrived by boat at Magadan, and from there were transported to the inland:

> Prisoners tried like the devil to avoid going inland to the mines. They'd do anything. They'd wait until the lorries were being loaded. I remember a prisoner who asked to go to the toilet. He ran to the wooden toilet and jumped headfirst into the shit. Why? So they wouldn't load him. He had to be hosed down, and by then the trucks had gone. He was crossed off the list so he stayed on here. He'd won a month or a year, at least until the next transport. People were that afraid of the wilderness and the mines.[18]

But Gulag labour was only half as productive as free labour. Although the labour of the half-starved prisoners came cheap, supervision costs were high, as was the opportunity forgone for the work that could have been done by these people in the normal economy. At best it can be said that Gulag labour worked in conditions that free workers would not, but important though this was in some areas of construction and some regions overall, the Gulag, even at its peak, seems only to have provided at most 2 percent of output. A sense of how counterproductive the Gulag could become can be seen in the way that imprisoned scientists were set to work in what were called *sharaski* – essentially prison laboratories and design workshops.

THE TARGETS OF THE TERROR

As we have seen, in the first years of Stalin's terror several million peasants were exiled as kulaks, and oppositionists were arrested, including both intellectuals and politically active workers, and slung into camps or political isolators. When he was arrested in 1930 Ante Ciliga found in these camps the giants of the Russian Revolution that he had come to doubt existed when he arrived in 1926.[19] Repressed too were the specialists and any others who might question the dizzy drive forward, whether they were inside or outside the party. With a degree of recovery from the chaos of the first plan, collectivisation and famine in 1933-34, it seemed as if repression might be moderated. Kirov, the Leningrad party chief and loyal henchman of Stalin, briefly (probably without his active participation) became a symbol of a potentially more moderate 'Stalinism without Stalin'. He was murdered on 1 December 1934. Debates still continue about whether Stalin orchestrated his assassination. He certainly used it to his advantage. The 'enemy' had killed a loyal son of the new regime and had to be crushed. The secret police renewed their efforts and, fearing to stop lest this might point the finger at them, they redoubled their brutality and used torture to secure mass confessions. A series of show trials were put on to destroy the remnants of the old guard. In August 1936

Zinoviev, Kamenev and 14 others were tried as wreckers and fascists. Then in January-February 1937 Piatakov, Radek and 15 others were publicly tried. In May-June 1937 much of the General Staff was destroyed. This weakened army morale, disrupted the command structures, distorted war preparation and helped to pave the way for the defeats of 1941. The victims included Tukhachevsky, who Stalin feared quite wrongly might provide a further source of opposition. Around 35,000 officers were imprisoned or shot, including all eight admirals, most of the Supreme Military Council and all 11 deputy commissars of defence. Finally in March 1938 came the third and in some ways greatest show trial – that of Bukharin, the favourite of the party, and Rykov, Krestinsky and others, including Yagoda, who had headed the OGPU from September 1934 to September 1936. All were carried away.

The power of the secret police to break people was enormous. Bukharin in his testament talked of:

> ...an infernal machine that seems to use medieval methods, yet possesses gigantic power, fabricates organised slander, acts boldly and confidently... These 'wonder working' organs can grind any member of the Central Committee, and member of the party, into dust, turn him into a traitor–terrorist, saboteur, spy. If Stalin doubted himself, confirmation would follow in an instant. [20]

Some have doubted the extent to which fear penetrated the wider population. But the sense of terror was widespread. 'Russia, guiltless, writhed/Under the crunch of bloodstained boots/Under the wheels of Black Marias/Only a dead man smiled, glad of his peace,' said Anna Akhmatova in her great poem 'Requiem'. [21]

Once inside the infernal machine the secret police had limitless power. 'I was told that Kosior and Chubar were people's enemies, and for that reason I, as an investigator, had to make them confess that they were enemies,' said one investigator. [22] In the 1920s the GPU had used threats and pressure but not, it seems, systematic violence. In the 1930s this became commonplace, deliberate and calculated. It ranged from the crude sadism of beatings to the more sophisticated sadism of sleep deprivation and white light. Yet some people were still able to show enormous courage and refuse to bow down, as others were broken and humiliated.

But behind these trials were hundreds of thousands of other victims who were shot, and millions who were arrested and imprisoned. By late 1938, possibly partly from exhaustion and partly because of the indiscriminate nature of the terror, an attempt was made to rein in the secret police. In April 1938 the secret police chief, Ezhov, with whom the terror had become closely identified, was himself arrested and replaced by Beria. His methods were now used against him, and in February 1940 he was shot for illegal repression, spying and trying to assassinate Stalin. But this was only a partial moderation, and terror remained present at a high level through the war years. Then, between 1945

5.1. THE DEATH OF MEN AND THE DEATH OF IDEAS

The fate of Lenin's last (1923) Politburo

V LENIN	*Died of natural causes 1924*
L KAMENEV	*Murdered by Stalin's regime 1936*
G ZINOVIEV	*Murdered by Stalin's regime 1936*
M TOMSKY	*Suicide, fearing arrest, 1936*
N BUKHARIN	*Murdered by Stalin's regime 1938*
A RYKOV	*Murdered by Stalin's regime 1938*
L TROTSKY	*Murdered by Stalin's regime 1940*
J STALIN	*Died of natural causes 1953*
V MOLOTOV	*Died in disgrace 1986*

Stalin and his successors feared open discussion of the real nature of the new society they ran. They also feared any challenge to their claims about their continuity with the past. In the 1930s many old Bolsheviks who might dispute this were murdered or committed suicide. The Society of Old Bolsheviks was dissolved by Stalin.

The real history of the revolution and its degeneration had to be kept secret. The archives contained millions of documents hidden from what Stalin called 'archive rats'. Libraries had special stores where previously published works were kept from readers. The biggest was in the Lenin Library in Moscow. It held hundreds of thousands of books, and millions of copies of journals and newspapers. There were also secret translations of Western works done so that Russia's rulers could see what both left and right were saying about them. They even included a translation of Tony Cliff's **State Capitalism in Russia***, the book that has inspired some of the arguments here. In 1986 less than 5,000 readers (0.00002 percent of the population) had access to this special store in Moscow.*

What could be published about Lenin was severely limited and needed authorisation at the highest level. This helped support the regime's own myth of continuity. After 1991 this was often turned on its head to create a myth of 'evil' continuity. But it does not work. For example, Dimitry Volkogonov's increasingly shrill claims that 'Lenin is the source' sit uneasily alongside his no less frequent admissions that Russia's leaders knew little of Lenin: 'As for party leaders...the majority of those I have known never read a word of Lenin beyond the "party minimum".'[xiii] The same goes for their understanding of Marx or other socialist theorists.' The state even tried to control the sale of second hand copies of Lenin. 'It was a funny old Leninist world where Lenin had become a suspect author,' writes Robert Service. It was indeed. But this contradiction is never resolved by such writers for whom to confront it would be to confront the inadequacy of both the view that Lenin led directly to Stalin, and also the wider arguments about continuity.[xiv]

and 1953, it exploded again, and the camps reached their greatest scale as the regime tried to reimpose control after the Second World War. In an atmosphere born of isolation, war-induced xenophobia and growing Cold War paranoia, the experience of the 1930s was repeated. Several hundred thousand returning soldiers and officers went to the camps. An August 1946 decree attacking Anna Akhmatova and the humorist Zoshchenko began the bringing down of shutters on culture associated with Stalin's henchman Andrei Zhdanov. In science the pseudo-biologist Trifom D Lysenko was given the green light to persecute 'enemies of the progress of Soviet science and the Soviet people'. Biologists who resisted were marginalised or sent to the camps as 'unpatriotic fly breeders'. History became the ever more progressive role of the 'Great Russian people'. Jews were increasingly suspect as 'cosmopolitans'. In 1949-50 the 'Leningrad Affair' saw the arrest and shooting of Voznesensky (head of the State Planning Commission) and other key figures from the city. Then in 1952-53 Kremlin doctors were accused of plotting to poison Stalin, and it seems that it was only his death in 1953 that stopped a still more intense repression.

HOW MANY VICTIMS?

The prisoners themselves struggled to make sense of their numbers and situation. 'Every cell possesses at least one statistician, a scientific investigator of prisons [who] from...disjointed observations...manages to construct a composite picture of the surrounding reality,' said Gustav Herling, a Polish socialist who spent two years in Stalin's prisons and camps in 1941-42. But the prisoners did not have a clear idea of the scale of repression, and those who followed their accounts were often misled over the size of the camps. With the archives more open we can now better understand the real extent of the repression. The records are not perfect, but they were kept. 'Surely one of the greatest nightmares of the whole Soviet system is that mania for liquidating their victims with all legal formalities,' said one of Herling's fellow prisoners. Of course not everything was reliable, and least of all the charges themselves. For the secret police the issue was less the truth than 'a compromise whereby the accused allows himself to be convicted by choosing the most convenient fiction from a number of fictitious crimes'.[23] But the basic quantitative records seem more or less reliable, and are broadly consistent with one another and the evidence of population change.

The most extreme penalty was execution. If we date the Stalin era from 1929 to 1953 then we know with reasonable accuracy that there were 790,000 executions for what the regime defined as overtly political offences, most concentrated in 1937-38. There were, of course, other executions for 'non-political offences', and other 'political' executions such as those of Polish officers in 1940. This would seem to suggest a maximum figure of direct state executions of just under

1 million. Those found guilty but not subjected to the 'highest penalty' faced five possible punishments. At one end of the scale was corrective labour involving no detention but penalty wages while effectively on probation. As we saw in the last chapter, millions of workers suffered this because of 'crimes' against labour discipline. Detention had four main forms – prison, corrective labour camps for sentences of over three years, corrective labour colonies for sentences of one to three years, and exile to special settlements which people could not leave but in which they were not formally detained. Together these made up the Gulag, though formally this applied to the camps and colonies. Table 5.2 sets out the numbers caught up in this system at different points.

In terms of numbers we know most about the operations of the secret police. Between 1928 and 1933 they sentenced more than 800,000 people, and a higher number must have been arrested. The prisons became so full that the authorities had to temper repression in 1934, when only 68,000 arrests were made. Then the full terror exploded, with 1.7 million arrests between 1935 and 1940, 80 percent of them in 1937-38. Around 2 million sentences were handed out in these five years, the higher numbers reflecting the re-sentencing of prisoners in 1935-36. Arrests fell to 690,000 during the war, with 525,000 sentences. But then the regime extended its grip again between 1946 and 1953.

TABLE 5.2. THE CHANGING SIZE OF STALIN'S GULAG (THOUSANDS)[24]

	1933	1937	1939	1941	1944	1953	1958
Prisons	800	545	351	488	na	276	na
Camps	334	821	1,317	1,502	664	1,728	948
Colonies	240	375	355	420	516	741	
Special settlements	1,142	917	939	930	na	2,754	49
TOTAL	2,516	2,658	2,962	3,348	na	5,499	na
POPULATION (millions)	162.9	162.5	168.5	195.4	na	188.7	208.8
PERCENTAGE	1.54	1.63	1.76	1.71	na	2.9	na

na: not available

But the numbers in the table are snapshots at particular dates. The camps, said Solzhenitsyn, were in 'perpetual motion'. Sentences did end – every year

20 percent or more were released. Others escaped, still others died. The numbers going through the camps were therefore at least twice as high as the 1953 figure, and possibly three times higher. Numbers were exceptionally reduced during the war. This was partly because there were fewer arrests, and partly because the death rate shot up, while perhaps 1 million men were released to the Red Army, and early release was granted to half a million pregnant women, and the old and sick of both sexes. But from 1946, as the table shows, the Gulag swelled to its greatest size.

How many were criminals and how many political prisoners? The question can be answered formally by looking at those convicted under Article 58 and related political articles in the criminal code. On this basis it is clear that 'politicals' only formed a minority of those in the Gulag. In 1950-51, for example, they were a quarter. But this is not a sensible approach. Crime of all kinds has social roots, which is why it varies between societies and over time. Similarly the treatment of crime has political roots, whether in terms of definitions of criminal acts or the operation of policing, the law and punishment. One example of the broadened and punitive definition of criminality would be the introduction of the death penalty or 10 years hard labour for the theft of state property that we noted in the previous chapter. Another was the decision of 7 April 1935 to place juveniles under the control of the courts, and to apply 'all penal sanctions' from 12 upwards. This brought large numbers of boys into prison, where they gave 'themselves up passionately to the only two occupations of their lives – theft and self-abuse'.[25] The growing alienation and exploitation, and the gap between what the regime claimed and what it actually delivered, all created ample conditions for crime to flourish. Moreover, if a regime lacks wider legitimacy, so too will its punishments. This is not to say that we should romanticise criminality under Stalin. People – perhaps desperate, perhaps greedy, perhaps brutal, perhaps all three – grabbed what they could, and often at the expense of others no more fortunate. But they remained a product of the regime. And this regime claimed to be superior to other states. One standard of judgement is therefore to compare its imprisonment levels to those elsewhere at the same time. Equally we could compare what came later with the years of NEP. The result is much the same. For a society with Russia's population, something of the order of 200,000 people at most should have been in jail – by this standard most were political prisoners.

RESISTANCE

Resistance did not die in the camps, but it was difficult. The Gulag reduced and degraded people. Here was 'the world of the insulted, humiliated and executed'.[26] For many it was triumph enough to survive where so many succumbed. Survival involved a physical struggle against hunger and disease.

Malnourishment was the norm, and starving prisoners were vulnerable to illness and infection. Over the period 1936-50 camp death rates averaged around 61 per 1,000. This was many times the civilian level for groups in the prime of life. Only towards the end did conditions improve, and in 1952 death rates fell to six per 1,000. The full extent of the emaciation that many experienced was only apparent during the irregular visits to bath houses while prison clothes were deloused. There were 'shadowy forms, with drooping testicles and fallen stomachs and chests, their legs covered with open sores and joined like two matchsticks to thin hips'. 'Hunger is a horrible sensation,' remembered Gustav Herling:

> The body is like an overheated machine, working at increased speed and on less fuel, and the wasted arms and legs come to resemble torn driving belts. There is no limit to the physical effects of hunger beyond which tottering human dignity might still keep its uncertain but independent balance... If god exists, let him punish mercilessly those who break others with hunger.[27]

Conditions deteriorated catastrophically during the war. In 1942-43 the death rate rose in the camps to more than 170 per 1,000. Overall in the war years some 800,000 were carried off by hunger, illness and exhaustion (including several thousands executed in the panic of 1941). Herling experienced the beginnings of this really intense hunger. To survive he gathered flour and dust from the floor of the wagons he unloaded. This was then made into a thin paste, and moulded around the sagging breasts of a female prisoner so she could smuggle it past the guards to fill out what was more or less a diet of bread and water.

Alongside the physical struggle was the psychological struggle. Hopelessness in the face of incomprehension, degradation, boredom and overwork was all too easy. Here there could be few heroes. Some lived by making victims of victims. They denounced others. Before the war some one in 50 were said to be informers. During the war the ratio may have been one in 12. Others bullied, some scapegoated. 'No one who has not lived in a Soviet labour camp can realise the extent of anti-Semitism in Russia,' said Herling.[28] His account too brings out the sexual exploitation – open homosexuality in single sex camps (the Gulag was overwhelmingly male), heterosexual sex in camps where men and women were in neighbouring units. Physical debility reduced sexual feeling, but it did not stop rape or brutalised couplings in snatched moments: 'Women were treated like prostitutes and love like a latrine.' For some sex could give protection for a time with the right guard or prisoner. Pregnancy could be a means of temporary escape, with claims that some women even inseminated themselves with semen passed to them.[29]

Relief from the regime of constant work could also come with mutilation – a finger, a toe, even a whole foot or arm. To stop this the NKVD in 1940 began to consider accidents at work sabotage unless they were authenticated. But illness could also be simulated or manufactured for real – cuts infected, blood poisoned, lungs injured with inhaled substances.

What of escape? Between 1934 and 1938 300,000 escapes are recorded. Recaptures numbered 190,000, so perhaps 40 percent got away, but this was significant. One of them was Ante Ciliga, who left a memorable account of how he did it.[30] But control of the camps was quickly tightened. In 1939-40 there were only 24,000 escapes, and recaptures ran at 80 percent of this number. During the war escapes remained low at 32,000 (though proportionally this was higher than in 1939-40), and they were even lower absolutely and proportionally between 1945 and 1953, when only 22,000 managed it, though with recaptures only just over 50 percent this number.[31]

As the numbers rose, conditions in the camps and colonies deteriorated and repression intensified, but at this stage there was still some fightback. The most important instance came at the Vorkuta camp complex in the north which mined coal for Leningrad. Here Trotskyists who had refused to capitulate to Stalin at the start of the First Five-Year Plan led an heroic hunger strike. It lasted 132 days, from October 1936 to the spring of 1937. Their indomitable will forced concessions to improve conditions, but the gains were shortlived. In the whirlwind of repression in 1937-38 these Trotskyists were taken out in groups onto the tundra to be shot by the secret police – out of sight of their comrades in the camps, but within hearing distance of the gunfire.[32]

But many of the reported revolts were, if not fabrications, gross exaggerations, as was their attribution to the work of 'Trotskyists'. Between 1941 and 1944, for example, 11,000 were shot for being organisers of underground camp groups, of which some 600 were uncovered. But this was a time, wrote Herling, when 'the slightest infringement of regulations is treated as the most serious offence if it has the appearance of an "organised conspiracy".' The intense hunger increased desperation. It felt 'like a savage war dance in which the two warring groups [guards and prisoners], divided by the barrier of fire in the middle sway for hours to the rhythm of a drum, staring at each other with mistrust and gradually increasing fury'.[33] Some real revolts did break out, such as one at Vorkuta in January 1942, when over 100 prisoners seized weapons, and there were nearly 100 deaths before order was restored and a further 50 executed.[34] But revolts on a mass scale would eventually come in 1953-54, and they helped to bring much of the huge camp regime to an end.

THE GREAT REVOLTS

On 5 March 1953 Stalin died. Tens of millions had grown up thinking of him as a godlike figure. Horrific confirmation of the power of Stalin came quickly as crowds gathered in central Moscow to mourn his passing, and a still unknown number were crushed to death. 'The souls of hundreds of trampled

✸ 5.2 *THE CULT OF STALIN*

The 'cult of Stalin' grew with the terror, and reached its peak between 1945 and 1953. Writers, poets and artists were expected to engage in obscene adulation. In December 1949 the Tretyakov Gallery in Moscow held an exhibition in celebration of Stalin's 70th birthday. The star painting was Shurpin's **The Morning of Our Motherland** *— a model 'Socialist Realist' fantasy. The art magazine* **Iskusstvo** *described it as follows:*

'On a bright early morning Comrade Stalin is seen working in the vast collective farm fields with high voltage transmission lines in the distance, wearing a white tunic with his raincoat over his arm. His exalted face and his whole figure lit with the golden rays of springtime sun. One recollects verses by the people's poet Dzhambul: "Oh Stalin, the sunshine of springtime is you!" He walks triumphantly towards the new dawn. The image of Comrade Stalin is the triumphant march of Communism, the symbol of courage, the symbol of the Soviet people's glory, and a call for new heroic exploits for the benefit of our great motherland. In this image are immortalised the features of a wise, majestic and at the same time amazingly modest and unpretentious man who is our beloved leader.'

Not all portraits of Stalin had such a 'happy' fate. In 1953 Picasso was asked by a French Communist journal to do a commemorative drawing. His slight sketch of Stalin as a younger man provoked condemnation for failing to show Stalin in the right light. When a party intellectual was sent to talk to him, Picasso explained the dilemma of the artist:

'Can you imagine if I had done the real Stalin, such as he has become, with his wrinkles, his pockets under his eyes, his warts…? A portrait in the style of Cranach! Can you hear them scream, "He has disfigured Stalin! He has aged Stalin"? And then too I said to myself, why not Stalin in heroic nudity? Yes, but Stalin nude? And what about his virility? If you take the pecker of the classical sculpture…so small. But come on, Stalin, he was a true male, a bull. So then if you give him the phallus of a bull, and you've got this little Stalin behind this thing, they'll cry, "But you've made him into a sex maniac! A satyr!" Then if you are a true realist you take your tape measure and you measure it all properly. That's worse — you've made Stalin into an ordinary man. And then, as you are ready to sacrifice yourself, you make a plaster cast of your own thing. Well, it's even worse. What do you take yourself for? Stalin? After all, Stalin, he must have an erection all the time, just like the Greek statues… Tell me, you who knows — Socialist Realism, is that Stalin with an erection or Stalin without an erection?'[xv]

fellow citizens formed a funeral wreath,' wrote a later Soviet poet.[35]

The one place in the Soviet Union where unrestrained joy at Stalin's death could be found was in the camps. At the huge Vorkuta camp complex, when loudspeakers announced the death of Stalin, prisoners fell to their knees weeping with joy. At Norilsk free workers (many of whom were ex-prisoners) were heard singing, and when the prisoners asked why they were told: 'Everyone should be singing. The tyrant is dead!' As the news spread in the Norilsk camps the prisoners threw their hats into the air, shouting. 'Everyone was ecstatic,' wrote one prisoner. Bottles were found from their hiding places and opened to celebrate. But revolt soon followed.

After 1945 new groups had been dragged into the system. Few prisoners had a simple story to tell. Some were imprisoned as spies simply because they had been captured by the Nazis. Others were true collaborationists, and still others had joined the dissident General Vlasov in his Liberation Army, while others still came from the borderlands which had been integrated into the Soviet Empire as the Red Army had moved west. The share of Russians in the camps fell from 63 percent in 1941 to 52 percent in 1951. Ideologically many of these were committed nationalists when they went into the camps and, if not, they became so as they looked around for a simple explanation of their plight.

Sometime in 1947-48 a revolt did break out in the Vorkuta complex. A prison army took control of some of the camps and then began to march on the town of Vorkuta, but it was massacred on the tundra by the troops and planes of the secret police. Solzhenitsyn says the revolt soon took on a legendary character. But it seems clear that the leaders of the revolt saw success in terms of an unrealistic military victory, perhaps with the hope of linking up with Western forces as the Cold War developed.

But the problem was to find a unity that might be the basis of a larger scale action. One valuable reconstruction of the 1953 revolts is by Andrea Graziosi.[36] He argues that forced labour to some extent turned prisoners into workers and encouraged them to develop a degree of unity. This process was assisted by a small improvement in material conditions after 1948. Gradually the character of relations in the camps began to change. Collaboration between the guards and the criminal elements broke down in some camps. Foremen and informers might now occasionally be found 'in fresh concrete, badly mutilated or even dismembered'. Tree trunks sent from timber camps were found with messages carved on them asking when the Stalin regime would fall. Low productivity began to slump further.

The prisoners were having to begin to create a political consciousness of their own and their own programmes. The authorities responded by increasing the number of guards and informers. Prisoners were moved, but this only helped to spread organisation. So too did the separation of criminals from political prisoners. Clandestine organisations, usually on a national basis, began to overcome their mutual suspicions, and small protests and revolts began to be recorded in 1951-52. Then Stalin died.

Jacob Scholmer, an imprisoned East German Communist who had already been a victim of the Gestapo in Nazi Germany, wrote that Stalin's death was awaited 'with an intensity which must be almost without parallel in the annals of human desperation'. When the news finally came the relief of the prisoners was matched by the disorientation of the guards. The anger and expectation of the prisoners was increased when Stalin's henchman, Beria, almost immediately released several hundred thousand criminal prisoners.

The first major explosion came in the Norilsk camp system in May 1953. Nervous guards fired on prisoners. This led to camp after camp spontaneously striking. By the end of May 20,000 were on strike. A temporary truce was arranged. But then in June the authorities appeared to backtrack, and many of the Norilsk camps came out again. Signallers went onto roofs. One camp appealed to the inhabitants of the town of Norilsk by flying kites. The striking camps were heartened by rumours of support from the town and solidarity signs from passing train drivers. The authorities hesitated to act, and both they and the prisoners awaited the arrival of a commission from Moscow.

It was in late July that strikes at Vorkuta began. The Vorkuta camps held 100,000 prisoners, whose initial clandestine organisation was probably better than that at Norilsk. Here news of the eruption of protest against Stalinism in East Germany in June 1953 was an important boost to morale and a trigger to revolt in the most radicalised camps. Communication was limited. Prisoners had to deduce what was happening by watching for changes in movement or reading messages scratched on railway wagons. To prevent the Vorkuta strikes spreading the authorities quickly improved conditions in the complex, but by the end of the month 12,000-16,000 were on strike there, awaiting their own commission from Moscow.

The strikes were run by elected committees that reflected the national composition of the camps. The authorities tried to split the strikers, but they were not always successful. Some former collaborators and ex-Nazis made good stoolpigeons. Others came over to the strikers. The committees tried to stop the lynching of informers who were then forced to write out strike propaganda. The prisoners' demands focused on political freedom, improved conditions, and the national question in the different parts of the Soviet Empire. Plays and concerts were put on. Funerals were held to bury and honour those killed at the start of the strikes as 'martyrs to freedom'.

Camps that struck were immediately surrounded by machine-gun nests. But the authorities' nervousness meant that they lacked a clear capacity to act. Nowhere did the guards feel confident to cut off supplies. Both sides were really waiting for the commissions from Moscow, which would hold the real power. When they arrived their tactic was to try to break the strikes by concessions. How many accepted these is unclear but at both Norilsk and Vorkuta some camps held out. At the end of July and the beginning of August at Norilsk the order was finally given to storm these. The last camp to fall was Number Three, with perhaps 80 dead and 280 wounded – a sign of the fight put up. Some strike leaders killed themselves rather than be captured. At Vorkuta at more or less the same time, the last camp to hold out was also bloodily stormed, and the months of turmoil came to an end.

There would be one more large-scale revolt in the camps. In 1954 at the Kengir camp in Kazakhstan another great revolt took place which lasted for 40 days. One of the participants was Alexander Solzhenitsyn, who would later describe it in his *Gulag Archipelago*.[37]

But the authorities' real victory over the prisoners was limited. The new and shaken leadership moved to improve conditions in the camps. Strike leaders were beaten up but not shot – a sure sign of the changed mood. Mass releases now began of political prisoners – some 90,000 were let out in 1954-55 before the emptying of the political camps associated with Khrushchev's de-Stalinisation policy of 1956. The freedom to breathe freely, said Solzhenitsyn, was precious: 'No food, no wine, not even a woman's kiss is sweeter to me than this air steeped in the fragrance of flowers, of moisture and freshness'.[38]

But the revolts in the camps also have a wider significance, for they indicate to us something about the nature of social relations in Stalin's Russia. When Jacob Scholmer asked one old Communist in the camps what he thought of what was happening he simply said: 'The history of all hitherto existing societies is the history of class struggle'.[39]

REDUCING THE TERROR

Stalin's death released a blockage in the system in another sense. A modern industrial society cannot depend in the long run on coercion alone. The army, police and secret police cannot be everywhere all the time. Nor can managers and foremen always be standing behind the back of the worker. Development needs a degree of positive engagement from workers, and it also needs a degree of stability and routine. Much of this was missing in Stalin's Russia, and especially in the last years of his life. At the very top, so long as he remained alive, no one had the courage to challenge his despotic whims. 'When Stalin says dance, a wise man dances,' said Khrushchev after he was made to do a folk dance for Stalin's amusement.[40] It was also often unwise to challenge despotic actions carried out by officials in the wider state. Who knew what was an individual whim and what had support from above?

Irrationalities also abounded in society at large. The scientific work in the Gulag, for example, now included perhaps half the atomic energy research for

Russia's nuclear programme, which was seen as essential to boost the military position.[41] And with the workforce as a whole, the squeeze on living standards and conditions had been pushed down so far for so long that the struggle to survive precluded interest in much else. Edward Crankshaw saw this first-hand as a journalist in Russia in the immediate post-war years:

> Soon after the war...life was at such a low ebb throughout the Soviet Union that in the remote areas — and in some not so remote — it was often impossible to tell a free citizen from a prisoner... There were prisoners being marched about, doing fatigues, or manhandling heavy trunks, or trying to break up frozen soil to sink foundations. And next to them came free labourers, with nothing in their appearance or the work they were doing to show the difference. Nobody cared — they were all half-dead with hunger anyway.[42]

Once Stalin was dead the new leadership moved to set in motion a 'thaw' which led to the process of de-Stalinisation in the 1953-64. The small group of leaders needed to protect themselves by drawing a line against the past. This also meant making sure that the secret police did not turn against them, so Beria, their former chief, who seems to have initiated the thaw, also became its most important victim. There was also a desire for a degree of stability at the top, not only from the leadership itself but the layers beneath it who wanted a space to breathe. Beyond this there was also a recognition of the need to build some kind of bridge to the population, both in terms of gaining wider political support and more narrowly creating positive incentives in place of the unproductive terror regime.

De-Stalinisation involved unspectacular reforms in many aspects of Soviet society, but its most visible sign was Khrushchev's 'secret speech' at the Twentieth Congress of the Party in February 1956.[43] More quietly the camps began to be emptied and many closed down, as can be seen from the data in table 5.2. Another liberal push was given in 1961 at the Twenty Second Congress, and Stalin's body was removed from its place of honour in Lenin's mausoleum. In this situation it became possible to have wider discussions about the past and the present – even statistics began to reappear, albeit without the most interesting ones. But the biggest impact was perhaps made by the publication of Solzhenitsyn's novel *One Day in the Life of Ivan Denisovich* in *Novy Mir* in 1962 describing prison camp life. But there were limits – even to a literary exploration of the past, present and future. Nor was the liberal movement all one way. In 1958-61 there were new codifications of the criminal law. New procedures insisted that there must be a crime before there was a charge, that there should be no torture, and that the law should be applied equally by an independent judiciary and procuracy. But particular articles still made some ordinary acts political, and these 'political acts' criminal – flight abroad (Article 64), religious practices (Articles 142 and 227), anti-Soviet agitation (Article 70), and the very serious anti-state crimes (Article 72). New elements were added too. In 1957 a law against 'parasites' was passed, the death penalty was introduced for economic crimes in 1961, and zealous party members were encouraged to criticise youth whose dress and appearance belied the approved image of the Soviet young.

These limits and contradictions were not simply a product of Khrushchev's whim. The regime remained caught in the web of the Cold War, facing not only enemies to the west but to the east as well. The ability to make concessions was limited therefore by continued pressures on resources and the need to sustain, both economically and politically, the core military-industrial complex built up under Stalin.

Nor was there any desire to throw the baby out with the bathwater. The Soviet system appeared to be working. The economy was progressing. Militarily it was closing the gap with the West. This suggested the need for moderate reform. The self-confidence of Russia's rulers was reflected in the comment of the party ideologist Suslov to the novelist Vasilii Grossman that his epic but critical war novel *Life and Fate* would not be published 'for 200 to 300 years'.[44]

Beyond this the leadership and wider ruling class was itself a product of Stalinism, and the more radical the critique, the more dangerous the challenge to its position. This was why when Khrushchev condemned Stalin he limited his attack to the period after 1934, leaving 'pure' the building of the foundations of the regime in the revolution from above of 1928-34. He also, of course, pushed all the responsibility for the crimes onto Stalin personally and 'the cult of the individual', in order to avoid pointing the finger at himself and those around him. Boris Pasternak said that in 1956 'the cult of personality' gave way to 'the cult of hollow words...the cult of faceless Philistines' beneath which 'the cult of evil, and the cult of uniformity, are just as ever present as they were'. Sooner than he realised he would feel this personally when his novel *Dr Zhivago* was suppressed. Worse than a pig, said Semichastny (then head of the KGB), Pasternak 'had befouled the place where he lives'.[45]

More fundamental reform was also difficult because of the nature of the system itself. The ruling class that developed under Stalin was heavily bureaucratised in its structures. Bureaucratic resistance could always stymie bureaucratic change. Moreover there were tactical differences at the top over how far to go. In the years immediately after 1953 this led to infighting from which Khrushchev emerged the victor, but only after he had appealed to the Central Committee in 1957. This act showed that a clear dispersal of power had taken place, but it also showed that it still remained highly concentrated.

It was these newly empowered but narrow groups at the top who would bring Khrushchev down in 1964 when his approach finally offended them too much. In 1957 Khrushchev had tried to break up the high degree of centralisation of the economy, partly to introduce more flexibility into the system but also to break up the power base of any potential opposition. He also tried to purge sections of the upper party. In 1960-61, for example, most of the regional party bosses were removed in a bloodless purge. But he was not able to capitalise on these moves. Reorganisation had only a limited economic effect, and in some ways confused things even more. Khrushchev himself often appeared erratic in his attitudes and demeanour, both inside and outside Russia. What those at the top wanted was both progress and stability. What was called 'harebrained scheming' came to be seen as something that they could do without. In 1964 he was replaced by the non-scheming Brezhnev, who headed the Soviet Union until his death in 1982.

MAINTAINING REPRESSION

With Brezhnev the shutters came down on further liberalisation, and in some respects the net of repression tightened a little more. The change was signalled by the sentencing of two writers – Siniavsky and Daniel – to prison for a satire which was condemned as 'anti-Soviet propaganda'. Then in 1967 Articles 190-1 and 190-2 were added to the criminal code to allow imprisonment for anti-Soviet fabrications (published criticism) and violations of public order (demonstrations). But the feared Stalinist renaissance never materialised. The position was effectively that Stalin should be neither praised nor condemned but avoided. Khrushchev became an unperson and was able to write his memoirs in secret. Politics and society now operated in well established channels. Natural death by old age was the major means of exit from political life. When individuals fell out of favour (and relatively few did) they were rarely disgraced in the old way. 'In Stalin's time,' said Yeltsin, 'ex-politicians were shot. Khrushchev pensioned them off. In Brezhnev's "era of stagnation" they were pushed off as ambassadors to distant countries'.[46]

This stability produced an underlying complacency. In November 1972 Brezhnev told the Party Secretariat that 'everything is going alright, everyone is on the job working hard and fruitfully, in general and overall, all tasks are being dealt with in time and correctly, and both routine and problematical issues are being resolved'.[47] But, as long as things worked, technocratic improvements seemed all that was necessary. When some liberal supporters of the regime like Andrei Sakharov, Roy Medvedev and, initially, Alexander Solzhenitsyn went further and argued that in the interests of the system itself the leadership should continue with more fundamental changes, they were marginalised and pushed into more oppositional dissent. But even here the pressure was much less than it had been in the past.

After the initial wave of de-Stalinisation Khrushchev could claim in January 1959 that 'there are no political prisoners in the Soviet Union today'.[48] This was never true. Russia remained a society with one of the biggest prison-industrial complexes in the world. But what was true from the 1950s to the late

1980s is that the numbers imprisoned for blatant political reasons were now quite a small component of the total. In 1975 Amnesty International estimated that there were some 10,000 political prisoners in the USSR – around 1 percent of the prison camp population. The figure seems likely to have remained at this level until 1988-89, when most 'politicals' were released.[49]

The fact that the regime could not forgo repression completely was a sign of weakness. So too was its continued suppression of the most basic information about many aspects of daily life, and the sometimes relentless persecution of those who challenged the authorities. Alexander Solzhenitsyn, for example, was finally deported in 1974. Andrei Sakharov was exiled internally. Others were subject to hard labour. Some, like Anatoly Marchenko, died in prison. But it is important to recognise that there had been a shift to a much lower level of repression than in the past, even if the authorities could now to some extent rely on an inbuilt caution in most people born of half-suppressed memories of earlier nightmares.

'In the 1960s and 1970s...my mother still trembled with her whole body when somebody rang the doorbell,' said Alexander Latsis whose father, an old Bolshevik and Cheka official, had died in prison in 1938. 'To preserve her peace of mind I permanently disconnected the doorbell'.[50]

In the context of the Cold War some were reluctant to admit the change. This was part of the psychology that led intellectuals to line up either in favour of Washington or Moscow, and condemn unequivocally the other side while ignoring the blemishes of their own. In the West this helped obscure the fact that 'Western democracy' was the privilege of the few, and that capitalism in the West could be as barbaric as state capitalism in the East. In 1984, for example, Amnesty reported that in at least 117 states out of over 150 sovereign states there were political prisoners who had been killed, tortured or degraded, and perhaps 1 million had died over the previous decade directly at the hands of their governments or with their collusion. Gabriel García Márquez suggested that the population of those forced to flee repression in Latin America was greater than the entire population of Norway, and in Central America, with a population of some 25 million, hundreds of thousands were murdered by Washington-backed regimes with rates of repression perhaps comparable to high Stalinism.

To say this is not to detract from the internal suffering inflicted in the name of the Soviet regime after 1953 (nor its actions abroad), but it is to stress that high Stalinism had been modified and scaled down to much lower levels. Of course, sometimes even the most innocuous activities could get caught up in the continued repression. A British judge once remarked that the law should not be used to break a butterfly upon a rack. But this is exactly what happens in even some of the most liberal states. In repressive systems the broken butterflies can include poets like Joseph Brodsky, arrested in 1964 as a 'parasite', or Irina Ratushinskaya, jailed in 1983, whose rhymes, however inadvertently, gave offence to those in power.

The targets of repression in these last decades came from five main groups. The biggest appears to have been religious – evangelical Christians, Baptists, Buddhists, Muslims, Jehovah's Witnesses, even True Orthodox all fell foul of the laws on church, state and schooling. A second group were national rights activists from the different republics. A third were Jews trying to leave, though as a result of international pressure between 1970 and 1989 several hundred thousand were allowed to go (including some for whom Jewishness was a flag of convenience).[51] A fourth group were human rights activists, who became a special target with the unauthorised production of *A Chronicle of Current Events*, detailing state repression, and the creation of a monitoring group to check the adherence of the regime to the Helsinki accords. Then there were those who took a more systematically political stance. Here the real offence continued to be challenges that tried to take the regime at its formal word and compare its reality to the dream of socialism, even if only to reform it. 'Attempts to investigate history and the contemporary situation with the aid of the Marxist method...provokes the harshest measures of repression,' wrote one dissident, Lev Kopolev, in the 1970s.[52]

Once political proceedings were initiated there was no way out: 'There has never in Amnesty's experience been an acquittal of a political defendant in the USSR.' This partly flowed from the very top, but it also reflected confidence lower down in the KGB. The local authorities were unlikely to be criticised for being brutal. Not every political offender ended up in court. Between 1969 and 1975, for example, Amnesty identified 120 cases of psychiatric confinement for political and religious reasons, including the hospitalisation of the scientist Zhores Medvedev, left wing general Pytor Grigorenko, mathematician Leonid Plyusch, and Vladimir Klebanov, a worker who tried to protest against work conditions and establish a free trade union. 'You're not well known like Solzhenitsyn,' one dissenter was told. 'For his opinions they sent him out of the country. But they'll put you in a psychiatric hospital for your statements and opinions.' Diagnosed illnesses included 'an obsessive mania for truth-seeking' and considering the invasion of Czechoslovakia in 1968 'to have been an aggression'. Victor Fainberg, who was hospitalised for this in 1968, was told: 'Your disease is dissent. As soon as you renounce your opinions and adopt the correct point of view, we'll let you out'.[53]

Conditions for those imprisoned in the camps, whether for political or criminal offences, continued to be bad. Prisoners were subjected to four different regimes – ordinary, intensified, strict and special – defined by limitations on conditions, rights and food. Further dissent could result in the punishment isolator or *shizo*, 'the standard Soviet camp method of torture by cold and hunger' wrote Ratushinskaya, who calculated that she spent 8 percent of her sentence there. Malnourishment continued to be a problem – the only time when good food was available was during hunger strikes as part of the authorities' tactic to break them. The struggle to survive against the system and informers also carried on to the end – 'never believe them, never fear them, never ask them for anything' was a basic rule. Among non-politicals simulated illness, mutilation, bribery and, for women, pregnancy were still used to achieve some relief (and are still used this way today). Those known as 'goats' curried favour with the guards, while 'rejectors' refused them any recognition. Organised revolt, however, was now very difficult, though this did not stop Ratushinskaya and her fellow women political prisoners celebrating wildly when news came through in 1984 of the death of the Soviet leader and ex KGB chief Yuri Andropov.[54] But the fact that Andropov had been able to become Soviet leader was less a reflection of the power of the KGB than the way in which, alongside the repression and eventually displacing it, new institutions and mechanisms of control had developed. It is to the nature of the social group that controlled these that we have now to turn.

At the centre of the picture is the head of the Moscow Metro. His full dress, military style, gold braided uniform

6 RULING CLASS

Few aspects of the system created by the revolution from above after 1928 produced more confusion than the issue of class. The official story was simple. Russia had been a class society – there were even classes in NEP Russia – but with the coming of state-directed accumulation classes disappeared, or least antagonistic ones did. The idyll of social harmony was set out in the 1936 constitution. The new Russia had two non-antagonistic classes, workers and peasants, and a stratum, the intelligentsia. This remained the official version until the end. Even when it became possible to suggest that some antagonistic contradictions did exist, it could never be allowed that these were of the kind found elsewhere. To make that step, to see the USSR as a class society in Marxist terms, was to invite arrest and imprisonment.

Looked at from the outside, it was always possible for those not taken in by the propaganda to see the basic contours of power and privilege, although here also perhaps too much credence was given to the official version. Could the levels of inequality really be as sharp inside Russia as outside? Alexander Yanov certainly thought so. In one essay he described a visit to the countryside home of one of the 'top thousand'. Here was one room dominated by Old Masters and the finest 18th century antiques, a second filled with the most modern electronic equipment, a living room with a bar loaded with the finest French cognac, a cellar done out in medieval splendour, a study with a fine library that included the banned works of Solzhenitsyn, and so on: 'I have seen a great deal since then. I have been the guest of a well to do American colleague and have attended a reception given by a Texas lady millionaire. But in comparison with the owner of that astonishing house, all of them – including the lady million-aire – are proletarians who have nothing to lose but their chains'.[1]

However, the fundamental confusion was less about the facts, nor even about Soviet Russia – it was a confusion about class itself. Those who showed enormous care in analysing the working class in capitalism, in debating the role of white collar workers or discussing whether or not there was an under-class, showed no such discernment when it came to the ruling class. It is not too much to say that when the issue of whether or not there was a ruling class in Soviet Russia was discussed, the theory of class seemed to have more in common with a TV costume drama version of 19th century capitalism. Here capitalists are men who control capital as their private property, owning it per-sonally or in the form of vast aggregations of shares. These individuals use their wealth to consume conspicuously and then pass on what is left to their children through inheritance, so allowing capitalism to reproduce itself over time. This costume drama did not fit Soviet Russia. Here was a state-controlled society – formally property lay in the hands of the state itself. There was no sig-nificant private ownership, no vast holdings of shares, and no direct inheri-tance mechanism whereby enterprises were passed from father to son. Soviet Russia, it was said, could not have a ruling class. The only problem was that in these terms neither could the West. Even in Victorian England this costume drama view was far from exhausting all the different forms of capitalism as it actually existed. To see class in these terms, therefore, is to miss its deeper logic and the way that class control can operate through varied forms. Over time these forms have become more varied still, so that it now makes no sense as an image of class anywhere. Nor does it help to argue that the parts where the model doesn't fit – for example, the rise of state production – are only cap-italist because they remain dominated by the parts where it does fit. The rea-son is simply that it is the more varied parts which are increasingly the dominant ones.

Here two developments have been crucial. One has been the rise of the manager-controlled company, where there is a separation of formal ownership and control. Some big companies remain in the grip of personal owners. But the core of global capitalism is now manager controlled, and even when these managers remain nervous of shareholders, those they worry about tend to be the institutional shareholders – the banks, the pension funds and the insur-ance companies that are themselves manager controlled.

No less important has been the rise of state industry which, despite privati-sation, remains an essential part of modern capitalism. Here too there is no private ownership in a narrow legalistic sense – it is the state which is effec-tively in charge. There is no legal inheritance mechanism, but this does not mean that there is no class rule, no exploitation, no alienation of power from one class to another. What counts, whether in the manager-dominated com-pany or the state enterprise, is the way a class of people emerges to control and administer the competitive accumulation of companies and states. It is this competition which determines the nature of the system and the class relations within it. The reproduction of capital determines the reproduction of capital-ists, not the reproduction of capitalists the reproduction of capital. At times, indeed, the power of the state in the West has equalled that in Soviet Russia, as the private sector has been constrained and directed the better to defend the interests of the 'national capital'. This happened in Nazi Germany, but it was and is a feature of all war economies. 'It meant in the end the extension of the administration into almost every aspect of social existence, and a total priority for "war" production over every aspect of "civilian" production,' said one eco-nomic historian of the Second World War. In the US 40 percent of output went into the war effort, and in Britain over 50 percent. Some 59 percent of employment in US manufacturing was devoted to military production, and 66 percent in the UK.[2] As this happened the power of the great and the small at the centre grew. In Britain after 1940, for example, it has been said of Churchill that he was 'the nearest thing to a dictator which Britain has owned since the days of absolute monarchy'. In the US J K Galbraith tells how he and his fellow economists controlled prices across the economy, with the military even setting the price some brothels could charge to troops.[3] Economic and military competition forced a basic symmetry of forms the world over.

Those who control capital use their power to divert income to their own con-sumption. No less do they try to use their control to secure a future for them-selves and their dependants, and the mechanisms that are so developed become part of the way in which the system adjusts over time. But it is important to see which way the causation runs – what is central and what secondary. Personal consumption is a secondary drive to the development of capital. To the contrary the idea of an 'ascetic bourgeoisie' in the form of the Protestant ethic disparag-ing those who did not put everything into accumulation was part of the original ideology of the rise of capitalism. Marx, we should remember, said that 'the pri-vate consumption [of the capitalist] is a robbery perpetrated on accumulation'.[4]

Similarly the idea that capitalism must provide a space to include those with the best skills rather than just the children of the existing rulers has also long been a part of the system. It was after all in Napoleonic France that the idea of a 'career open to talents without distinction of birth or fortune' developed as part of an attack on the legacy of an aristocratic past. With these ideas in mind we can now begin to develop our analysis in the direction of a more realistic understanding of the nature of the ruling class in Russia after 1928.

We suggested in Chapter 4 that the essence of the revolution from above was that it turned those who had risen to the top in the 1920s into a new ruling class because it solidified new relations of production. Workers and peasants were now subordinated to the unhindered pressure of accumulation, while those above them emerged as a state bourgeoisie administering this process. This structural relationship of control of the means of production on the one hand, and subordination to them on the other, was the objective base of the power of the Soviet ruling class. But class is not only a relationship to the means of production. It is also a relationship between people, and its full development is often only expressed in movement, when classes interact.

It is sometimes suggested that to focus on class control in the USSR is unhelpful because at the lower ends the issue of who had power remained fuzzy.[5] But this situation was hardly unique to the USSR. In all but the smallest examples of private enterprise 'owners' have to share power with 'managers' and 'administrators'. Moreover, there are many common institutions that are considered class institutions – the army, church, universities, hospitals – where the chain of hierarchy creates the impression that there is a gradation of power and control. These issues are ultimately not resolved by drawing dividing lines with more or less finesse. They are resolved dynamically, as classes interact and polarise. Consider, for example, how industrial conflicts transform a situation in a workplace. Here hierarchies begin to divide in a systematic way as one group withdraws its goodwill or labour and the smaller group at the top refuses to or is instructed not to participate. No less on a national level, in a revolutionary crisis, lines become sharper. The more impressive the challenge from below, the more people will be pulled over, but this does not alter the structured way in which institutions and society divide. We have already seen clear elements of this in 1917 as part of the wider process of class conflict developing at that time.

In tracing the contours of the ruling class in Russia after 1928 we have therefore to begin with this general sense of how the means of production were controlled – who the real bosses or *nachalniki* were. Two misleading ways of thinking about this have been common among writers on Russia. One has been to focus on the 'elite' with the highest incomes. If we are interested in the scale of inequality (as we will be later) this can be helpful. But, as in the West, the highest incomes can sometimes be at a tangent to real power. They include some we may want to exclude – think of footballers, film stars and musicians. They can also exclude some we may want to include – in Russia for example, the salaries of enterprise directors (though this is less true of their wider privileges) were more restricted than some other top groups.

A second misleading approach has been to focus on the *nomenklatura*. This refers to the way in which the Communist Party developed a system in which only approved people could be elected for certain posts. The *nomenklatura* (or establishment) list identified the position, the people eligible, and who had the authority to make the appointment. To be on the list was therefore a sign of party trust, and perhaps the larger part of those in the ruling class were part of this system, which covered perhaps some 750,000 posts. But there were still others, some enterprise managers for example, who were not always part of the party *nomenklatura*.

PARTY RULE AND THE INTERNAL BALANCE OF POWER

Marx at one stage used the term 'hostile brothers' to describe the capitalist class. What he meant by this was. that, like brothers, they were united when the interests of the family were under threat – when the workers or the servants threatened to dispossess them. But they were also disunited among themselves by the competitive struggle for profit. It is in this contradiction that we find an important part of the explanation for the political structures that develop alongside the economic ones in capitalism.

To manage competition and unite these hostile brothers in their common interests requires organisation – informal and formal. Businessmen come together in clubs and societies, they form trade organisations and political parties. States, too, partly develop to manage, organise and resolve potential conflicts of interest. They also help provide things like education and health systems which capitalism needs to continue, but which are more difficult for private capitalism to produce on a sufficient scale to meet the wider system's needs. Most importantly, the fact that capitalism exists as a world of competing states gives the state itself what has been called a 'Janus face'. It looks inside to preside over the internal interests of the national capitalism, and outside to defend and extend its power on a more global scale.

At the level of the productive economy a pattern of power and influence emerges that reflects the relations of the different units of capital. Big capital tends to dominate small. Finance, industry and service companies compete for influence. The more dynamic and competitive the economy, the less fixed the balance of power. The less competitive, less dynamic and more institutionalised it is, the more fixed the balance of power becomes.

In the Soviet Union the balance of economic power was fixed in the 1930s by the basic competitive drive to accumulate. This created the conditions for the predominance of the military-industrial complex for almost all of the Soviet period. The continued external pressures reinforced this, but just because the system was a bureaucratic one it was also institutionalised from within. Internal attempts to challenge the priorities of this complex – to stress, for example, light consumer goods industries – never really succeeded. The power and influence of those who were based in this sector were sufficient to block any radical reorganisation. 'Beginning in the late 1950s, one got an increasingly clear picture of the collective might of the military-industrial complex and of its vigorous, unprincipled leaders, blind to everything except their "job",' said Andrei Sakharov.[6] His frustration with it helped to push him towards more open criticism, and to become the figurehead for the liberal dissident movement in the 1980s.

But the Soviet system also developed as a single-party state and one, in the first instance, ruled by a brutal dictator. One result of this was to inflate and elevate the role of the organs of repression. This, of course, made even bureaucratic politics dangerous under Stalin, though elements of it continued, as is obvious from any memoir account. Ultimately though fear extended to the very top, as we saw in the previous chapter. Once Stalin was out of the way, however, the leadership moved to ensure that more ordered relationships developed, and this did allow a greater degree of bureaucratic politics within the bureaucratised ruling class. It was the Communist Party and its Komsomol youth organisation that were the site of these bureaucratised politics. They existed alongside the normal system of government. Indeed, it was the Communist Party Politburo that was the real executive force in the Soviet system rather than the 'parliamentary body' – the Supreme Soviet and Council of Ministers. A second consequence was to ensure that 'politics' outside of the Communist Party took place under its closest supervision. 'The smallest organisation, even a club of dog lovers or cactus growers, is supervised by an appropriate body of the CPSU,' said the dissident Roy Medvedev in the early 1970s.[7]

This did not mean that the party, as a mass organisation, had a significant impact on those at the top. Rather, it was one of the instruments through which they ruled. Control was always a top-down process. No party congress was held from 1939 to 1952. Meetings of the Central Committee were rare. There was a brief flurry of CC activity under Khrushchev before meetings declined under Brezhnev, and in 1974 and 1979 the CC managed only a single resolution at its brief meetings.[8] Indeed, the party that developed from the 1930s not only had no real contact with 1917, it was even a new party compared to that of the 1920s. By 1939 70 percent of members had joined since 1929. Moreover it was these new members who filled out much of the hierarchy too. At the Eighteenth Party Conference in 1941 78.4 percent of the delegates were aged 40 or less (and therefore under 18 at the time of the revolution). Only eight (1.8 percent) were more than 50, and therefore over 25 in 1917.[9]

Stalin expressed the top-down character of the party in militarised terms. In 1937 he told the Central Committee plenum that the party had 3,000-4,000 generals, 30,000-40,000 officers and 100,000-150,000 NCOs.[10] The job of the party was essentially twofold. Partly it helped to organise the ruling class, and ensured that the decisions of the leadership and their priorities and policies were carried out. Partly it helped to socialise, mobilise and supervise society at large. This was explicitly also the function of the huge youth section – the Pioneers and the Komsomol – which operated as a state-run Scout organisation. Indeed, the Komsomol was initially developed against the influence of the Scouts. Its motto was also 'Be prepared'. But for adults, too, the party was supposed to play this role. Under Stalin the party became a managerial organisation. Workers 'at the bench' by the end of the 1930s were probably less than 10 percent of the membership – a figure that even the British Conservative Party could have bettered. Those with managerial positions were estimated to have made up 50-70 percent of the party. Although not every manager was a party member, nearly 100 percent of factory managers were. After the death of Stalin, however, the base of the party was broadened to try to make it less managerial – a process likened by one historian to an established bourgeois regime turning to extend its influence by offering a degree of incorporation based on an image of 'consensus' after the initial turmoil of the development of new class forms.[11]

ROOM AT THE TOP?

The drive to industrialise Russia opened up new possibilities for people to find 'room at the top'. New enterprises needed managers. So did hospitals, schools, universities and research institutes. The expanding party state needed new layers of senior administrators. Beneath them, intermediate layers of white collar workers, professionals, doctors, teachers, engineers and architects had to be filled out. The desperately low level of overall education had to be dealt with. The fact that capitalism is always in movement creates some capacity for people to move up to the top. But the leap forward begun in Russia in the 1930s vastly expanded these opportunities. In the years 1926-37, for example, while the numbers of workers doubled, the size of the intelligentsia (a smaller group) grew 3.8 times, and within it the number of scientific workers increased 5.9 times, and engineers and architects 7.9 times. Hidden in these occupational categories are parts of the new ruling class. They can be found too amongst the numbers of managers of enterprises, small and large, and collective farms, whose numbers grew 4.6 times.[12] The war also kept the system more open. Many of those who had already made it never saw service at the front. But so bloody was the war that it could not stop a section of the emergent ruling class losing their lives alongside the millions of workers and peasants. Stalin's son, for example, was a victim. After 1945 the speed of expansion began to moderate and a more stable pattern began to emerge, with the top groups beginning to reproduce themselves in a more typical pattern, ie disproportionately but not exclusively from within. Indeed, the bureaucratic character of the system not only helped to create economic rigidities but social ones, so that the new ruling class was able to begin to enjoy its privileges and grow old, resisting change, to the dismay of more insightful reformers.

The impression is often given that the combined impact of industrialisation and the purges was to create a wholly new ruling class in the 1930s. This is not true. The rapid changes opened up possibilities for mobility alongside those who had already established themselves before 1928. The impact of the purges also seems to have been far more selective than was once thought. Once the immediate aims of destabilising specialist opposition to industrialisation had been achieved, Stalin was anxious to preserve the place of loyal professionals. 'It would [now] be stupid and unwise to regard practically every expert and engineer of the old school as an undetected criminal and wrecker,' he said in June 1931. He later made the same point in respect of family: 'Sons are not responsible for the offences of their fathers.' Of course, when a person was arrested their families did suffer, but this should not mislead us as to the overall position. The limited data that we have suggests that there was only limited downward mobility at this time.[13] The new ruling class was socially a merger of old and new elements, united by their more or less sincere belief in the new system and their desire for its rewards.

The system of promotion from the bottom up was known in Russian as *vydvizhenstvo*. Some, known as *pratiki*, achieved this by being promoted on the job. But there was a need for more developed formal education and higher education. In 1928 only 1 percent of party members had completed their higher education, and there were only 138 engineers in the party. Crash courses of higher education and training were therefore developed alongside the campaigns to eliminate illiteracy, raise skill levels, and train machine operators, tractor and combine drivers, and so on. Between 1928 and 1941 some 600,000-700,000 graduated from higher education, many of them in engineering, reflecting the needs of industry. At the Eighteenth Party Congress Stalin boasted that more than half a million party members had been promoted since 1928. But if you were loyal you did not have to join the party, and many others rode the escalator upwards.[14] In May 1935, for example, Stalin stressed the value of what he called 'non-party Bolsheviks'. Bukharin took a more cynical view, seeing those riding up on the back of Stalin as zombies who 'can be turned in any direction like a lump of wax'. To Boris Pasternak, the literary bureaucrats he met were lackeys who 'happily walk over corpses to further their own interests'.[15]

Loyalty, competence and pliability produced spectacular examples of promotion. Some rose, like Icarus, towards the sun, only to burn out at an early age. At the age of 33 Grigorii Nosov was made chief engineer of the Kuznetsk Iron and Steel Combine, then chief engineer at Magnitogorsk and, from 1940 until his death at the age of 46 in 1951, he was its director, lauded with honours.[16] Others became the great survivors. Consider three well known cases. In 1930

Aleksei Kosygin (aged 26), Leonid Brezhnev (aged 24) and Dimitri Ustinov (aged 22) were all drafted into higher education. Like tens of thousands of others they graduated in the mid-1930s, in time to be beneficiaries of the purges. Kosygin graduated in 1935, became a director of a textile plant and, aged 35 in 1939, commissar of the whole textile industry. Ustinov headed a defence plant, and then in 1941 became the commissar of armaments at the age of 33. At this point slowest to rise was Leonid Brezhnev, but he nevertheless managed a high level regional appointment before the war. These were examples of what one observer called 'the hard-faced men who had done well out of the purges'.

Opportunities were also created in the peripheral areas of the Russian Empire. Once again for those with ambition, provided they were loyal and spoke Russian, it was possible to get to the top. Stalin, after all, was a Georgian. Women too could rise. This was not liberation in the sense understood in 1917 and the 1920s. Indeed, the Women's Department (*Zhenotdel*) of the party was a victim of Stalin's revolution from above, and was closed down early in 1930. Thereafter the broader feminist agenda disappeared for decades, and when a group tried to raise it they were arrested in 1979. But for a period, as with the nationalities, opportunities were created by rapid industrialisation for wider social mobility which was sometimes ahead of the West. Of course, in both cases substantial patterns of inequality remained. Women, for example, were concentrated in light industry, food processing, teaching and health. They usually had low grades, low skills and lower pay. In 1956 only 1 percent of enterprise directors were women. By 1975 the figure was 9 percent. But the highest political office was denied to them. By 1986 only 3.5 percent of Central Committee members were female, and only two women ever made it to the Politburo or became Soviet ministers.

The net effect of these changes was to create perhaps the youngest ruling class in the world in the late 1930s. Once Stalin died, its members were anxious to ensure that their positions were safe, and that they would not again be threatened by the whim of a dictator.

But the fact that they were part of a state bourgeoisie meant also that class reproduction had to depend on wider formal and informal social mechanisms than simple inheritance. These were in no sense peculiar to the Soviet Union. In any society a privileged education is an important means of class power – so too is the ability to work the informal systems to your advantage. What differs between countries, even in the West, is the balance between these different mechanisms of advancement. The privileged lifestyles of those at the top of Russian society gave them and their children opportunities unavailable to peasants and workers lower down. No less than elsewhere, opportunities for those at the bottom were limited by the daily grind of inequality. But in Russia this was accentuated by the poverty and the petty restrictions. The special passports peasants needed to leave the village, and the residence permits needed for anyone to move to big cities and the capital, were more easily available to some than others. But it was the education system that was the central mechanism by which the ruling class as a social group allowed privilege to be passed on from one generation to the next.

Under capitalism the education system allows the identification and nurturing of potentially talented outsiders while giving the children of insiders the possibility of a head start. In Russia after 1928 the system was structured so that beneath the rhetoric of equality this second element operated as intensely, possibly more intensely, than in most Western societies, for as one observer put it in 1965 the unwritten rule was that 'a worker's son will go on to higher education provided he has the ability and desire to, but the son of one of the new class will go on always'.[17]

Experiment in the educational curriculum was stopped dead in its tracks in the early 1930s. But the need to fill out positions in the new ruling class initially led to a widening of recruitment into higher education. By the mid-1930s, however, access began to reflect the emerging contours of the new class. Even party membership was no longer as central, with Stalin's endorsement of 'non-party Bolsheviks'. Table 6.1 shows how the formal composition of the student body shifted. The socially conservative pattern at the end of the 1930s is clear – so clear, in fact, that from 1938 information ceased to be published about the social composition of the student body. Then on 2 October 1940 a decree was passed abolishing free education in the upper school grades and universities. Scholarships mitigated some of the effect of this for those at the bottom, but the clear aim was to allow those at the top to buy (formally and informally) educational advance.

TABLE 6.1. THE CHANGING PERCENTAGES OF SOCIAL COMPOSITION OF THE STUDENT GROUP IN THE 1930s[18]

	1928	1932	1935	1938
Workers	25.4	58.0	45.0	33.9
Peasants	23.9	14.1	16.2	21.6
Employees	50.7	27.9	38.8	44.5

Moreover, as in any education system, there was a dropout rate that was socially structured, so that the social composition of those graduating was even more biased to those from the top groups.

AN AGEING AND RIGID RULING CLASS

After Stalin's death there was a retreat from the most grotesque examples of inequality – tuition fees, for example, were abolished in 1956. But the underlying mechanisms remained well established, and those at the top were resistant to any change. Even at the turn of the 1960s they were still a comparatively youthful group. Indeed, one commentator wrote that they were 'probably...the youngest aggregation of men of such illimitable power in the world'.[19] But over time they aged in their posts with little sign, at the very top, of wanting to leave. One minister, Patolichev, was in the same post for 27 years. Baibakov was head of Gosplan for 20 years. Half the Politburo at the start of the 1980s were survivors of the 1930s generation. Kosygin, for example, had two strokes. The Politburo rejected his attempts to resign and kept him in his post until he died.[20] When Chernenko replaced Andropov as leader a new joke did the rounds: 'In February 1984, at the age of 71, after a long illness, and without regaining consciousness, Konstantin Chernenko became the leader of the Soviet Union.'

'Stability of cadres' was the policy of the Brezhnev regime, and the rate of turnover on the Central Committee was the lowest ever. Brezhnev himself became increasingly detached from day to day issues, leaving them in the hands of the administration. The Party Secretariat would meet on a Tuesday, and the Politburo on a Thursday for an hour. Brezhnev would then spend a long weekend at his palatial dacha at Zavidovo and indulge his passion for hunting. In this situation the system became flabby, and corruption developed on the periphery and close to the centre, including Brezhnev's own family. Andropov sought to reduce the corruption but was himself part of this group. To help him and to the general relief of the Politburo a hidden escalator was built to enable their arthritic legs and failing bodies to get more easily to the top of Lenin's tomb for official appearances.[21]

Beneath the top, other elements of growing rigidity could also be seen. In 1980, for example, Filipov, a Soviet sociologist, could brutally state that 'the systems of vocational, specialised and higher education are nothing but an extension of the existing social structure. Each educational track is tied to a corresponding class, social group or social stratum'.[22] The implication of all this is that over time the pattern of social rigidity and rates of social mobility became comparable to those in more mature Western societies. Indeed, they may have become worse. Such comparisons are notoriously difficult, but by the late 1970s the French sociologist Basile Kerblay suggested that the chances of a worker of working class origin gaining promotion to become a senior manager were 15 percent greater in France than the USSR, three times greater in Japan and five times greater in the United States.[23]

INCOME AND PRIVILEGE AT THE TOP

But was this a ruling class that could capitalise on its privileges to live a life of luxury? The picture drawn by Alexander Yanov at the start of this chapter certainly suggests so, but doubts remain about the contours of Soviet affluence and its nature. To make sense of these we need to distinguish wealth from income. Wealth refers to a stock of assets – land, a company or company shares, money in the bank, etc. Income refers to what is earned by work or in the employment of these assets – wages, salaries, rent, profits, etc. Because the Soviet economy was state controlled there was little private ownership of wealth, but we have already seen that in the West this is not always central. What effective control of these organisations and enterprises does allow is the establishment of a flow of income, which helps to make their managers a class apart in terms of distribution as well as control of production. This is what happened in Russia on a national scale to such an extent that the class income and consumption gaps were quite comparable with those elsewhere. This statement may come as a surprise because historically many observers failed to observe an elementary distinction. This is the difference between the individual and the group. The income gap between the richest Western billionaire and the poorest worker was probably greater in the West than any comparable gap in the USSR. But in a class analysis what matters is the systematic pattern of inequality between classes – not the individual extremes. We have no direct way of measuring this, but a crude approximation is to compare the incomes of, say, the top 1, 5 or 10 percent to the equivalent group at the bottom. When this is done, and proper allowance made for income in kind, then the Soviet pattern reveals a ruling class using its power to preside over a pattern of inequality no different from that in other states.

With the revolution from above Stalin immediately moved to attack old ideas of equality. In June 1931 he condemned what he called 'equality mongering' (*uravnilovka*), arguing that wage payments should create incentives and rewards, and 'the more boldly we do this the better'.[24] As these ideas were implemented pay scales were stretched, creating huge income differentials. These were supported by the incorporation of formal markers of inequality. In the army, for example, regular ranks were reintroduced in 1935 and extended in 1940. The same year badges of rank, gold braid and epaulettes came back with a vengeance. The special military officer cadet schools were set up (named after Tsarist heroes such as Suvorov and Nakhimov). Uniforms became more elaborate, and military medals were regulated by rank – subconsciously reflecting the view that history was made by those at the top while it was the duty of those at the bottom to 'do and die'. In the war the highest military got the order of 'Victory' while junior officers and men got the order of 'Glory'. In the state bureaucracy the concern for hierarchy and position led to gradual reintroduction of civilian uniforms in these years, and they were used until 1954. This was justified by its contribution to order and discipline and, as in the Tsarist period, the different levels could be distinguished by the style, colour and quality of the uniform.[25]

But what of earnings more directly? The most important part of incomes in the Soviet Union came in money form. To this was added privileges and fringe benefits, and the higher you went the more there were. Looking at how money wages and salaries changed over time, we can see first a dramatic rise in inequality in the 1930s, which peaked around 1946. At this point there is good reason to think that the gap, between say the bottom 10 percent and the top 10 percent, was wider than in any other advanced country. This is all the more likely since the data we have exclude the poverty-stricken rural sector. Thereafter the regime reduced the levels of inequality, partly by raising the appallingly low standard of living of those at the bottom and partly by cutting back on some of the high incomes at the top. By the 1960s and 1970s wage and salary inequality had returned to levels that showed 'a rather striking similarity' between the USSR and the West. Inequality was less than in countries like the US, Spain and Italy but greater than in Japan and Sweden. One survey, for example, suggested that whereas the poorest 10 percent of households got 3.4 percent of income, the top 10 percent got 24.1 percent – seven times more. Then, from the late 1970s on, it appears that the level of inequality began to rise again, stretching the gap between top and bottom. It should be remembered too that in the Soviet Union income tax did not play an important role – it was only mildly progressive and in the mid-1970s raised less than 10 percent of the state budget.[26]

Of course the top 10 percent of earners are still a large group, and within this there was great differentiation. Firstly, many top people had more than one source of income (leaving aside the question of often related earnings of family members). Membership of the Academy of Sciences, for example, awarded for both scientific and non-scientific reasons, brought an additional monthly stipend of two to three times the value of the average monthly wage. There were also some super-incomes which, as we suggested earlier, were at a tangent to the real class structure. In 1936, for example, 14 writers had monthly royalties of more than 1,000 roubles (at least 43 times the then monthly wage), and even in the more equal 1960s and 1970s successful writers were immensely well off. But more significant than this is the fact that the closer people rose to the core of the ruling class the more their money incomes were supplemented by the fringe benefits of power. Box 6.2 gives some indication of the access to wealth that came with a position at the very pinnacle of power – in the Politburo.

Fringe benefits were not specific to the Soviet Union, but they played a more important role there, partly because they were a way of 'hiding' incomes (in the same way that occurs in the West when incomes are formally controlled) and partly because they were a method of ensuring loyalty. In 1960 it was revealed that one third of all retail sales were in special stores to which the mass of the population had no right of access.[27] They were especially important in helping to boost the incomes of people like enterprise managers. With power went special privileges at work. There were special waiting rooms at stations and airports for those at the top. Power brought cars (sometimes chauffeur driven), a better home, a good dacha. There was access to privileged holidays, trips abroad and so on. All these were official. But at the top, too, people had better access to the more expensive private farm markets, to the black market and to moonlighting service provision, and above all they could deploy *blat* to get special favours done. Real *blat* was concentrated at the top. In one survey, for example, 55 percent admitted to using 'favours' to get food and medicines but only 40 percent for the acquisition of consumer goods and 10 percent for privileged access to holidays and hospital treatment. And, of course, a favour from a shop assistant or pharmacist was quite different from that which got you a car or a stay at a Black Sea dacha.[28]

A RULING IDEOLOGY?

These class patterns were also reflected in the development of a highly conservative ideology. Formally the names of Marx, Engels and Lenin were evoked to justify policy, even though reality belied their whole analysis. Some critical commentators therefore concluded that ideology was simply used to legitimise policy that was decided on purely pragmatic grounds. There was undoubtedly much of this quotation mongering. But it is a mistake to discount ideology completely. The need is to understand it. Ideology operates at two levels – what we can call the formal and the lived. By formal we mean the way in which ideas were codified. By lived we mean the way in which these ideas became transformed into everyday assumptions guiding behaviour.

It is by no means unusual for conservative and privileged states to lay claim to a continuity with a different past. For nearly 2,000 years the rich Christian churches have evoked the ideas of a penniless carpenter who despised worldly wealth. In France successive governments have laid claim to the heritage of 1789, even having the slogan 'Liberty, equality and fraternity' chiselled into their buildings. No less in the United States the supposed heritage of the American Revolution remains a totem even to the extent that one of the most conservative social organisations calls itself 'The Daughters of the American Revolution'. In each instance, of course, the past is no guide to the present. What is important is the way that the past is selectively appropriated and manipulated in a safe form into the ruling ideas. In the USSR even a most cursory examination shows the same process at work. It is even apparent in the publication figures. Of the 17 billion books published in Russia between 1918 and 1954, for example, 706 million, or over 4 percent, were by Stalin. This was two and a half times more than those of Lenin, and nearly 11 times more than those of Marx and Engels. And to these must be added 'a vast torrent of literature reflecting Stalin's views on the theory and history of socialism' and the 'indecently large editions of people close to Stalin'.[29]

It can also be seen in the fate of those who took the past seriously enough to try to use it as a basis for a critique of the present. Thus the starting point for any analysis of formal ideology has to be the texts of the regime itself – Stalin's *Problems of Leninism*, the *Short Course History*, etc, and the way that the leadership understood and interpreted these in its more general declarations. Given that the USSR was a one-party state, this formal ideology was ruthlessly enforced. People were expected to make open demonstrations of their party-mindedness (*partiinost*), their ideological maturity (*ideinost*) and their popular national outlook (*narodnost*).[30] After the death of Stalin these codewords for the limits of official thinking were policed by men such as Mikhail Suslov, the chief ideologist, and Boris Ponomarev – in charge of relations with foreign Communist parties and who, according to Khrushchev, was 'as orthodox as a Catholic priest'. Indeed, Khrushchev nicknamed him 'ponomar', which is the Russian word for the sexton who looks after the church and the churchyard.

But ideology also has an informal element where it becomes part of the everyday thinking, and this 'lived' element can then feed back to the formal level. With any social class a sense of this informal ideology – the commonplace values and assumptions which are often revealed unwittingly – is crucial to an understanding of action. When, for example, the ghost writer of Leonid Brezhnev's memoirs wrote on his behalf (or perhaps these were his own words?) that, 'a man who does not love his mother, who has given her life to him, fed and brought him up – such a man is suspect to me, personally. Not for nothing do the people say mother country. The person who is capable of rejecting and forgetting his own mother will also be a bad son of his native land,' we see here the unwitting demonstration of his nationalism and the conservative image of the role of the family that he shared with other members of the Soviet ruling class.[31] We see this as lived ideology both because the expression of these conservative sentiments comes naturally to the author and because the expectation is that the Soviet reader will be impressed by them, and share them approvingly. The fact that the memoirs were ghosted for effect makes them all the more telling in what they reveal about the assumptions of the regime.

In trying to unravel some of these connections we will limit ourselves here to showing the essential conservatism of the real ideas of the ruling class and the way that they affected social relations. The concept of nation played a key role here. Competitive industrialisation was a vision of national development. The degree of overt nationalism varied over time. During and after the war it culminated in what Kopolev called 'an orgy of xenophobia'.[32] But the basic assumption of the centrality of the nation was a constant. In 1934, for example, Molotov insisted that 'the defence of the fatherland is the sacred duty of every citizen of the USSR'. The novelist Count Aleksei Tolstoy went further at the high point of the purges: 'Any citizen who does not love his motherland is a Trotskyist, saboteur and spy'.[33]

Formally what was important was Soviet patriotism – the patriotism of an empire. The parallel with imperial British patriotism is obvious. But within this there was a tacit acceptance of the central role of Russia and Russianness. A degree of open racism even received the support of parts of the regime. Lev Kopolev was struck by the way that:

> To concern oneself seriously with Marxism is no less dangerous here than to disseminate Samizdat [dissident literature] or to join the Zionists. the Baptists, the Jehovah's Witnesses, the True Orthodox faith, the Buddhists or to defend the Crimean Tartars who still remain in forced exile. On the other hand, the crudest abusers of 'Khokhols' [Ukrainians], 'Yids', etc, at worst hear fatherly reproaches and receive symbolic, cursory punishment.[34]

This identification of those at the top with nation also took place at a more subconscious level and could have a protective quality for them (and others). Stalin's daughter was typical in reflecting, as she considered the harm her father had done: 'What is good in Russia is traditional and unchanging too, even more than what is bad. And perhaps it is this eternal good which gives Russia strength and helps preserve her true self'.[35] Only with a sense of how commonplace this mystical idea of nation was does it become possible to understand how after 1991 parts of the Communist Party could merge into a semi-fascist Red-Brown alliance.

Within this national framework the ruling class developed an image of itself that had at its centre a 19th century vision of work, family and culture. The earlier radicalism of the revolution did not fit with the counter-revolution, but the fact that the regression went so far is explained by the parvenu character of much of the ruling class. Legitimacy for them appeared to be an identification with earlier bourgeois forms albeit now labelled 'socialist'. Avant-gardism and experiment were denounced. Music, art and literature now had to be uplifting – they had to express an optimistic romanticism similar to that found in the more commonplace art and literature of the 19th century. The doctrine was called 'Socialist Realism', but it was neither socialist nor realist. The aim was to uplift the masses and present an image of an idealised world in which they, and Russia's rulers, could bask. Life was to be seen more as it should be than as it was. In painting, for example, woe betided the artist whose realism became too realistic. In the 19th century the French artist Millet had scandalised Paris when he dared to depict rural labour as backbreaking toil in his painting 'The Gleaners'. In Russia in the 1930s Soloman Nikritin went one step further to capture some of the reality of Stalin's courts on canvas. But it was seen as too brutal a depiction. 'What a dreadful nightmare!' said one contemporary. 'This picture should not be accepted – we should protest against it. After looking at such work one finds it dreadful to be alive for a month, in spite of all the gaiety of our life'.[36] What was needed, whether in writing, music or painting, Sholokhov later said, was 'art which actively helps people in the construction of a new world – [this] is the art of Socialist Realism'.[37]

The ideology of family, femininity and sexual chastity can illustrate the way in which an almost 19th century style conservative ideology emerged in wider social life. We know, of course, that the reality of the 19th century middle class family belied its image, but this does not mean it was simply an ideological device developed to control the lower classes. This is part of the function of a ruling ideology, but Foucault has pointed out that the 'bourgeois ideal' also served as an ideology of self-definition – this is what we, the bourgeoisie, are, this is how we live, this is why we are what we are, and this is what you should aspire to, even though you may never be capable of achieving it.[38] The avalanche of conservative social measures in Russia in the 1930s functioned in the same way. There was a clear deployment of these ideas to stabilise life below in the interests of the regime but there was an element also of self-definition in the ideology that informed policy.

The rise of social conservatism can be traced in policies, behaviour and attitudes in the early 1930s. New laws were soon implemented to consolidate and reinforce these. The burden fell especially on women. The regime still needed them as workers, so whereas the Nazis emphasised 'Kitchen, children and church' the Soviet regime emphasised 'Kitchen, children and the factory', or even 'Kitchen, children and the army'. 'Every girl must be treasured not only as a textile worker, a bold parachute jumper or an engineer – but as a future mother. The mother of one child must be treasured as the future mother of eight,' it was said in 1936.[39] The point was that women were expected to carry out both a traditional role and a work role. Between 1943 and the early 1950s even coeducation was abandoned in favour of 'a system by which the school develops boys who will be good fathers and manly fighters...and girls who will be intelligent mothers competent to rear the new generation'.[40]

Abortion was banned by a decree in 1936 and remained illegal until 1955. The underlying aim was to boost population growth to provide a new generation of workers and soldiers. But the justification that was given reflected the deep social conservatism of the new ruling ideology. 'Mass abortion resorted to for egoistic reasons cannot be tolerated. The Soviet state cannot countenance the fact that tens of thousands of women ruin their health and delay the growth of a new generation for socialist society,' said one propagandist.[41] One foreign Catholic bishop said: 'God, looking from heaven, may be more pleased with Russia than with us.' If this is thought extreme, we should note that by the end of the 1930s the formal ideology of the regime had become so sexually repressive that one Soviet psychologist even argued that 'it is desirable that sex relations, as far as possible, take place without resort to contraceptives and with a view to conception'. Partners, with a nod to women's equality, should also get mutual pleasure, but 'certain contraceptive devices are not a matter of indifference, and coitus interruptus is especially undesirable. The sex act should produce complete psychological as well as physical satisfaction, but pleasure should not be overextended as prolonged coitus may also carry certain dangers'. Too little lovemaking, however, was not dangerous: 'Many mistaken notions and scientific misconceptions are encountered in this area, not only among laymen, but in medical circles as well. As a result, over-anxious parents often marry off their children as soon as they manifest any sign of nervous symptoms [but] there is...no reason to believe that sexual abstinence in itself can cause any serious mental disturbance, let alone a psychosis'.[42] In 1944 Motherland Glory medals were introduced – first class for bearing six children, second for seven, and so on, with 'heroine mother' status for 10 or more children.

Of course, sexual relations inside and outside marriage continued. For men power brought (and bought) women. 'Beria's deputy Vladimir Dekanozov... liked to drive around the streets of Moscow looking for women. He would rape them in his limousine in the presence of his bodyguards and chauffeur. Beria was less crude... He would walk near his house...and point out women to his bodyguards, who would force the women to have sex with him,' said Sakharov.[43] Beria's victims possibly included a 14 year old who reportedly committed suicide. But the hypocrisy should not blind us to the social role of these formal images, many of which survived until the end. The relaxation of Stalin's laws from the 1950s – the allowing of divorce, abortion, etc – still left this formal ideal in place whatever the real situation.

The sociologist Lewis Coser, still influenced by a youthful Marxism, saw the conservative function of these ideas in a penetrating but neglected study of the changes in Soviet family policy in the 1930s and early 1940s:

> One arrives at the startling conclusion that the economic basis for a stable family life, such as is required by the new Soviet ideology, can be found only among the families of the upper strata. The top bureaucrat can allow himself the luxury of a stable family life and of a Victorian morality. He has enough housing space, his wife does not have to work full time, his household equipment is more adequate and modern, and he can engage domestic help. To maintain a family that comes up to the official standards is a leisure class activity.[44]

Servants were widely used in the early 1930s only to be renamed as domestic workers. Soviet Russia was run by leaders, Trotsky ironically said, who 'have long ago forgotten how to shine their own shoes'. It was a skill that it seems unlikely their descendants ever regained. 'It was commonly known that the party and the army elites, artistic and scientific intelligentsia had a housekeeper and a cook,' says a more recent account.[45] In the 1930s Trotsky quoted the French newspaper *Le Temps* on the transformation, but stumbled himself on following up their conclusion:

> This external transformation is one of the signs of a deep change which is now taking place throughout the whole Soviet Union. The regime, now, definitely consolidated, is gradually becoming stabilised. Revolutionary habits and customs are giving place within the Soviet family and Soviet society to the feelings and customs which continue to prevail within so-called capitalist countries. The Soviets are becoming bourgeoisified.[46]

But over time this articulation of class ideas, culture and behaviour became even more firmly implanted. 'The Soviet manager is a dignitary,' wrote one outside observer in 1977:

> ...this celebrity inevitably encroaches on his private life, in which public opinion takes an interest. His living standards and privileges — official car, house, and personal dacha, travel facilities, and so on — set him apart, like a nobleman under the old regime. His private life must comply with the standards of Soviet morality.[47]

The conservative values were also reflected in the regime's criticisms of the 'licentious West' and the way that, from Vyshinsky to Andropov to the coup plotters of 1991, a frisson of sexual fear and fear of spontaneous human relationships marked the charges against opponents of the regime. When the writer Boris Pasternak died, for example, the vindictiveness of the regime extended to his secretary Olga Ivinskaya (the model for Larissa in *Dr Zhivago*) and her daughter. She was sentenced to eight years imprisonment for fraud. Justifying this Surkov, the secretary of the Writers' Union, attacked her private life, denouncing her as 'a 48 year old woman... The last mistress of this elderly man... Despite her advanced age she did not stop to have many parallel and frequent relations with other men.' Other charges included sleeping with the deputy editor of the magazine *Ogonyok* for the fees for articles that others had written, stealing Pasternak's royalties, and so on.[48]

Whether these liaisons were real or imagined is neither here nor there (though most likely every accusation was false). The important thing is the confidence of the assumption that we will be shocked by the sexual ones, and endorse the view that they establish the degeneracy of the person who has fallen foul of the regime. This was a far cry from the hopes of Alexandra Kollontai that in the revolution the winged Eros would take flight, and a still further cry from the radical groups of the earlier 1920s who astonished passers-by removing all clothing in demonstrations against shame.[49] In fact, at the high point of Stalinism, the display of the human body in the wrong context was as much an object of shame as in Victorian Britain. William Campbell, a British migrant to Stalin's Russia who achieved honoured status as a top Soviet clown, remembered trying to sell a valuable French bronze nude statuette to help raise money to buy a car in 1952: 'Nobody wanted to buy a nude figure. One woman declared it would be a disgrace to have such a thing in the house. Only after a present of a packet of Gillette razorblades did the [commission] shop manager agree to keep it hidden away in the shop and to show it only to connoisseurs... Three months later it was still unsold'.[50]

AN IDEOLOGY OF ACQUISITIVENESS

It was sometimes suggested that Russia could not have a real ruling class because those at the top could not openly display their privileges. This argument, however, involves several mistakes. Ostentatious display was not frowned upon only in Russia. Nor was it even true that there was no ostentatious display in that country – indeed, at various points a *'jeunesse dorée'* has been identified. But more important is the fact that inequality and the enjoyment of it, if linked to the functioning of the system, was seen as legitimate, and rejection of it as dangerous radicalism. Members of the ruling class had a right and a duty to live unequal lives. From the 1930s on the argument was that unequal rewards reflected unequal contributions – 'from each according to his ability, to each according to his work' was the slogan. This material acquisitiveness underpinned Stakhanovism and the vision it offered to the workers. In December 1935 a Stakhanovite, Vinogradova, boasted at a meeting: 'Since July, I bought a good bed – paid 280 roubles [applause], bought a winter coat – paid 400 roubles [applause], paid 180 roubles for a summer outfit, 180 roubles – for a watch [applause], 165 roubles – for an autumn coat [applause].[51] Just as Western managers believe that it is their effort that creates wealth and justifies their rewards, so their counterparts and acolytes in Russia believed that their income was underpinned by the practical and moral value of the contribution they made. This became part of the formal and informal code of the regime. Pavel Dybenko, a revolutionary in 1917, but by 1937 trying to stay alive by ingratiating himself with Stalin, unwittingly showed this inversion of values in an attack on Yan Gamarnik, the head of the political directorate of the army: 'That Gamarnik! He pretended to be a pure as Jesus Christ! Never had an extra stick of furniture in his house... We've been saying all along these bluebloods are sticking together. Wouldn't give us a chance to move up!'[52] In this new world, asceticism – not to enjoy privilege – was a symbol not of a true revolutionary but of an 'aristocrat' standing in the way of new rulers who could enjoy what they earned the right to. Although producer goods were generally emphasised at the expense of consumer goods, a pattern of supply of goods to the new ruling class was quickly established, and it can be easily traced in the plan and output figures. Newly produced goods, even if of questionable quality, marked their homes. This was reflected in their dress which came to embody a social distance between people. They even made them smell better. Whereas soap production was only planned to increase 2.5 times between 1927 and 1936, cosmetic production grew 4.7 times and perfume production 4.8 times. The detail belies the claim that these products were for everyone. 'The most expensive

🦋 6.1 NATIONALISM, POWER AND EAST-WEST COMPETITION

When F J Erroll, a Tory MP, visited Russia in 1954 he was shown the Moscow Metro. 'Not bad for a race of peasants, eh?' asked his guide. Erroll, an engineer, was suitably impressed.[xvi] It was what Russia's leaders wanted. They believed that they should have the biggest and best of every-thing. National power is about economic and military might, but it is also about prestige. The US monopoly of atomic weapons, for example, challenged not only Russia's ruling class but also Britain's. 'We have got to have this thing over here, whatever it costs...we have got to have a bloody Union Jack on top of it,' said Ernest Bevin, the Labour foreign secretary in 1946. Russia's leaders felt the same way, but they did not only apply this thinking to nuclear bombs. They wanted it to be seen that they were a global force. Matching the achievements the US and Western Europe across a whole range of areas was seen as an economic and military necessity, and a symbolic one.

When Russia's leaders and diplomats travelled abroad, for example, they felt humiliated if their planes seemed inferior to their Western counterparts. But when Khrushchev flew non-stop to Washington in an Aeroflot TU-114 and the Americans did not have a set of moving stairs to reach it he was delighted. Now the embarrassment was theirs. From the plane door he could lit-erally look down on them.

Such competition went further still in the non-military sphere. In the 1960s, for example, Russia's leaders decided that if Britain and France were going to develop the Concorde then they had to have one too — Concordski, as it was called in the West. The best designers where put on to it and the best resources followed. Whatever the technical achievements of both planes, they were economic disasters. They were the subsidised playthings of those with power, East and West. But they reflected the symmetrical national competition of the Cold War years which led each side to try to match the other.[xvii]

The competition extended to leisure. In sport a 1948 resolution of the Central Committee declared that the state's aim was 'to spread sport to every corner of the land, to raise the level of skill and, on this basis, to help Soviet sportsmen win world supremacy in the major sports in the immediate future'.[xviii]

The national flag had to be seen, whether it was painted on a rocket rolling through Red Square, or held aloft by an astronaut, or an athlete given the best resources to compete in the Olympics.

kinds of eau de cologne and perfumes are produced in much greater quantities, and so are creams in glass jars and metal tubes, while the output of cosmetics in small tin containers has remained at the same level and in some cases fallen,' said one propaganda article, unwittingly giving the game away.[53] 'Limousines for the "activists", fine perfumes for "our women", margarine for the workers, stores "de luxe" for the gentry, a look at delicacies through the store windows for the plebs – such socialism cannot but seem to the masses a new refacing of capitalism, and they are not far wrong,' said Trotsky.[54]

The extent to which this right to consume became part of the everyday ideology of the regime is beautifully brought home by Vera Durham in her study of the popular literature of Russia in the late 1940s and early 1950s. Precisely because this was mass literature for the relaxation of the new upper and middle classes, its implicit assumptions and aspirations – the marks of distinction that it values – are so revealing. In one story a young worker rejects the idea that he should respond to crude material incentives. The trade union chief tells him: 'So, perhaps, we don't need to pay you wages either? Is that it?... Why, to give you a room today, we had to make a revolution, sleeping on the bare ground and holding our rifles tight. And you, you wave it all aside! Some gentleman you are!' As with Dybenko's comment above, the rejection of the materialism of the rulers poses a threat. Their attitude is summed up in the motto of another character in the same story: 'Thousands of roubles, that's reality. If you live better, you work better. If you work better, you live better'.[55]

Russian workers and peasants were not so lucky. But so ingrained did ideas like this become that people who voiced them often did not appreciate the unconscious humour in their defence of their 'rights' and the 'toil' that produced them. In a debate in the Writers' Union in 1967, for example, one regime writer took offence at the suggestion of Solzhenitsyn that it was they who enjoyed easy access to the West with trips to Paris, Rome, Berlin, London and beyond. Infuriated, the writer replied: 'You have sarcastically referred to trips abroad as if they were pleasant strolls. We travel abroad to wage the struggle. We return home from abroad worn out and exhausted, but with the feeling of having done our duty'.[56]

In these terms it is not surprising to find that the official paper *Literaturnaia gazeta* should be able to go even further and print an 'Ode to a Businessman' working for the system:

> In the old days, my uncle used to be called a kulak because he owned a cow and two horses. Today where is there a home without a television?... What is the harm in people saving to buy a car or carpets, since they have earned their money by honest labour – show me a rich man today. Let him serve as an example.[57]

The implication is obvious. Just as the honest labour of the worker enables him to buy a car (actually the cost of a car at this point was equivalent to four to five years' salary for the ordinary worker!), so it is the honest labour of the businessman/manager that gives him the income and influence to get his better house, his dacha, his car, his holidays, the privileged consumer goods, trips abroad, and so on.

This mentality gained a new edge from the 1970s, and it helped to pave the way for the changes at the turn of the 1990s. Selected Russians were able to travel more widely in Eastern Europe. In 1960 100,000 Soviet tourists visited Eastern Europe. In 1976 the figure was 1.3 million. Comparing themselves to the upper classes there they often returned chastened about the pressures on consumption in Russian state capitalism and their own position.[58] They were more present too in the Third World, with diplomatic, journalistic and business postings. Detente enabled some to have wider access to the advanced West, where the higher levels of development allowed military spending, accumulation and a degree of consumerism to flourish side by side in contrast to the more austere forms in Russia. The privileged groups who had sight of this were no radicals. Their acquisitiveness was perfectly compatible with loyalty to the system, as we shall see later. What they wanted was to capitalise more openly on their power and position at home. This was even more an aspiration of the rising generation of the ruling class. As they became enterprise managers or their deputies, business-oriented officials in the party, KGB or Komsomol, so their progress was marked by an intensified consumerism at home. Characters satirising them began to appear in Russian literature in the late 1970s and 1980s. Disdain for 'Soviet snobs' with their Western goods, their antiques, even high status pets like well groomed setters was widespread in intellectual quarters.[59] But, ironically, acquisitiveness was no less present in many within this intellectual milieu. Indeed it was in some of the most exclusive Moscow institutes that the gilded youth of the regime – the *zolotnaia molodozh* – being trained for high office, began to express similar tendencies in their behaviour even as they sneered at it in others.

THE RIGHT TO RULE

But the texture of class relationships can also be seen in the sense of 'them and us'. This sense emerges not just in workers' responses to those above them, but also in the texture of relations from the top down.[60] Stalin horrified many Russians when in June 1945 he toasted the role of ordinary people in the war as *vintiki*, 'the cogs': 'If any cog ceases to work – it's the end.' And so it would have been. But the condescension in his apparent praise of 'the people who have few offices and whose status is unenviable' spoke clearly of the gap between rulers and ruled.[61] Big bosses in the Soviet system gave orders to middle ranking bosses who passed them on to their juniors and foremen. 'I was brought up in the system. Everything was steeped in the methods of the "command" system and I, too, acted accordingly. Whether I was chairing a meeting,

6.2. 'FANTASIES OF PROPERTY, PLEASURE AND MEGALOMANIA'

This was how Boris Yeltsin described the lifestyle of the Soviet Politburo.[xix] Privileges included:

WORK: palatial offices, large staff. Guarded, Central Committee canteen with gourmet cooks.

MOSCOW HOUSING: large flats, houses in selected parts of town. Accommodation large enough for family, including grown up children and relations. Domestic staff.

CONSUMPTION: supplied under direction of Ninth Directorate of the KGB. Subsidised Kremlin rations of high quality, often unobtainable goods. Special reserved section in GUM store on Red Square. Closed shops, including special Kremlin grocery store. Home delivery to ensure quality and safety. Special workshops, dry-cleaning, and services including tailor made clothing. Official gift catalogues for presents including for wives.

MOSCOW RELAXATION: theatres and concerts. Closed Kremlin sports facilities on Lenin Hills — outdoor and indoor courts, swimming pool and saunas.

WEEKEND RETREATS: large, waterside, marble lined dachas with gardens, tennis and other courts. Numerous rooms, each with a TV, including a dining room with a 10-metre table and a billiard room. 'I lost count of the number of bathrooms and lavatories.' A personal cinema with a projectionist on duty Friday to Sunday. Three cooks, three waitresses, housemaids and garden staff.

HOLIDAYS: summer break and two-week winter break. Special dachas in places like Valdai Hills (between Moscow and Leningrad), Pitsunda and Gagry on Georgian Coast of Black Sea, Theodosia in Crimea. 'Summer dachas are as luxurious as the all year round residences.'

TRANSPORT: Zil and escort for personal use with all traffic cleared ahead by police. Chauffeur-driven Volga for family. Personal plane — IL-62 or TU134. No public walking necessary, even to beach in the summer.

HEALTHCARE: supplied by the Fourth Directorate of the KGB. Daily medical examinations by own doctor. All medicines imported and personally vouched for by a doctor. Treatment in Kremlin Hospital with 'huge suites…porcelain, crystal, carpets and chandeliers', 'the medicine and equipment…all imported'. Treatment by teams of five to 10 top doctors.

BODYGUARDS: personal bodyguards, as well as bodyguards at different homes.

running my office, or delivering a report to a plenum everything that one did was expressed in terms of pressure, threats and coercion,' Boris Yeltsin later said.[62] Some tried to leaven these relationships with a degree of humanity and common courtesy, but the overall image of the Soviet manager was of 'a hard man, harsh and irritable with a fondness for shouting', and, we should add, swearing.[63] It is in this form that he stalked the pages of Soviet literature, but it was also often the image that the Soviet boss preferred for himself. In the 1970s the magazine *Literaturnaia gazeta* ran a series of articles on Soviet management styles. The tone throughout the discussion was much the same, but one study expressed the general view more clearly than others. A Lithuanian academic had surveyed 119 'assistant directors', chief engineers and others working closely with top management. He divided managers into liberal, democratic and autocratic, and those questioned put 13.5 percent of their bosses into the liberal camp, 20.5 percent into the democratic and 66 percent into the autocratic group. What was interesting was not just this grouping but the thinking behind it. The autocrat was thought to be personally unpleasant to work with, but he was also 'considered energetic, diligent, bold and able to formulate arguments clearly'. The attraction of traditional factory autocracy could not be clearer. And then, with an unconscious insensitivity born of an implicit acceptance of the need for workers to feel the firm hand of management while 'professionals' were treated with respect, the group said that 'although the autocrat was acceptable as an executive in factory conditions, we concluded he should not head an educational, research or public organisation'.[64]

Orders and reprimands were 'pumped out' (*nakachka*). The disparaging *tu* form of the language became widely used with subordinates – the instruction was 'davai' – 'do it!'[65] The reward for following these orders was that the boss might demonstrate a sense of paternalism, and protect and reward you. And from the point of view of the boss this made some sense in that the enterprises might hit blockages where he needed the additional cooperation of the workforce. But paternalism rests upon a shared sense of inequality in which both sides tacitly recognise their different positions, and in which the inferiority of the recipient – dependent on the discretion of the boss – is clear. And the other side of this 'generosity' of the boss is his frustration that it is the workers who do not respond or do not respond sufficiently who are ultimately the source of the problem. Sometimes, indeed, this class sense was so strong it could take your breath away. One is reminded of George Orwell's account of the way in which the Edwardian middle classes said quietly to one another: 'The lower classes smell.' Even before more open expressions of it emerged in the *perestroika* phase it was evident for those who opened their eyes and ears, and it was displayed as much by liberal reformers as conservatives. Consider, for example, the implicit view of class in Tatiania Zaslavaskaia's comments on the 'human factor' in the report that she wrote in the early 1980s to encourage the process of reform:

The social mechanism of economic development as it functions at present in the USSR does not ensure satisfactory results. The social type of worker formed by it fails to correspond not only to the strategic aims of a developed socialist society, but also to the technological requirements of contemporary production. The widespread characteristics of many workers, whose personal formation occurred during the past five-year plans, are low labour and production discipline, an indifferent attitude to the work performed and its low quality, social passivity, a low value attached to labour as a means of self-realisation, an intense consumer orientation, and a rather low level of moral discipline.[66]

Workers and factories were encouraged to compete against one another. This factory noticeboard from the earl...

7 WORKING CLASS

In 1936 the new Soviet constitution announced that 'the exploitation of man by man has been eliminated', but workers and peasants over the decades saw little of the wealth that they created. 'Capitalism is the exploitation of man by man,' said perhaps the best known Russian joke from the pre-1991 era. 'Under our socialism it's the other way round.' But it was more than a joke. Just as in the West, Russia was a society built upon the alienation and exploitation of generations of workers. As the regime went into crisis at the end of the 1980s, Gorbachev was forced to admit that there were 'ever-increasing signs of man's alienation from the property of the whole people' (though this formulation betrayed the class thinking we noted in the previous chapter – it was not man that was alienated from 'the property of the whole people', but 'the property of the whole people' that was alienated from man).[1] When the end came in 1991, whatever the confusion about the future, one thing was clear – there was no enthusiasm to defend the old. To see why, we will first look at who the workers and peasants were, before exploring some of the ways in which their changing situation reflected the pattern of alienation and exploitation.

We have already outlined the way in which workers were subordinated to the new competitive logic of the system in the 1930s. But that revolution from above also helped to mould what Stalin in 1936 called 'a completely new [working] class'.[2] Rapid growth required a new urban industrial workforce. In the short term this could only come from mass migration from agriculture to industry. The speed of this shift was unique: 'No other economy has remotely matched the Soviet labour influx rate at comparable stages of development, especially during the period of the first three long term plans'.[3] Over time, as the urban industrial share of the population increased, the growth of the working class would come to depend more on natural increase, on the children of already existing workers. But until the 1980s a very sizeable increase in the number of workers continued to depend on migration from the countryside.

The most obvious measure of the speed of this change is the rise in the level of urbanisation noted in Chapter 4. The three sources of this growth are set out in table 7.1. This clearly reveals the limited role of natural increase until late on. The most rapid period of migration was between 1926 and 1938, when the urban population grew from 26.3 million to 56.1 million. So rapid was the shift that, combined with the impact of the 1932-33 famine, it caused the size of the rural population to fall absolutely from 120.7 million to 114.4 million. Since most migrants were of working age, the size of this group in agriculture fell even more, from 72 million to 35 million, leaving a countryside disproportionately inhabited by the young, the old and women. Even in the Second World War the shift continued, and it grew again after 1945. Then, until the end of the 1960s, the absolute size of the rural population stabilised at around 108 million, suggesting that out migration was equivalent to the rate of natural increase.[4] Thereafter it fell to 95 million in 1990.

TABLE 7.1. SOURCES OF INCREASE OF URBAN POPULATION[5]

	INCREASE IN URBAN POPULATION (millions)	PERCENTAGE DUE TO		
		Migration	Urban spread	Natural increase
1926-39	29.8	62	20	18
1939-58	39.2	62	18	20
1959-70	36.0	40	14	46

The huge wartime mobilisation and losses further churned up the working class that had begun to form in the 1930s. In the immediate post-war years large numbers of new recruits were again pulled into an urban workforce whose conditions remained at rock bottom. In 1948, for example 58.5 percent of workers in Leningrad quit their jobs to look for better ones in a city still wrecked by the war. Overall by 1950 only 25.7 percent of Russian workers had an unbroken work record of more than five years. It was worse in a city like Leningrad. In 1948 only 37 percent of the city's workers had an unbroken period of work of more than three years, compared with 43.5 percent nationally, and by 1951 only 11.4 percent of the city's workers had a 10-year work record.[6] In the 1950s a more stable pattern of growth and a larger hereditary urban working class began to develop, as the urban population grew from 33 percent in 1939 to 56 percent in 1970 and 67 percent in 1989. But, as table 7.1 shows, it would take a whole generation after the war before the larger part of urban growth would come from the natural increase of the town population, and even then a large inflow of rural dwellers still continued throughout the 1970s.

Why move? The answer is simple – however bad urban conditions were, and they were very bad, rural conditions were worse. Attempts were made in the early 1930s to limit and direct the movement. Roadblocks were even set up in the first stages of collectivisation, and this is the reason why peasants were denied internal passports until the 1970s. Organised recruitment was also tried in order to channel the movement to industry. But most of the movement was spontaneous. As the pressure to industrialise drove up the demand for labour, those who could escape took their chances. At the end of the 1960s, for example, it was estimated that only 30 percent of peasant youth doing military service would return to the villages from which they came.[7] In the 1980s only 49 percent of the rural population was of working age, compared with 60 percent in the towns.

But the new working class was not simply formed from the peasantry. Industrialisation also absorbed the surplus of the unemployed of the 1920s. Most craft industry was destroyed, and artisans turned into factory hands. Women, predominantly urban women, were pulled into the labour force, their share in large-scale industry rising from 28.7 percent in 1928 to 43.4 percent in 1939 and to a peacetime peak of 51.2 in 1980.[8] Part of this new working class was formed in the old industrial areas. Moscow, Leningrad and the Donbass grew. There was a doubling of the population in the 25 largest cities between 1926 and 1939 from 8.8 to 18.1 million. But everywhere new factories were built and old ones reconstructed. In January 1935 three quarters of industrial capital was invested in plants where at least half the investment had taken place since 1928. New industry also meant new cities and new communities. Tsarist Russia had 700 significant towns, the USSR in the 1980s 2,000, in some of which new migrants were still the dominant social group. People also migrated to new regions. Between 1926 and 1939 3 million moved to Siberia and another 1.7 million to Central Asia, and this eastward movement continued and increased for some areas after 1945.

No place symbolised the new more than Magnitogorsk. 'This was the

Magnitogorsk in 1933,' wrote the American engineer John Scott:

> ...a quarter of a million souls — Communists, Kulaks, foreigners, Tartars, convicted saboteurs and a mass of
> blue-eyed Russian peasants — building the biggest steel combinat in Europe in the middle of the barren Ural
> steppe... Men froze, hungered and suffered, but the construction work went on with a disregard for individu-
> als and a mass heroism seldom paralleled in history.[9]

But such heroism is not so unusual. Throughout history, whether directly as a result of fighting, or indirectly in the battle for production, it has been, from the pharaohs onwards, exactly what those who rule have demanded of those they rule over.

PEASANTS OR WORKERS?

Despite the speed of urbanisation it was only in 1961 that the balance between town and country tipped in favour of the town, and even in 1990 some 19 per-cent of the workforce was directly dependent on agriculture, to say nothing of the wider agro-industrial complex. What, then, of those who stayed behind in the countryside? Often these are spoken of as peasants, and in 1926 this is what they were. But collectivisation began a transformation that brought many of them nearer to being poverty-stricken workers. Over time a large group of non-agricultural workers was formed in the countryside, engaged in tasks such as building, transport or various white collar jobs. Within agriculture, too, jobs became more specialised. Indeed, from the 1950s the numbers of col-lective farmer-workers – *kolkhozniki* – declined faster than the rural popula-tion as a whole, until at the time of the 1989 census there were only some 11 million left.[10] But it was these who remained the core of the rural population, and it was here that the worst conditions were found.

By 1937 40 percent of the population lived in the 242,500 collective farms, which had an average of 78 families and 316 people in each of them. Survival often depended as much on what was produced on the private plots that were legalised in the 1930s and which could never be done away with: 'Millions lived in wretched huts, feeding themselves from their tiny plots of land (on which they grew potatoes, cabbage, cucumber, beets, turnips and onions) and their cow'.[11] Others were connected with the state farms or the machine trac-tor stations where much of the equipment was concentrated for hire to the *kolkhozy*. For this rural population the worst point was the famine of 1932-33, but conditions remained pitiful for long after on all but a few model *kolkhozy*. One writer remembered his childhood in these terms:

> We had bread baked with sawdust, with clover heads, and when it was made with ground potatoes — that was
> a holiday. But the most disgusting thing in childhood was going to the lavatory in the yard because all this saw-
> dust and undigested grass scratched the anus until it bled. Of course, one year to another was different, some

years it was better, but beginning in 1932 (this famine I remember clearly) we rarely ate our fill. Good har-
vest or bad harvest — the difference was not great, it was necessary to feed the state, until in the end even the
feeders fled away in all directions.

Another asked: 'What was there left for the *kolkhoznik* to do? It's clear what. Either leave or go out stealing. This is what they did, depending on what they were able to do'.[12] If you stole, however, or even scavenged in the fields you had to be careful. One peasant woman described how:

...all spring you'd go and work hard there... But when pay day comes, they give you 100-150 grams of grain
per working day — it came to 15-20 poods [24-32 kg] — nothing to take home! I nicked more from the
kolkhoz than I earned. We worked hard for nothing. So we had to take grain or whatever from the fields. It
was the only way to get by. The chairman was svoi [one of our kind], he just warned us not to take too
much. He used to say: 'Hey babes, you'd better be cautious so that I wouldn't account for you.' But apart from
that he turned a blind eye.[13]

Conditions remained bad during the war, and worsened again immediately after 1945. In some parts this was due to the establishment of the collective farm system in new areas or its reinforcement in those that had been occupied. But the situation was made worse by the bad harvest of 1946. Even Khrushchev in 1956 condemned Molotov's foreign grain sales in 1946-47, 'while in some regions people were swollen with hunger and even dying from lack of bread'.[14]

Thereafter it became obvious that conditions had to be improved. The logic was spelled out in a later story by the rural writer Fyodor Abramov where a party secretary says: 'As a *kolkhoz* boss I can't do anything but crack the whip. I've nothing to give people. But a horse needs oats to make it go. What good is a hungry man as a worker?'[15] The huge gap between town and country was therefore partially closed. Agriculture began to absorb a larger share of resources, as attempts were made to overcome the heritage of backwardness and bitterness, but progress was slow. The 1959 census showed that 70 percent of the rural population lived in centres of less than 100, many of them lacking the most basic facilities. It is not surprising then that in 1961 the hundredth anniversary of the emancipation of the serfs passed without significant rural celebrations for, as Lev Kopolev put it, 'no one dared remind the passportless peasants of their ancestors' fate'.[16] By that point the income of collective farmers had been increased to 70 percent of the average of other workers. In 1970 it was 80 percent, and by 1986 it had been pushed up to 92 percent.[17]

Even with the continuing rise in rural incomes, by the end of the 1980s *kolkhozniki* were still worse paid and spent more of their income on food but still consumed 24 percent less meat, 18 percent less milk, 12 percent less sugar and even 4 percent fewer eggs than town workers. Much of the food that they did consume came from their private plots. The right to have these had been recognised in 1935 and, despite attempts to cut them back, successive

❧ 7.1 THE REGIME OF DOCUMENTS

One measure of the extent to which Russians were controlled can be seen in the documents that they had and still have to have. Those without the appropriate documents were second class, which is why the status of the peasants was so low for so long. Documents marked your status, but they also gave the state power over you. Before 1991 only the privileged or the very lucky could get foreign passports to travel to the West. But within Russia all adult Russians depended on a variety of documents in addition to birth certificates, marriage certificates, driving licences and pension books. All Russians eventually came to have, and still have, an internal passport. This contains details of name, nationality, date of birth, marital status, spouse's name and names of children. The existence of the internal passport was one of the things that made it easier for the Nazis to spot Jews in the occupied lands in the Second World War. These passports continue to function as identity cards. They are used for a variety of tasks, from collecting parcels from the post office to registering your permanent residence with the police. At the start of the 21st century they are even needed to use tickets on trains and planes, which are issued with the buyer's name to stop speculation.

*The internal passport will have a residence stamp — the **propiska** or **registratsiia**. Rights of residence in some places have always been restricted — in Moscow, for example. Without the stamp other rights are not enforceable, and people can be moved on by the police.*

*The work book or **trudovaia knizhka** was another crucial document. It was gained with the first job and passed from employer to employer. It measured your length of service (on which pensions used in part to depend). It recorded bonuses and work medals awarded. And it recorded disciplinary offences which therefore stayed with the worker throughout their career. Employers could also demand a reference or **kharakteristika**.*

*In addition males at the age of 18 will get a notice of their eligibility for call-up, a **pripisnoia svidetelstvo**, and after they have served in the army they will have further documents if they are in the reserve in the form of their military papers, the **voennaia knizhka**.*

Forms always demand a mass of information. But under the old system they had a special paragraph, paragraph five, which required people to state their nationality. This was how, on occasion, discrimination took place against certain groups like Jews.

governments had to endorse them. They produced a disproportionate amount of output by value, but this is somewhat misleading as they were really private market gardens. But their importance is shown in the fact that at the end of the 1980s *kolkhozniki* still got all their milk, potatoes, vegetables and 74 percent of their meat consumption from their private plots as well as a surplus to sell in the legal *kolkhoz* markets in the towns.[18]

Overall the rule was clear – the countryside was poorer, its facilities were fewer, of poorer quality and had less qualified staff. In schooling, for example, at the end of the 1980s 17 percent of rural pupils had to be educated in a second shift (especially in Central Asia and Kazakhstan), and 2 percent in a third shift. But a wider measure of the problems in the countryside was the fact that in 1988 the rural death rate was 30 percent higher than the urban one, a gap only partly to be explained by the age structure of the population. The weak infrastructure and poor housing had an inevitable impact. Deaths from respiratory problems, for example, were twice as high as in the towns, TB deaths 40 percent higher, and typhoid and paratyphoid outbreaks were by no means restricted to the much more backward periphery. None of this should be surprising when it is realised that only 9 percent of villages had a centralised water supply and 'in practice sewage systems do not exist in the villages of the Central Asian and Caucasian Republics'. When illness struck, a significant part of the rural population lacked easy access to medical aid, and what there was lagged seriously behind:

> More than half the district hospitals and more than 70 percent of local hospitals and independent rural poly-clinics and surgeries are situated in adapted buildings, and approximately half of these buildings are not satisfactory for their purpose. Nearly half the district hospital buildings lack hot water, a fifth sewage and 12 percent running water. In eight out of 10 local hospitals there is a lack of hot water, in a half sewage systems, in a third running water.[19]

Nevertheless, the rural-urban gap had partially closed, and as this happened it became more apparent that what separated the mass of the rural population from the urban workers was less a difference of kind than one of degree. In 1966 Arutunian, a Soviet rural expert, perhaps not noticing that his words pointed not merely to the horizontal unity of the countryside and the town but the implicit class differentiation above, said: 'The social distance between workers and peasants is already now less significant than between the social groups internal to each class, connected with this or that quality which distinguishes one type of labour from another'.[20]

THE SHAPE OF THE WORKING CLASS

Table 7.2 shows how the wider structure of employment changed as the Soviet economy industrialised. The relative decline of agriculture, the rise of industry and services is clear. The pressure to produce created a full employment economy similar to Western war economies. It is not true that there was no unemployment at all. What is called frictional unemployment – workers out of work while they changed jobs – was at similar levels to the West but not counted. Significant pockets of unemployment and underemployment also existed in some backward and rural areas. But in general high pressure growth led to the labour surplus being soaked up. In this context workers had a lot of freedom to move – 'nazhmut uidy', or 'if they put the pressure on, I quit' was a popular saying. Attempts were made in the 1960s to set up labour exchanges to assist this, but most workers, 68 percent in 1976, were simply hired by managers 'at the gate'.[21]

TABLE 7.2. THE CHANGING PERCENTAGE STRUCTURE OF EMPLOYMENT[22]

	1913	1940	1960	1980	1989
Agriculture and forestry	75	54	39	20	19
Industry and construction	9	23	32	39	39
Transport and communications	2	5	7	9	7
Non-productive spheres and management	14	18	22	32	35

Table 7.3 shows the distribution of workers into three main groups. These figures are based on relatively crude Soviet categories, but the growth of an urban industrial working class is clear, and alongside it can be seen the rise of the office-based working class. By the 1970s and early 1980s the USSR had one of the biggest, if not the biggest, working class in the world.

TABLE 7.3. MAIN CATEGORIES OF THE SOVIET WORKFORCE IN MILLIONS[23]

	1940	1960	1970	1980	1989
Collective farmers	29	21.8	16.6	13.1	11.6
Manual workers	23.9	46.2	64.9	78.8	78.7
Non-manual workers	10	15.8	25.3	33.7	36.7
TOTAL	**62.9**	**83.8**	**106.8**	**125.6**	**127.0**

It was a working class whose educational level increased rapidly from the 1930s. By the 1980s the majority of workers had been born of urban parents and had completed their primary education, which had itself been extended over the previous decades. Skills levels rose and vocational training increased. Both helped reduce differentials between different kinds of labour. The number of people with higher education also grew. In 1939 there had been 1.2 million with complete higher education. By 1989 the figure was over 20 million. But this increase in education and skill was often combined with a continued dependence on manual labour and brute force which reflected the uneven development of the economy.

The pattern of Soviet development also moulded the working class in another sense. This was the preference for large plants employing huge numbers of workers – a trend that developed to such an extent that people spoke of 'gigantomania' in the 1930s. But even in the post-war era this preference for large plants continued as can be seen in table 7.4.

TABLE 7.4. SIZE DISTRIBUTION OF RUSSIAN AND AMERICAN PLANTS BY WORKFORCE[24]

	RUSSIA		US	
	c1960	c1985	c1960	c1985
Less than 100	2.7	2	27.9	22
101–1,000	35.5	24	42.4	47
More than 1,000	61.8	74	29.7	31

Before 1917, as we have seen, there was a high concentration of labour in Russian plants and this helped to forge solidarity. But workers then, even under Tsarist repression, had more chance of independent organisation. After 1928 the larger plants operated more like company towns, fiefdoms of the plant managers, which gave them a degree of authority not only over workers in the workplace but outside it as well.[25]

THE GRIND OF WORK

In the 1930s and during the war administrative attempts were made, alongside the forced labour of the Gulag, to allocate labour more widely. But these were not successful. A labour market of some kind always existed in Russia, though the level of constraint was considerable during the Stalin era. But ultimately, whether working through the market or centralised direction, what determined the overall allocation of labour were the same competitive pressures that we have argued were at the root of development as a whole.[26] Wage scales were set centrally and differentiated by industry, by grade according to skill, and by region (so that workers in the far north, for example, got a supplement). But directly or indirectly these rates broadly reflected market pressures. Scales were worked out in 1931 and then modified under pressure of shortages. They basically remained as they were until 1956. As we saw in the previous chapter, this was a period of widening differentials. Differentials between industries also changed as the balance of the economy was shifted to a heavy industry base in the 1930s. Coal mining leapt from 14th to first place, iron and steel from ninth to second, and oil from eighth to third in the scales, while in industry workers in the light and consumer industries fell back.[27] In the 1950s the general pressure to improve conditions led to a wage reform in 1956. Some of the differentials were rationalised, and attempts were made to tie wage differences more closely to work norms. This led to a general contraction of industry differences similar to that seen in the West. The revised pattern broadly reflected the changing balance of supply and demand for particular kinds of labour. The regime had now to try to encourage a more positive commitment, and this was also reflected in the reduction of the share of industrial wage earners paid by the piece from 76 percent in 1956 to 58 percent in 1965.[28] The broad pattern of industrial differentials created in the 1930s remained, because the economic structures which had underpinned them also remained a constant feature of the economy until 1991. These structures also incorporated a significant degree of discrimination against women. Formally pay was equal, but despite their widespread employment women came to be concentrated in 'feminised' sectors or in lower grades, where they were held back by less complete education, experience and home pressures, so that on average women earned only around two thirds the amount earned by men.

The more interesting question relates to the overall squeeze on the level of wages created by the continual pressure to accumulate, build up the arms sector and divert wealth to the expenditure of the ruling class. Because real wages were effectively cut in half in the years of the First Five-Year Plan, even when they began to rise they remained pitifully low. In 1940 the overall real wage level was still below that of 1928. Wages were then forced down again, and in 1950 they had still only risen to 60-85 percent (depending on the method of calculation) of the 1928 level. Only in the mid-1950s did they finally crawl above the 1928 level, and then, although real wage levels significantly improved and minimum wages were established, overall real wages were still held back by the continuing diversion of resources away from satisfying the needs of the mass of producers. A minimum wage was established in 1956 and raised in 1965, 1968 and 1975, but at this time, despite it being set below official poverty levels, some 10 percent were not even paid this.[29]

At least until 1988-89 the terms of employment were not the outcome of any collective bargaining element but were set by the state and enterprise managers. Immediately after 1945 there was a short term intensification of labour repression, but from 1950 this was lifted, and in 1956 most of the earlier legislation was repealed. But this did not stop the state watching closely what happened. Under Andropov in the early 1980s, for example, police checks were even made on queues and cinema audiences to identify people who should have been at work. But the most important continuing constraint was that workers could not organise freely. Trade unions remained state instruments, administering social benefits, and occasionally taking up the cases of aggrieved workers as individuals. But their real job was to support the exploitation of workers and this was embodied in their statutes: 'The principal task of the trade unions is to stimulate the initiative of the masses, to foster involvement, in order to strengthen economic power, the over-fulfilment of the plan, the mobilisation of reserves, the raising of the material and cultural level of the workers.' At one stage the overall head of the trade union movement was Alexander Shelepin, a former head of the KGB. One response to this came in 1978 with a small-scale attempt to set up a Free Trade Union Association. But this was immediately repressed, and one of its leaders, Vladimir Klebanov, was detained in a psychiatric hospital (having already enjoyed a previous five years of prison and psychiatric detention for his protests).[30]

But workers remained dependent on managers in other senses. Often benefits (including some housing) were tied to the length of time at an enterprise, so dismissal might be a serious threat. People lacking a residence permit to large cities were especially vulnerable. Around Moscow lived an army of *limitchiks* – cheap labourers with no residence rights. Yeltsin said that these were:

...in essence...slaves... They had practically no rights at all. They were bound like serfs, to a factory or an enterprise by their temporary work permits... Their employers could do anything they liked with them — break

*the law, for example, or disregard the health and safety regulations — simply because they knew that the wretched **limitchiks** would never complain and never write letters to anyone in authority.*[31]

Plant benefits also reflected managerial power. Russian health resorts and sanatoriums were the preserve of the minority rather than the many. Workers in one steel plant might have had access to them once every six years had the places been distributed equally, reported one commentator. Needless to say they rarely if ever were so distributed. Sometimes even the press took up complaints. 'Year after year,' said one Donetsk worker of his workplace in 1978, 'the same people enjoy the privileges of spells at health resorts'.[32]

Despite what we have said, some commentators have argued that the degree of exploitation of the Soviet workers was mitigated by the paternalism of the bosses or a strong degree of workers' resistance from below. We see no evidence, however, that what happened in Soviet plants was significantly different in degree or kind from what can be found elsewhere. Paternalism, for example, has been a standard managerial practice throughout the history of capitalism and, as we suggested in the previous chapter, it depends on a fundamentally unequal relationship. But plant studies carried out by Soviet sociologists do not suggest a high degree of confidence and trust in Soviet bosses. One study of the Urals in the early 1970s showed that only 34.2 percent of workers felt that the regime's collective trade union/management agreements reflected their needs and interests, and only 25.5 percent felt that plant management carried out their part. Not all plant managements were equally bad. In the best plant, Sverdlovsk Plastics, 45.8 percent thought the collective agreements reflected their interests, but even here only 36.6 percent believed the management kept to them. In the worst plant, Urals Cable, these figures were 20.9 percent and 14.3 percent. Not surprisingly, 35.9 percent of those in this plant told the investigators that they felt no personal interest in improving labour discipline. And all of this comes from a survey publicised for Western consumption, where all the pressure would be to exaggerate the degree of satisfaction of the workforce.[33]

Nor is there strong evidence that workers had an unusual capacity to create a degree of negative control by building slack into the system. Workers did resist, and the process of work involved a continuing battle over control that we will explore later. But there is no evidence that this played a qualitatively greater role than it has done at times in the West. Many of those who looked at the Soviet plant from above or from the outside certainly played up this aspect, but this was part of the 'blame the workers' culture. Tatiana Zaslavskaia, for example, suggested that only 32 percent of workers tried to do a good job, and in lagging industries it was only 17 percent. But to stand what was called 'the human factor' on its head and see it as the central contradiction of the regime makes no sense. And there is one fairly compelling piece of evidence against this view. If workers had so much more workplace power than workers in the West, then why did they allow the system to kill and maim them so much? Soviet industrial death and injury rates long remained a secret, but when the evidence did come out it suggested a picture of comparative carnage. One sign was that in the mid-1960s 58 percent of the industrial labour force was classified as doing arduous or dangerous work.[34] In 1989 agricultural (and *kolkhoz*) work was the most dangerous, with 218,000 reported injuries and 3,900 deaths, an average of 85 injuries per 100,000 workers, though in some regions the figure rose to 142 per 100,000. Industry recorded rates of over 70 injuries per 100,000, and several thousand more deaths. Overall in that year alone (supposedly a 25 percent improvement on 1980 and even more on the decades before) this meant that there were up to two thirds of a million industrial injuries and thousands of deaths, to say nothing of the unrecorded thousands whose lives were annually cut short through industrial disease.[35]

Here is a measure of the extent to which an alienated and exploited workforce were victims of loose labour codes and managements that would push people to the limit when the system they ran needed it. The case of the mine worker Vladimir Klebanov is telling. He fell foul of the authorities for trying to get managers to honour the labour code over hours and wages, to record injuries properly, and to pay the appropriate compensation as well as refusing, as a foreman, to send his team into unsafe conditions. Lest it be thought he complained unnecessarily it was revealed in 1989 that during the time of the Afghan war (1979-1989) 10,000 Soviet miners died, a figure only just under the number of troops killed. Each million tons of coal was reckoned to cost one life, and around 700-800 million tons were mined a year in the 1980s.[36] In the light of this it is no surprise to learn that one of the demands raised by striking miners in 1989 was that silicosis and anthracosis should be acknowledged as work-related diseases. Overall, said one commentator, as new light began to be thrown on working conditions at the end of the 1980s, in Russia 'workers live on average six years less than their class brothers in the other developed countries'.[37]

MYTHS OF THE 'WORKERS' STATE'

But outside of work too the Soviet working class experienced long and difficult periods. Regime propaganda claimed that good social provision compensated for failings elsewhere. But much of the good social provision was a myth. Take housing – this demands infrastructure investment but, as we know, everything was pushed into industrial investment in the 1930s. While cities exploded, instead of the 17 percent of capital investment that went into housing in the 1920s only a 9.1 percent share was devoted to housing in the first plan, 11 percent in the second and 8.1 percent in the third. The resulting housing crisis was then made much worse by the wartime destruction. It should be remembered that the official sanitary norm was 9 square metres per person, but as the table below shows the average housing space fell far further below this, and only began to exceed it in the 1960s.

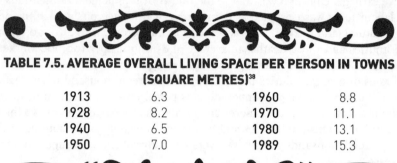

TABLE 7.5. AVERAGE OVERALL LIVING SPACE PER PERSON IN TOWNS (SQUARE METRES)[38]

1913	6.3	1960	8.8
1928	8.2	1970	11.1
1940	6.5	1980	13.1
1950	7.0	1989	15.3

But these average statistics obscure a huge variation and the often dire situation of many working class families until quite late on. Workers lived in several different kinds of housing. Most primitive, used in the war and on vast construction sites in the 1930s, was the *zemlianka* – a dugout supported by a few planks. Then there were large dormitories which were used to house single workers and some couples. In new areas families were often put in the *barak* – a long, low building made of clapboard, and divided into a corridor and rooms by thin partitions, where 10 to 20 families and even animals would cluster for warmth in the winter. Boris Yeltsin claimed that he was kept warm during his childhood in the 1930s by having the family goat sleep in the room. A sense of the longevity and scale of the *barak* in some areas can be seen in the Sverdlovsk province, one of the larger industrial provinces. At the turn of the 1980s Yeltsin, as provincial party boss, tried to get rid of the *baraks* and had to suspend all other housing construction for a year to devote two million square metres of new housing space to rehousing the *barak* families there.[39] In older cities housing also took the form of the *kommunalka* – the communal flat that was shared by several families, again divided by partitions or even curtains, and sharing the same kitchen and toilet. And finally there was a degree of privacy in the mass housing blocks – 'feverish sprawls of featureless glass and concrete boxes' one novelist called them.[40] These began to be built under Khrushchev at top speed and with limited concern for quality, in order to try to deal with the accumulation of problems. It was these blocks that allowed the improvement in space per person shown in the table above. But, as with Western housing blocks, the liberation they brought was limited. Quantity and quality remained a problem, as Gorbachev found when he undertook public walkabouts in the late 1980s. In September 1988 in Krasnoiarsk, for example, one Russian told him: 'Just look at the brand new houses here, Mikhail Sergeyevich, it's impossible to live in them. Within a month there are huge cracks in the floor, and the doors don't shut. It's dreadful, leaks everywhere – when it rains you get water all over the flat – and that's not the end of the story'.[41] The failure to build to standard could have more tragic consequences. In December 1988, for example, 25,000 died in an earthquake in Armenia, many in buildings not built to specification.

Providing the wider urban infrastructure, – water supplies, sewage, gas mains, transport systems – was also expensive. Moscow and Leningrad were developed as show cities. Everybody visits and admires the Moscow metro, though not the graves of the many workers who died building it. But it was different in the suburbs of these cities and even more so elsewhere. In 1941 only 460 towns and cities had water supplies, 140 sewage systems and a mere six gas. The first thing that the young Edward Crankshaw noticed when he arrived at Archangel in 1941 was the stench of raw sewage.[42] Even in big cities water was drawn from pumps, rivers and ponds, and sewage collected in cesspits until the developments of the 1950s onwards. Even then the record remained uneven. Money was poured in, but the urban infrastructure often remained underfinanced, with too little capacity as cities grew faster than were planned. Even the idea that the regime was committed to bringing great art and culture to people on a mass scale needs to be treated sceptically. When Yeltsin took charge of Moscow, for example, he found that the number of theatre seats per head of population was actually less than in 1917.[43]

LAGGING CONSUMPTION

The day to day consumption patterns of families also reflected the priorities of the system. In the 1930s consumption fell less than real wages because, with more women forced into the labour force, many families had two incomes. Two incomes continued to be an essential requirement for most working class families. Here there was a major social contradiction. Soviet workers needed their families, including not only the mother and father but also the help of the grandmother, the *babushka*, because creche and kindergarten places were only ever available for a minority of children. But the housing and general conditions put enormous pressure on married life. One consequence of this was the speed of the fall in the birth rate, especially in towns. Given the lack of contraception, this was largely achieved through abortion, both legal and 'backstreet'. When abortion was banned, the latter was all that was available. The abortion ban was in part a panicked response to the falling birth rate, and its rescinding a recognition that there were limits to state control. But the leaders of the regime continually worried that slow population growth meant fewer soldiers and fewer workers. In January 1955 Khrushchev had said that 'if about 100 million were added to our 200 million, even that would not be enough', but when it became obvious that this would not happen 'a state of near-panic among sociologists and their politician bosses' became obvious in public discussion.

The worst point for workers' consumption (apart from the war) was in the early 1930s. Bread rationing was introduced in 1929, and by 1940 40 million depended on centralised bread allowances and another 10 million on local. But in 1932-33 rationing extended to a wide range of goods.[45] It is a sign of how desperate things were that even in Moscow industrial plants were ordered to raise rabbits. Victor Serge has left a vivid description of the situation of workers at this time, 'hemmed in by the police, by poverty, by lies':

> One must picture the worker preoccupied with obtaining, stamping, checking, and reregistering a bread card, which is refused to half the workers on various pretexts; the housewife, running from one empty store to another, and registering in a queue at the doors of the fish stall early in the evening, pauper no 778, in order to wrangle the next morning over a ration of salt fish; the worker coming home to comment at the table on the arrests made the night before; finding rhymed apologies for the death penalty in his paper; not knowing where he can get a spare shirt; fearing to be driven out of the big city by being refused a passport, because his son is married to the daughter of a former small merchant; wondering what risky combination to resort to in order to get hold of a dollar and buy some precious medicament at the Torgsin [hard currency store].[46]

Food surveys show that most workers ate less meat, fewer vegetables and less dairy produce, and filled out their diets with potatoes. Only in the late 1950s was there a sustained improvement in diets that took them beyond the levels of the late 1920s (or 1914). Thereafter as wage levels rose so did food consumption levels. Some of the basic national data is set out in the table below, from which the scale of the improvement is clear, although a more detailed class analysis needs to be made to isolate the consumption of different groups.

TABLE 7.5. ANNUAL FOODSTUFF CONSUMPTION PER HEAD OF POPULATION (KILOGRAMS)[47]

	1913	1950	1965	1975	1989
Meat and poultry	29	26	41	57	67
Fish	7	7	13	17	17
Milk and dairy	154	172	251	316	363
Eggs	48	60	124	216	268
Potatoes	114	241	142	120	98
Grain products	200	172	156	141	129
Vegetables	40	51	72	89	95
Fruit	11	11	28	39	41

The share of workers' income spent on food declined from 54 percent in 1940 to around a third in the 1970s, so there was the possibility of spending more both absolutely and relatively on other consumer goods. But it needs also to be remembered that many workers depended on a degree of home production. Sewing machines were frequently in use, and much food came from a growing number of allotments on which many ordinary Russians lavished time, not only gardening for essential food but scrimping and scavenging to build their own small summer dachas. The dacha allotment took off in many parts of Russia. For the powerful a dacha could mean a palace. For most Russians it was more a glorified allotment on which a wooden summer chalet could be built and precious food grown. In Leningrad, with a population of 4 million, for example, there were 850,000 dachas in the 1970s, from which every autumn a significant part of both the bulk and variety of foodstuffs could come.[48]

Then there was also the erratic nature of the supply system, which became infamous and continued to mark the lives of ordinary people. People carried an *avoska* – a string bag – because you had to be prepared to queue to get what you could when it was available.[49] Even in Moscow, the best supplied city, shortages of basics occurred, and these were made worse by the fact that as much as 15 percent of supplies were siphoned off into the black market (to say nothing of those officially removed for those above).[50]

Brezhnev spoke in 1979 of 'interruptions' in the availability of 'medicine, soap, detergents, toothbrushes and toothpaste, needles, thread, nappies and other goods produced in light industry'.[51] He might also have added the endemic shortages of toilet paper in many areas and the lack of production of sanitary towels. It is worth pausing a moment on this list. Although it by no means exhausts the range of deficit goods, the lack of each of these items is in its own way a measure of a basic human indignity. Governments and systems that fail to meet people's needs in such basic things as toilet rolls and sanitary towels eloquently express the real value they place on the people in whose name they claim to rule.

One way of measuring the impact of all this is to look at the relationship between living conditions and health indicators like death rates, life expectancy, the birth weights of babies and even adult height – all of which bear the imprint of success and failure in a social system. During the Stalin period attempts were made to compensate for the health impact of shortages by making a little go further. Food rationing was one example. Campaigns for cleanliness and rationing of healthcare were others. But these could not mask the short term impact of famines or the medium term impact of poor nutrition on, say, the low birth weights of babies, always a sensitive indicator of maternal health, which fell significantly in the 1930s and 1940s. But in the longer term the benefits that industrialisation eventually brought, combined with public health improvements, did increase life expectancy from 44 in 1926-27 to 48 in 1938-40 and 67 in 1955-60. This looks impressive compared with past examples of industrialisation. It is rather less impressive when compared with what has been achieved in Third World countries in the last half century. Moreover, the regime should really be judged against what it claimed, and the fact that it had to hide the evidence here for so long is telling. Moreover, the difficulties in the situation of the mass of the population were underlined by the fact that from 1960 the life expectancy grew by only small amounts. Just how great the problem was emerged in the *glasnost* era. In 1988, for example, the then health minister revealed that in terms of relative health spending the Soviet Union was ranked only between 60th and 70th in the world. In infant mortality it was 50th – below countries such as Mauritius and Barbados – and in life expectancy only 32nd.[52]

PROTEST AND CONFLICT

Why, then, did workers not protest more? There are two connecting explanations. One is the continual social turmoil in the working class created by the speed of urban and industrial change. The second is the impact of repression. Lenin once said that workers had to be boiled in a factory pot before they could begin to develop a stronger sense of class consciousness. One aspect of what he meant was simply the time it takes for a rural migrant to adjust to the shock of the new urban-industrial ways. But he was also referring to the learning process in which new workers take on and use existing channels of organisation and militancy to help give their grievances direction. It takes time, even in the best of circumstances, to acquire a capacity for sustained organisation and action. A merging of pre-industrial and industrial traditions, and the struggle to establish and sustain organisations are part of the labour history of all countries. Without it discontent often has a sheet lightning character, shooting across the sky but not leaving an immediate organisational legacy.

In Russia the circumstances workers found themselves in after 1928 made this development incredibly difficult. Take social change. We have already stressed the social turmoil within the working class. Even late on the speed of development in some towns was striking. In Togliatti, for example, the development of a new car plant caused the population to expand from 250,000 to 400,000 in the years 1970-74. In the same years in Naberezhaniye chelny, the centre of the Kama Motor Plant, the town grew from 48,000 to 160,000.

This did not mean that Soviet workers formed an inert mass, but organised resistance and independent activity were not possible. This was the result of the second element – the past history of repression and, as we saw in Chapter 5, its continuing legacy that was only broken in the late 1980s. An understanding of the real nature of earlier traditions had been wiped out in the 1930s. The great struggles of the past had become distorted lessons in the history books. The more informal class memory carried by individuals died in the camps. When surviving inmates were released in the 1950s no space was allowed for their experience to be communicated. One former camp inmate put it this way:

> As prisoners we would talk about anything. Once we were free we had padlocks on our mouths again. We'd thought that when the camps came to an end we'd be free, and tell everyone everything about our sufferings and pain. But we emerged into a real world where you couldn't talk. Again we were afraid. We were shackled by fear. [53]

And, of course, the regime's ideological control allowed it to continue to batter people with its formal claims to be 'socialist', deluding some into working with the system rather than against it.

The picture that we now see of the mood of Russian workers as the Stalin era continued is one where, in Sheila Fitzpatrick's words: 'A degree of scepticism, even refusal to take the regime's serious pronouncements fully seriously, was the norm... The antithesis of 'us' and 'them' was basic to Soviet subaltern mentality in the 1930s.' The term 'subaltern mentality' is an affectation designed to dissuade the reader from thinking in the class terms that this historian rejects. But the evidence she and others adduce from the spying of the authorities speaks strongly of a sense of class division. 'Life has become better, life has become more cheerful,' said one woman, echoing Stalin's official propaganda. Then she added: 'Everything for the bosses.' The target of her anger is clear. For others it was more confused with some workers blaming

Jews or other ethnic groups, or even 'Trotskyists'.[54] We now know that even after the first resistance to the industrialisation drive was crushed occasional strikes did break out. As the Nazi armies advanced in 1941, for example, workers in Ivanovo-Voznesensk struck. They had been provoked by more real wage cuts, and fear that equipment and bosses, but not workers, would be evacuated. Some individuals and small groups, often struck by the contrast between the regime's claims and reality, made more political gestures. One small group of workers, then in higher education, protested against Stakhanovism in 1935. The physicist Lev Landau wrote a leaflet that got him jailed in 1938, which said: 'Socialism cannot be found anywhere except on the pages of newspapers, which are absolute liars'.[55] This was part of a thin stream of 'red dissent' which, usually unnoticed by the outside world, never completely died out.

But the everyday resistance of workers was normally expressed at a more basic level until the post-Stalin repression lessened, and even then workers had to be careful in what they did. Many workers responded to poor conditions, and feelings of alienation and exploitation, by quitting their jobs and moving from plant to plant. Turnover rates in the First Five-Year Plan were astronomical, but even when they settled down in the next decades turnover continued to reflect the widespread alienation that workers felt.[56] Of course, changing your job was only a short term solution, since conditions in the next one might not be much better. Some workers found a more permanent solution in drink. Vodka was what one dissident called 'The number one commodity'. The Russian population had a high alcohol consumption rate, and the pattern of binge drinking, then as now, is clearly related to 'drowning your sorrows' and seeking relief. Here too was something the authorities frowned on but were forced to tolerate. They complained too about the extent of absenteeism and pilfering but gave only glimpses of its extent.

However, the response of workers also took forms which, while not openly confronting the authorities, did depend on a degree of informal cooperation and unity. The most widespread was the way in which there was continual battle over work norms. Everywhere the posters proclaimed 'Today's record – tomorrow's norm'. But, if this was the case, why go for the record? As one worker said: 'What's happening is that they are squeezing more blood and sweat out of the worker – and they're paying him less.' The obvious response was to try to hold down norms, and since it is workers who must operate the process of production, the powers of management to overcome this were limited. This is a familiar tactic in the West too, especially in piece-rate systems. We have seen that in the 1930s Stakhanovites who broke norms were sometimes attacked and even killed, and later on overenthusiastic workers might still be taken aside. 'Grassing' about 'weak labour discipline' and 'inflated production figures' did not make you popular.

But this did not stop managers putting on pressure and changing norms upwards on an arbitrary basis. Some workers responded to this over time by go-slows, 'Italian strikes' where they came to their plants but did little or no work. In one reinforced concrete factory in Moscow workers demanded that old norms be restored and when there was no response, then for two days:

> ...the workers sat about in the shop doing nothing. The shop foreman begged his men to get to work, threat-ening them with legal action, but they demanded to see the factory director. The director, terrified by the strike, was afraid to enter the shop. At one point one of the strikers telephoned the local party committee and announced the strike. The local party secretary came straight to the factory with a promise to lower the norms, and the conflict was over.

But it was when conflict spilled out into the street, whether in an open strike or demonstrations, that it became more dangerous for the authorities, and a small but telling pattern of more open conflicts began to emerge in the 1950s as repression was relaxed. These were sometimes straight industrial conflicts but sometimes, in peripheral areas, work grievances, social grievances and national conflicts intertwined in complex ways.

There were a number of significant clashes within Russia in the Khrushchev era. The story of Novocherkassk printed itself on the folk memory as rumours of it spread through Russia. Nationwide food price rises combined with local work problems to cause an explosion in the town. Striking workers demon-strated with their families, and students and schoolchildren, and were met with troops and gunfire that left 24 dead and 69 severely wounded, with many minor casualties.[57] One worker who emigrated in the 1970s from a town over 1,000 miles away from Novocherkassk said that he was told by his workmates that there was no point in protesting: 'If the whole town protests they'll sim-ply mow us down with machine-guns as they did in Novocherkassk in 1962'.[58] But the leadership was also shocked by the incident, and the memory of it and the desire not to have it repeated was one of the factors that encouraged them to hold down food prices in the next decades. But Novocherkassk was not the only example of open protest. In 1956 Tbilisi in Georgia was in the hands of demonstrators for several hours. In the same year mass demonstrations took place in Lithuania. In 1959 thousands of construction workers rioted in Temir Temu in Kazakhstan. Then in 1960 there were demonstrations about food shortages in the coalmining town of Kemerovo in the Kuzbass area of Siberia. In 1961 a riot led to the police station in Murom being attacked, and after Novocherkassk there are records of conflicts in other cities in 1962-63.

We now know a lot about the Novocherkassk shootings, because when the system collapsed oral and archival evidence became available. But we know much less about more minor incidents and their patterns, because the overall evidence remains to be sifted from the national and local archives. But from information that came out to the West it seems that there may have been a reduction in more open conflict after the fall of Khrushchev that could have been related in part to improving conditions, though even here the national question could prove an additional impetus to conflict. In 1965 disturbances were reported in Yerevan, the Armenian capital. In 1967 in Chimkent, an industrial city in Kazakhstan, major riots were reported, and in the same year there were riots in Priuluk and a serious strike in Kharkov in the Ukraine. In 1968, on Lenin's birthday, exiled Crimean Tartars demonstrated in Uzbekistan, and bread riots took place in Khorol, near Vladivostok in the Far East.

After 1969 reports on strikes became more widespread, and nationalist riots and demonstrations appear to have continued to break out.[59] The extent to which there was a rhythm to this movement remains unclear. Most conflicts appear to have been localised, with local demands. But on the other hand the regime could not stop them occurring and, in some instances, apparently spreading to nearby towns.

The analysis that has been done of the evidence of this conflict suggests that most of it took place away from the Moscow-Leningrad regions because conditions were better there and the authorities could not be seen to allow it to take place there. But it was certainly not the case that conflict was limited to the periphery and areas with stronger national grievances. And even in an area like the Ukraine the stimulus to a number of conflicts seems to have been purely industrial. A dramatic example of conflict near to the centre came in the new car city of Togliatti in 1979, when bus drivers walked out. They did so again in 1980, and this led to walkouts too in the main car plant producing the new Fiat-based Lada. At the same time workers in the Gorky car and truck plant also walked out.

Four immediate causes of conflict recur in the information we have – concern over food supplies, arbitrary increases in work norms, housing, and police brutality. The latter cause does suggest that there were strikes when workers were prepared to confront the authorities. One strike in Leningrad in January 1979, for example, was over the death of a worker after being arrested and beaten by the militia. Even when the strike ended the workers made a point of going en masse to their workmate's funeral. The extent to which these cases were sparks or symptoms of deeper grievances, however, await investigation. But the pattern suggests something of a 'flash fire' effect, where conflicts could suddenly ignite once they got out onto the streets.

The response of the authorities to these flash fires was 'fire brigade actions' to stamp out the possibility of their spreading. So long as things had not got out of hand, the immediate policy was one of concession followed by attempts to remove 'troublemakers' (or officially 'the hooligans') who were thought to have instigated the conflict. The power of the authorities here was very real. In the 'Italian strikes' that were referred to earlier, those who had participated 'voluntarily' left their jobs sooner or later, perhaps with their *kharakteristikas* marked by comments on their 'labour discipline'. Leaders of more open forms of conflict could be dismissed and removed from the area, imprisoned or put, like Klebanov and some dissidents, into mental hospitals – who, after all, but a lunatic would protest about work conditions and wages in the workers' paradise?

Ultimately, however, the capacity to hold back discontent depended upon the ability of the regime to maintain control and give some concessions. The explosion of discontent in Poland in 1980-81, when more than half the workforce joined the opposition Solidarity organisation, was a warning that fire brigade actions might not be able to contain wider discontent. But it was not until the end of the 1980s that the workers began to move on a larger scale. The most significant action they took was the great miners' strike of 1989.

This strike began in July 1989 in the Kuzbass in Western Siberia, the source of one fifth of Soviet coal, and spread to the Donbass where another third was produced. Some 400,000 of the million or so miners of the USSR were involved in the first genuine mass working class action since the revolution. It was, as we shall see in the next chapter, an important stage in *perestroika*, but it was also a culmination of resentments developed under the old order, and it shone a clear light on the real position of workers under the old regime.

Coal was a core industry, its workers supposedly part of the top of the working class, but mining was stagnating due to underinvestment and worsening geological conditions, and unresponsive local and national authorities. Miners worked in dangerous conditions with old equipment, and they often depended on hand labour. One figure more than any other seemed to capture their situation – their soap allowance was just 200 grams per month, and it had not changed since the 1920s. Pay was high in Soviet terms but still poor, and holidays were inadequate, pensions low despite early retirement ages, and so on. Outside of work things were no better, with familiar shortages. Housing was poor, with considerable overcrowding. 23 percent of miners of lived in housing with less than four square metres per person and half between four and nine square metres. The atmosphere was poisoned. In the Karaganda, in Kazakhstan, it was estimated that four tons of pollutants per head were emitted. In Kemerovo, one of the centres of the strike, the rate of birth abnormalities was enormous, and 50 percent of newborn babies needed resuscitation. The polluted atmosphere affected the bosses too, but the rest of their life was different, with good housing, country dachas and gardens maintained by staff on the payroll of the pits.

Yet the miners had no rights to protest against any of this. When they struck, the chairman of the Donetsk Region Trade Union denounced it as 'an illegal act that remains an illegal act to this day, as we have no law as yet permitting such action'. Only in the act of resisting the so-called workers' state, only in the act of rebutting the so-called workers' organisations like the official trade unions, did the miners gain an element of that self-respect, dignity and confidence that must be the basis of any real alternative either to the system as it was then or the system as it would become. 'We feel good', said one Kuzbass miner. 'This is the first time we've ever done anything like this.' In Moscow Gorbachev did not see it this way – the strike, he said, was the 'worst ordeal to befall our country in all the four years of restructuring'. But he was wrong – the glimpse of a bottom-up alternative would fade again, and the next decade would prove a far worse ordeal for the mass of the population.[60]

PUTIN STOP THE WAR CRIMES IN CHECHNYA

Chechens demonstrate in London in 2000 against Russia's bloody wars in Chechnya. At first Western leaders turned a blind eye to the huge death toll and the refugee tragedy. Then they began to suggest that Russia had

⚸ TRANSITION

The previous chapters have tried to show how Russia after 1928 should be understood as a class society built on exploitation and oppression, dominated by the wider logic of capitalist accumulation. The peculiarities of the system there arose partly from its origins in the degeneration of a genuine revolution from below, and partly from the way that the tendencies towards state capitalism took such an extensive form in the Soviet Union and its satellites. The importance of this argument is not only that it helps us to understand the past of the system – it also offers a way of resolving the problems of the transition.

Making sense of the transition presents three great problems. The first is to explain what caused the system to both grow *and* decay. Earlier accounts had no trouble thinking of explanations for the spectacular growth. Later accounts had no more trouble in explaining the decay. The difficulty is to have an account that is capable of explaining *both*. The second problem is to explain the striking continuity at the top of Russian society. As we suggested in the introduction, if the transition was so deep rooted a change, how is it that the old order managed to ride out the storm as successfully as it did, converting its control of the old system into new accumulations of great wealth? The third problem is then to explain why the transition has been so chaotic without any of the promises of the transforming power of the market being realised. People were promised a short term transition crisis followed by a growth surge. What they actually got was a huge crisis in which the mass of the population experienced material immiseration alongside a new political freedom. But if life was better at the top, the manoeuvres of Russia's rulers still led to sharp splits over how to order the new political system.

The explanation of these issues lies in the way that pressures arose to change the form of Russian state capitalism to a looser market one. To use an image of Bukharin's, the ruling class was encouraged to try to shift its control from its 'state pocket' to a 'private pocket'. The shift was not a simple one. In the era of *perestroika* (restructuring) and *glasnost* (openness) in the late 1980s, political debate opened up in Russia and new social movements were created. But many of those holding power held back from committing themselves until they saw the likely direction of change. Ironically, with the exception of Boris Yeltsin, most of those who played a key role in Russian politics after 'the change' had not stood out in the battles before 1991. Those who did distinguish themselves at that time were now marginalised in the 'new' Russia. With hindsight we can now see more clearly what happened. The process of 'reform' from above got out of hand as pressures arose from below. But when the old Soviet Union crumbled in 1991 the policy of the new regime led by Boris Yeltsin was to be determined by a technocratic group, working with foreign advisers, that came largely from the gilded youth of the old regime. They were drawn from the Moscow institutes, the party youth organisation (the Komsomol), and the business-oriented sections of the old system. This was the milieu whose development we noted at the end of Chapter 6. Now its representatives, speaking fluent English, wearing good suits, and spouting the mantra of the market, which they had quietly been able to study because of their positions while others had been jailed for dissent, found an opportunity to have unparalleled influence. Their aim was not only to widen the role of the market but also to ensure that the beneficiaries of this were themselves and the existing members of the ruling class. The more able ones, leavened by some new entrants and a new role for those chancers under the old system who had played the shadow economy (often serving the needs of those in power), would emerge triumphant, their power re-legitimised by the 'new'.

However, the problem with looser organisation is that it risks the capacity of the centre to direct and control the process of competition and change. This is exactly what happened in the USSR at the turn of the 1990s. The pyramid of Soviet power did not collapse. It disintegrated into dozens of competing pyramids of power as the process of restructuring got out of control. The 1990s were characterised by a continuity of control of the productive resources but sharp changes in the political structures and organisations. To use a military analogy, Russia in the 1990s was like an army in which the officer corps remained in charge, ordering the troops around, but the command structure which had previously given it unified direction had collapsed.

THE NATURE OF THE CRISIS

The heyday of the Soviet economy was in the 1950s and 1960s, and, as we have seen, this encouraged Khrushchev to make grandiose claims for the future. In the 1960s growth rates began to slow. This led to discussions about reform and attempts to introduce more market elements, but these were all partial and limited. The strong pressure to try more fundamental change did not really arise until the 1980s as a response to the continuing growth slow-down. This slowdown is apparent in the official figures. These showed the economy growing at 10 percent in the 1950s, 7 percent in the 1960s, 5 percent in the 1970s and under 4 percent between 1981 and 1985. But everyone knew that these official figures were inflated. CIA specialists in the US laboured hard to produce their own estimates. They usually ended up with a growth rate half the official rate (apart from in the 1960s, when their estimates were just over two thirds the official figure). Even at this reduced level the CIA accounts still produced impressive growth figures for the quarter of a century after 1945. Things then became less impressive. Halve the official rates from the 1970s and early 1980s, and the figures look much less good. Worse, independent estimates suggest that the degree of distortion in both the official and CIA growth figures grew at this time, and if allowance is made for this then the Soviet economy looks more or less stagnant from the late 1970s.[1]

Most accounts of this 'Soviet failure' start by analysing internal contradictions. This is a mistake. The context of what happened in Russia at the end of the 20th century was the changes in the global system, and it is the interaction between internal and external factors that is important. The 1950s and 1960s were golden years, West and East. The 1970s and 1980s saw a generalised slowdown. Indeed, as we suggested at the end of Chapter 4, at first it appeared to the Soviet leadership as if the problems in the West were greater than those that they themselves faced. Only in the early 1980s did a sense of the scale of the Soviet difficulties emerge. With it came a significant degree of demoralisation at the top. When Gorbachev was elected as the new general secretary in 1985 he was reported to have said: 'We cannot go on like this.' But the growing crisis was underpinned by similar pressures to those affecting the West.

The vigour of the capitalist system is dependent on the general rate of profit. This varies in the short term boom-slump cycle of market capitalism. Elements of this appeared in Russian state capitalism, but they were mediated through the central control mechanism which helped to produce patterns of growth in the form of what some called 'planned cycles'. But the rate of profit also varies over the longer run. In the 1930s it fell, leading to fears of stagnation in the world economy. The response was massive state intervention, of which Stalin's Russia was an extreme example. After 1945 the rate of profit rose. The reasons are still argued over, but they appear to have been related in important ways to the nature of arms expenditure that had become generalised as part of the Cold War. However, as those who explored the role of arms spending argued, its capacity to help counteract pressures pulling down the rate of profit was not unlimited. These began to reassert themselves in the 1970s.[2] The result was that world growth slowed. Pressures arose to restructure capitalism, to shift investment into more profitable areas. This required greater flexibility. Policies were introduced in many economies, sustained by liberal market ideology, to widen the role of market forces. But, contrary to the myths of market liberalism, this did not result in a wholesale reduction in either monopoly or state power. The real picture was much more nuanced. But it did lead to greater global interpenetration rather than a retreat to the isolationism of 1930s-style 'autarkic' tendencies.

In Russia the economy remained trapped both by the pattern of global military and economic competition, and by its excessively bureaucratic internal structure. This made it difficult to restructure and take advantage of the potential offered by deeper integration into the global economy. Indeed, in some respects the weak external performance of the Soviet economy was even more depressing to its leaders than the slowing growth. Despite supposedly driving forward to modernity, the economy still relied on oil and raw material exports. The share of machinery in exports, even with the advantage of its own Comecon trading bloc, fell from 22 percent of exports in 1970 to 14 percent in 1985.[3] The confusion that this created affected all parts of the system. Kriuchkov, then deputy chairman of the KGB, said in 1988:

> The world of today is a tissue of discrepancies. On the one hand, the process of polarisation of political and economic forces continues, with the principal centres of capitalism developing in the United States, Western Europe and Japan. On the other hand, intercommunication and mutual dependence are leading to a confusion of interests, giving rise to unprecedented diversity, where demarcation and interaction displace and complement one another.

What Kriuchkov called 'cliches and stereotyped ideas' were now of little use in guiding policy.[4]

If the roots of the Soviet crisis were similar to those elsewhere, more specific elements did exist. One was the exhaustion of gains made from the switch from an agricultural to an industrial society. This had allowed for more easy growth by moving resources from less to more productive areas. A second factor was the continuing pressure of arms competition, the burden of which, as we have already seen, fell more heavily on the USSR than the US. 'To maintain our defence at the necessary level,' said Gromyko in 1985, is 'the holy of holies for us all'.[5] The knock-on effect of this meant that longstanding problems in areas like agriculture and housing were simply not being solved, and there was a lack of resources for new growth sectors too.

A third element was the problems that arose from central direction, and what Aganbegyan – a leading reform economist for three decades – called the 'restricted and deformed internal market' which we discussed in Chapter 4.[6] These difficulties generated enormous discussion inside and outside the Soviet Union, and this often led to the view that they were unique problems of the Soviet system. But, in the absence of any genuine system of social control, wherever competitive discipline is weak, problems like those identified in Russia arise, and if they are not discussed in economics textbooks in the West, they certainly are in business textbooks. These problems appeared everywhere in the Soviet economy but their extent varied. When it came to arms production itself one Russian writer said: 'We have to compare our product all the time with those produced abroad. What a pity this is not done in the case of civilian machinery'.[7] In fact in some areas it was, but the general point was valid. The greater the insulation from international competition, the greater the problem. It was made worse by the general shortages and the distorted price system, which meant that managers had an incentive to play the system rather than meet real needs.

There was a further element concentrating the minds of Russia's rulers – the changing pressures of the Cold War and difficulties within their own spheres of interest. We have seen that it was fears of instability in the south that were part of the incentive to intervene in Afghanistan in 1979. Then in 1980 the eruption of the Solidarity movement in Poland raised further questions about the stability of the Soviet sphere in Eastern Europe. Both of these events occurred against a background of the development of the 'Second Cold War'. Western and especially US policymakers responded to the increase in tension that followed the slowdown in the world economy by increasing arms spending and raising the global stakes. To spell out the full logic of this and its contradictions would take us too far afield here. But for the Russian leadership this military and economic challenge helped to concentrate minds. The fear was that they would have to respond in kind. US defence outlays rose sharply. In September 1983 Andropov said: 'If anyone had any illusions about the possibility that the policy of the present American administration would evolve for the better, then the events of the recent period have finally dispelled them.' Comments like that made by Ronald Reagan in 1985 in supporting his 'Star Wars' initiative were taken to heart: 'We want to develop as complex a weapons system as necessary to force the Soviet Union into bankruptcy if it should want to find a defence mechanism against it'.[8] Some US conservatives claimed that this is what happened but, as we shall see, it was the contradictions of the reform process itself that were to be much more important in explaining the way in which the Soviet Union eventually disintegrated.

❧ 8.1 THE ARMS RACE AND EAST-WEST COMPETITION

Before the First World War socialists began to analyse the increasingly militarised nature of modern capitalism. Some saw it as a monstrous aberration, and appealed to all sides to disarm in their own interests. Others, such as Rosa Luxemburg, Nikolai Bukharin and Lenin, saw militarism and war as intrinsic to the system, and therefore incapable of resolution within it. Capital and the state were merging in forms of state capitalism, with military competition supplementing and sometimes overriding other forms of competition. 'The anarchy of world capitalism…expresses itself in the collision of state organisations and in capitalist wars,' wrote Nikolai Bukharin. 'War is nothing other than the method of competition at a specific level of development…the method of competition between state capitalist trusts'.[xx]

But in the next decades militarism deepened, with frequent wars and huge peacetime military expenditures. The militarisation of the Russian economy after 1928 was a part of this process. But many on the left tried to wriggle off the hook by arguing that 'Soviet' militarism was different, or even that armed force was a neutral instrument. What mattered was which state wielded it. Thus the Western bomb was condemned amd the 'socialist bomb' celebrated. Perhaps foreign socialists should even welcome dying in a blaze of radioactive glory if Russia launched its missiles.

Any socialist state would have to defend itself. But there was a fundamental difference between the situation in 1918-21 and the systematic military competition that developed after 1928, with its focus on huge armies and nuclear stockpiles. The early Marxists had argued that the process of military competition expressed and perpetuated the nature of the capitalist system. States had to try to find ways of matching potential enemies in terms of the quantity and quality of troops and weapons, and they had to order themselves internally to do this.

There is no doubt that US and Russian levels of military expenditure after 1945 were closely related to one another. Nor is there any doubt that to keep up Russia had to devote proportionally a much larger effort to military production. 'The military sector became the strongest, most technologically capable part of Soviet industry. Its scale and predominance in the economy inevitably gave it powerful political influence. In short, the defence industry came to represent the very core of the Administrative System, the political and economic order,' said one expert.[xxi]

Gorbachev attempted to better adjust Russia's situation to its means, but the attempt badly backfired. The military core of the economy was badly disorganised. But militarism did not disappear. Nor did great power antagonism. A hope for a 'peace dividend' melted away, and the US led the world in finding new enemies and new cause to legitimise huge military expenditure. Russia followed, and an attempt was made to begin to rebuild the military sector at the core of the economy, creating a further element of continuity.

CHANGE FROM ABOVE OR BELOW?

In the first instance it did not seem that the prospects were good for radical change. Following the death of Brezhnev, Yuri Andropov was made leader. For Andropov and those around him, including Mikhail Gorbachev, the problems seemed capable of being solved by intelligent leadership, more discipline and a crackdown on corruption. Andropov died after only 15 months and was replaced by Chernenko. He was a sop to the old guard. He was supported by younger leaders such as Gorbachev in the knowledge that he would not last long. In fact their time came very quickly. Chernenko lasted 13 months, and for the last five of these he was effectively incapacitated. When he died in March 1985 Gorbachev was able to marginalise older rivals easily. Andrei Gromyko recommended him as someone who had 'nice teeth but an iron bite'. The implication was that he was a leader who would tighten up the system while acting in public with a style and finesse that the previous leadership had never been able to display.

This is exactly what happened in 1985-86. Gorbachev began to wrongfoot conservative leaders in the West. Their confusion increased as he pushed home his advantage. 'We find ourselves faced with a difficult question – if what is taking place is genuine in its nature, then do we wish Gorbachev to be attended by success?' said the head of the CIA in October 1987.[9] At home Gorbachev talked of *perestroika*, restructuring the system, and *uskorenie*, speeding it up. *Glasnost* – the idea of 'openness' – was a minor issue, and *demokratisatsia* did not figure. In fact one of Gorbachev's first disciplinarian moves was an attempt to limit alcohol consumption. Some health indicators improved, but so too did hostility to the authorities, and illicit alcohol production even created a nationwide sugar shortage.[10] There was therefore no clear policy of radical change, and even when this began to develop it was still assumed that the system would go on. In his explanation of 'the challenge of *perestroika*', written at the turn of 1988, Aganbegyan, then Gorbachev's economic adviser, said that it was a long term process that would last two to three decades, hopefully allowing the hundredth anniversary of the revolution in 2017 to be celebrated by Soviet productivity rising above that of its Western competitors.[11]

In the first instance what pushed the process of change on more quickly was Gorbachev's own desire to shake up the system. But this was affected by two deeper factors. One was that the old order was discredited by major blunders. In April 1986 the nuclear power station at Chernobyl blew up. A huge disaster zone was created, and the human and environmental legacy lives on. Then the prestige of the military for competence was hit hard when in May 1987 a young West German flew his light plane under the Soviet defence system and landed in Red Square. Gorbachev pointedly asked the humiliated generals if they had learned of the feat from the Moscow traffic police.[12] The second factor was the evidence of inertia in the system and the possibility that even moderate reform would again be suffocated as it had been in the past.

Instead of *uskorenie*, then, the central idea became that of *perestroika*. To achieve this discussion had to be opened up to generate new ideas and expose bureaucratic blockages through *glasnost*. The forces around Gorbachev were committed to this shift because they believed that the focus would be on forward movement. But *glasnost* raised all sorts of questions about the present and the past because, as Solzhenitsyn once said, the lie had become 'a pillar of the state'. More conservative politicians and forces which tended to gravitate around Yegor Ligachev were dismayed. As their opposition crystallised, Gorbachev's true nature as a man of the centre began to emerge more clearly.

It was Boris Yeltsin who first fell victim to this tension as Gorbachev bent to the conservatives. Yeltsin was a populist provincial leader disillusioned with much of the system. He had been put in charge of cleaning up Moscow. Much more than others at the top he felt the need for change, the strength of the opposition and Gorbachev's hesitations. In September 1987 he told Gorbachev that *perestroika* was nothing but 'inflated language for public consumption'. Then in October he resigned from the Politburo, only to be denounced and hounded. Gorbachev told him that he would never be allowed back into politics. But it was Yeltsin who became the focus of discontent and the carrier of the momentum for more radical change.

Gorbachev's difficulty was that even the original modest aims of reform were not met. He was therefore forced to encourage moves to open the system more to provide a counterweight to the conservative tendencies. But when this happened the agencies of repression themselves became disoriented, partly because, as in the case of the KGB, they had a clearer view of some of the system's weaknesses, and partly because they were uncertain whether they any longer had the full support of the regime. Gorbachev said in February 1987 that 'it is either democracy or social inertia and conservatism. There is no third way'.[13] At this stage what he meant was democracy within the existing structure. But the formal structures were as much a barrier to change as a vehicle for it. To get round them needed an even greater degree of democratisation and movement from below. At this point a controlled process began to give way to an explosion of popular discussion and action that changed the whole balance of power.

With *perestroika* turning more to *glasnost*, and *glasnost* to *demokratisatsia*, a wave of excitement and political engagement began to emerge from the bottom up. Suddenly life and politics became interesting. Magazine subscriptions shot up, banned books were published, huge queues formed to watch banned films, and people began to organise what were called 'informal organisations', no longer limited by control from above. It was estimated in what was claimed to be 'the first ever survey of [political] public movements in the Soviet regime' that at the beginning of 1990 there were 'between 2,000 and 3,000 so-called informal groups and associations with a membership of 2 or 2.5 million'.

These groups fell into three broad types: popular fronts of which there were nearly 140 (especially in the republics); clubs and associations ranging from organisations of the far right to 'democratic clubs and associations', voters' clubs, workers' clubs and independent workers' movements and organisations; and parties and 'proto-parties'.[14]

Change from above and change from below are very different things. Many people viewing this heady mixture misunderstood what was happening. The most common view was that this was a form of 'socialist renewal'. Since all other visions of socialism had been crushed, it is understandable that within Russia this should have been widely accepted. It is less understandable that many supposedly radical commentators in the West should have followed this view, some talking of the centrality of Marxism to the discussions of the Gorbachev era – even speculating that the turmoil might lead to a new 'golden Soviet future'.[15]

Here the arguments of those who had failed to see through the slogans about socialism, or only saw through them enough to consider Russia some form of degenerate socialism, fell apart. If socialism was being renewed, which way was Russia moving? Democratisation and *glasnost* suggested towards more socialism. If socialism was about centralised control and state property, then *perestroika* and the market suggested less. The desire to believe in renewal led commentators to emphasise the positive side of what reformers said. It also led to a failure to appreciate the nature of the reforms being proposed, and placing faith in individuals like Gorbachev and Yeltsin.

Reformers saw the economic issue as one of broader market relations and a closer link to the world economy. This would help to break up traditional centres of power and put pressure on poorly performing enterprises. Inevitably this meant more open unemployment. Some reformers, like Aganbegyan, suggested that this could be minimised. Others argued that long term unemployment would be a good thing. The needs of capital had to take precedence over the needs of labour, which was itself part of the problem. Those who boasted of their economic radicalism showed no insight into the extent to which workers were themselves pawns of the regime, victims of alienation and exploitation. 'Give us bricks and we will build you a good house,' said one worker. But for a reformer like Nikolai Shemlev, marshalling all the superior condescension that marked a section of the intelligentsia, 'rampant apathy, indifference, theft and lack of respect for honest work' characterised most Soviet workers: 'There are signs of an almost physical degradation of the Soviet people as a result of drunkenness and sloth'.[16] Yet as we saw at the end of the last chapter an entirely different picture of the Soviet workers was seen in the miners' strike in 1989. Elected rank and file committees provided safety measures in the pits. They developed self-policing by the striking miners to such an extent that alcohol consumption and crime both fell, and a basic civic and social pride re-emerged.

But this bottom-up vision was not the point of reform. Take workplace democratisation. In June 1987 Article Six of the new Law on State Enterprises provided for the election of managers and the creation of an elected labour council. Surely this was an attempt to reconnect with the spirit of 1917? It was no such thing. In Russia reformers well understood its limits. What was offered was the illusion of workers' participation, which it was hoped would encourage workers to support the regime, subject the bureaucracy to some public monitoring and, perhaps most importantly, as the social policy adviser Tatiana Zaslavskaia said, to 'substantially reduce the social tension that arises in the process of radical restructuring'. Since the essence of this restructuring involved 'sacrifices' by the workers, 'the reward for workers' activism might be the loss of one's job and all of the social benefits connected with one's employment'.[17] The correctness of this characterisation can be seen in the way that 'democratisation' was limited in the enterprise – the implicit choice would be between candidates from the top. That choice was subject to approval from above, and the works council could only have binding authority *to promote productivity*. Not surprisingly, a year later a survey found that only 3 percent of workers believed that 'self-management' was working. Another poll of 141 factories in the Urals in the summer of 1987 suggested, equally unsurprisingly, that 75 percent of workers had no idea of how *perestroika* would affect them in the workplace.[18]

The connection with 1917 came not with such controlled top-down manipulation, but with the uncontrolled movements that developed from below, and which culminated in the miners' strike of 1989. But the reaction to these exposed the limitations of *perestroika* as a supposed form of 'liberal socialism'. At the top there was deep ambivalence towards the idea of change from below. Many radicals around Yeltsin saw the workers' movement as an ally that was useful as long as it delivered support to them, but no more. Others could not go this far. It is not difficult to see why. The miners' actions of the second half of 1989 were hard to contain in established channels. In the autumn the focus of militancy had shifted to Vorkuta. A journalist interviewed a relatively moderate strike leader and their discussion gave a flavour of the anger that existed:

Q: There was an increasing escalation...of votes of no confidence which the strikers apparently passed indis-criminately – foremen, secretaries of party committees, pit managers, executive committees, city committees, regional committees – and when we finally found out that the Vorgashorskaia mine had demanded the government's resignation –

A: I know. At the time, I myself said that their next step was likely to be a vote of no confidence in Margaret Thatcher![19]

In October 1989 Gorbachev proposed a 15-month ban on strikes. He did not get this, but he did get a strike law that hedged the right to strike in such a way that most strikes remained illegal but for the fact that the law could not be enforced. Some, apparently to the left of Gorbachev, like Anatolii Sobchak, now appeared in a new light altogether.

> We passed a law providing measures for dealing with strikes that are found to be illegal — close the enterprise and fire all those who took part in the illegal strike. Remember how Reagan stopped the air controllers' strike. If a strike harms the interests of the people, decisive action must be taken, not by using the troops but by using the law.[20]

THE END OF THE USSR

The detailed political history of the years 1987-91 looks like a series of steps forwards and backwards. As this happened Gorbachev lost both popularity and key advisers. Control gradually slipped from the centre, and it was Boris Yeltsin who continued to grow as the focus for more radical change.

Several factors helped increase the turmoil. One was the collapse of Eastern Europe. Here pressures had also built up for change. The question was how the Soviet leadership would react. Within the Comecon bloc a degree of economic loosening had been long apparent. Romania had even been able to pursue something of an independent political line. But Russian security concerns had still set limits to what was possible. Now Gorbachev and his advisers began to consider that real security could not be preserved if the local populations felt oppressed and suppressed by the Soviet Union. Nor could the Soviet Union afford the costs of control, which included considerable trade subsidies to Eastern Europe. The relative weakness of the old USSR meant that the costs of empire and the wider Russian role had long been a significant drain on resources. 'Reform Communists' therefore no longer seemed such a challenge. When the pace of change speeded up in Poland and Hungary in the summer of 1989, and then spread to other countries, the Gorbachev leadership watched benignly. In places they gave change a push. One of Gorbachev's advisers said that the 'Sinatra doctrine' was in place. Eastern European countries could, in the words of the famous song, do it 'their way'. What they did not anticipate was the political and economic recoil which took place in the former Soviet bloc as new leaders saw their salvation in links with the West. Comecon quickly disintegrated economically, and the impact was to worsen the economic crisis in Russia.

Within Russia too there were challenges in the republics. These had an increasingly nationalist colouring. As we have seen, the USSR had never developed as a voluntary union. Within it Russia had always played the leading role. The image cultivated under Stalin and beyond was that of Russia as 'the elder brother of the Soviet family'. The reality, as we suggested in Chapter 4, was one of both uneven development and national oppression. The scale of the problem was spelled out by the reformer Yuri Afanasyev in 1990. The USSR, he said, was:

> ...*constructed like a single factory or conveyor belt where whole regions are like separate shops or units of the production line. For example, Kazakhstan was turned into an accessory supplying raw materials for all the other republics. Central Asia was given over to the cultivation of cotton. The result was an ugly deformation of the natural state of each region — mutilated land and suffering people.*[21]

But, unlike in Eastern Europe, there was no internal version of the 'Sinatra doctrine', or at least a barely heard one. Attempts to suppress national movements with violence stimulated more hostility. Sometimes troops were used at Gorbachev's command. In Vilnius in January 1991, when they killed more than a dozen protesters, he disclaimed knowledge, but few were convinced – and even if true it hardly spoke well of his own control of the situation.

A third source of turmoil arose from the internal problems of reform. Chaos was beginning to grow in parts of the economy, and conflicts were developing with conservatives over how radical a policy was needed to correct it. This widened the gap between reformers and conservatives. But there were also differences in the reform camp, although these were less clearly articulated at the time.

Among some intellectuals vying for influence a naive faith in the market grew. In 1990 one French journalist could write that it was in Moscow that one could find the 'the greatest concentration of Thatcherite economists on the planet'.[22] Some, taking the market message to heart, combined a more practical activity with speculation. Leaders of the Moscow Komsomol, for example, used their connections and privileged positions to import computers. They also helped to create one of the first 'private banks' for the 'new Russia'. But in the wider movement these ideas had less appeal. Here the issue was more one of exposing power, privilege and corruption, and the demand for social justice. Both the power of work-based militancy in this wider movement and the hesitations were well brought out in the interview with a miners' leader that we quoted earlier:

> *Q: Is there here not the seed of a situation in which the different parts of society come to oppose each other along class lines?*
>
> *A: No way at all! In our circumstances it would be criminal if the workers and the intelligentsia, or the workers and the co-operativists, or the workers and the scientists were opposed to each other... All I'm saying is that although the workers are not the most protected part of society, they are prepared not only to demand decisive changes but to put their money where their mouth is.*[23]

It is not surprising then that when Leonid Albalkin, then a senior Gorbachev minister, was asked about the events in Eastern Europe at this time, he said:

'I think we are rather more worried about what is happening in Vorkuta than in the GDR'.[24]

The overall strength of the reform movement also increasingly alarmed more conservative forces. Gorbachev tacked between these two groups in 1989-91. Late in 1990 he seemed to be moving towards the conservatives as he ditched some of his closest supporters to appease them. As he temporised he joked with reporters in December 1990 that he was not moving right but 'going round in circles'. Joke or not, it seemed to express his position.

In the spring of 1991 Gorbachev began to be pulled back by the pressure of opposition in the republics and that headed in Russia by Yeltsin. Gorbachev's fluctuating position reflected a degree of equivocation in the movement at the bottom of society. After the high point of the miners' strike in 1989 the popular movement subsided somewhat. But the miners remained angry, and in the spring of 1991 pressure was renewed. At this point Yeltsin, appearing statesmanlike, flew to the Kuzbass to persuade them not to strike, and to put their faith in him and his ability to lead further reforms that would improve their material and political situation. This was a strategic moment in encouraging the popular movement into safer channels. Instead of relying on themselves and building a mass movement, Yeltsin was effectively being delegated a degree of power to act on their behalf. Once again a political price was being paid for the confusion of labels and parties, the uncertainty over who represented what, and for the decades of lies and distortions over the nature of 'socialism' and 'trade unionism'. Reform hopes in Yeltsin rose further when he was elected president of the Russian Republic within the USSR, and now he appeared to be a countervailing force to Gorbachev, whose role was diminishing as he lost control of the key parts of the Soviet Union.

This was the situation in which a conservative group at the top began to plan their moves to impose order from the centre. On 18-21 August 1991 a 'State Committee on the Emergency' led a coup. Gorbachev was put under house arrest in the Crimea, where he was on holiday. Key figures in the coup included Kriuchkov from the KGB, Minister of the Interior Pugo, Pavlov from the economic bureaucracy, and Baklanov from the military-industrial complex.

The coup was a disaster. It was poorly organised. It had no real programme. It had little support (though many also watched with a degree of indifference). With hindsight it can be seen that it was not difficult for Yeltsin to organise opposition, defeat the coup and appear as Gorbachev and Russia's saviour. So, far from saving things, the backlash against the coup undermined the position of Gorbachev. It marginalised the KGB and the Ministry of the Interior, which were implicated in its organisation. It undermined the role of the Communist Party, and it helped lead to the disintegration of the USSR.

With the collapse of the coup a huge political vacuum opened up at the centre of the state and government. 'All the government bodies of the Soviet

Union were in suspension, and it was obvious that real power was in the republics, above all the Republic of Russia,' Yeltsin later said.[25] In Russia it was Yeltsin himself who capitalised on this, seizing control and pushing for more market-based reforms. In the other republics it was more often the existing leaderships that now saw the future in terms of consolidating their position through separation, perhaps with links through some new form of federation. Mobilising legitimate resentment in a nationalist direction against 'Moscow' helped to deflect attention from failings closer to home in Kiev, Minsk or elsewhere, and it helped to consolidate the old leaderships, revitalised in the same way that the Russian one had been. Victory over the coup plotters and Gorbachev therefore led to a double move in the autumn of 1991. Within Russia Yeltsin was able to impose a reform programme based on shock therapy. In the collapsing Soviet Union the Republican leaders and most notably those of Russia, the Ukraine and Belorussia were able to negotiate an agreement in December 1991 by which the old USSR was dissolved and replaced with the looser Confederation of Independent States. Yeltsin presented this as an 'anti-imperialist' measure. Given the past role of Moscow, and the more recent killings of demonstrators by Soviet troops in Tbilisi in April 1989 and in Baku and Vilnius in January 1991, this had a resonance. But Yeltsin also saw it as a move which would 'reinforce the centripetal tendency within the disintegrating Union'. Moreover, he said, having 'rid itself of its imperial mission' (sic), Russia could have 'a stronger, harder policy, even forceful at some stage, in order not to lose its significance and authority altogether and in order to institute reforms'.[26]

SELF-INTEREST AND CHAOS

In the autumn of 1991 Yeltsin, still covered in the glory of having 'saved Russia', told ordinary Russians:

> We must unreservedly embark on thoroughgoing reforms. The situation in Russia is difficult, but not hopeless... There is a unique opportunity to stabilise the situation over several months and to begin improving that situation... A one-time changeover to market prices is a difficult and forced measure, but a necessary one. For approximately six months things will be worse for everyone, but then prices will fall, the consumer market will be filled with goods, and by the autumn of 1992 there will be economic stabilisation and an improvement in people's lives.[27]

Yeltsin based himself on an alliance of three groups, the market-oriented sections of the ruling class (the commercialised *nomenklatura*), Russian radical market theorists and Western advisers. He increasingly detached himself from a popular base in the wider reform movement. 'Reform' in his terms was now to come from the top down, whatever people actually wanted, and whatever the cost. 'We had to forcibly introduce a real marketplace, just as potatoes were introduced under Catherine the Great,' Yeltsin later said.[28]

In fact the next years were a disaster for the mass of the population. But at the top those who ran the system before 1991 were able to grow fat in the new system presided over by Yeltsin, while Western states, most notably the US, became his 'cheerleader, accomplice and spin doctor'.[29] Why was Yeltsin's prediction so wrong?

Just as the disintegration of the larger Comecon bloc had increased chaos, so the same occurred with the break-up of the USSR. Disruption was inevitable, but it was compounded by the 'market madness' of the new government. In November 1991 Yeltsin got support to implement a reform programme under Yegor Gaidar. This had three main elements – price liberalisation and market relations, financial stability, and privatisation. 'The magic of property turns sand into gold,' Arthur Young, an 18th century contemporary of Adam Smith had said, and the aim was for it to work the same magic in Russia.

The opposite occurred. Price liberalisation (in a situation where there were de facto monopolies) led to massive inflation. Savings were wiped out. Chaos grew as links between firms began to break down. Privatisation meant a grab for property which further dislocated the system. At the same time there was a political shift from the centre, as regions tried to make their own way and state structures visibly weakened. In 1994 one influential regional leader said:

> The centre, aspiring as before to total control of the entire process of Russian existence, no longer possesses drive belts which would convey the impulses of its orders to the provinces. In the provinces, nothing at all remains of the archaic drive mechanism which existed in Communist society. Rupture, hiatus. The centre exists, the territories exist, but effective connection between them is destroyed.[30]

In the economy production collapsed. GDP fell by 40-50 percent in the early 1990s, industrial production by more. Agricultural production fell by less but rural poverty was worse, and the decline in livestock numbers created echoes of the collectivisation. No new basis was laid for economic growth. The level of capital investment fell by 75 percent. The Russian economy lurched downwards in the international division of labour. State industrialisation to support the military had created a larger industrial sector than was typical for an economy of the level of development of the Soviet Union. Without upgrading it could not exist, and much crumbled. Chaos simply made matters worse. To support the inflow of imports – often food and consumer goods – Russia became even more dependent on the export of oil and raw materials. In what sense was this 'a transition'? Even the United Nations Development Programme said that 'transition' was a euphemism 'for what in reality has been a Great Depression'.[31]

The military-industrial complex around which the old order had been built had already failed in terms of international competition. Consumer goods industries had been given such a low priority for so long that they were no match for foreign products. Expecting the Russian economy to survive in open competition was not far short of economic suicide. It was rather as if an age-ing boxer who has failed to win the heavyweight title is told to give up the ring, but that he has a great future in the decathlon and the first competition is next week. What was being asked of the Russian economy was like this, only per-haps even harder. The scale of the consequent crisis was disorienting. Many ordinary Russians did not know what had hit them, and disillusion became widespread. Newspaper readership declined by 80 percent between 1990 and 1994, partly because the news was so gloomy but also because people could not even afford to buy newspapers.[32]

The Communist Party experienced a shortlived ban after the failed coup in 1991. When it was lifted it remained a weakened but significant political force, drawing support from older people who looked back to the greater stability before 1991. But its leaders had no plans to return there. Other political par-ties were also formed, but membership remained uncertain and much less than was often claimed. Yeltsin and his supporters failed to build a parlia-mentary party that could dominate the parliament. Yet the other parties could hardly help but oppose his policies. When opposition arose from the parlia-ment in October 1993 Yeltsin had his tanks fire on it and smash resistance. Some 187 died and up to 500 were wounded, according to the dubious official figures. Yeltsin's words began to rebound regularly on him. He disparaged what he called 'the usual Russian overkill, sending out as many tanks and divi-sions as could be maintained', but something of this was involved in subdu-ing the parliament, and it would soon become even more evident in Chechnya.

Yeltsin's de facto 'democratic coup' in 1993 allowed him to introduce a new constitution which further increased the power of the presidency. In December 1993 it was ratified in a referendum that was almost certainly falsi-fied. But these manoeuvres did not enable Yeltsin to stabilise the system. In a wider sense, however, Yeltsin was forced to backtrack and to build a more sta-ble base for himself by bringing into his governments leaders of the power centres of the Russian economy. This involved a series of compromises as a result of which Yeltsin now began to have to share political power with the 'oli-garchs' who already controlled key sectors of the Russian economy.

This new relationship was symbolised by Victor Chernomyrdin – the head of Gazprom, the gas and oil giant – becoming prime minister in the mid-1990s. The links were leavened by even more corruption. As politics became dirtier, compromising material (*kompromat*) abounded, so that it is difficult to separate myth from reality. But at the top, said Yeltsin's aide Aleksandr Korzhakov after his dismissal: 'Yeltsin was very quickly compromised by all those things that accompany limitless power – flattery, luxury, absolute irre-sponsibility.' Certainly the oligarch Vladimir Berezovsky paid Yeltsin $3 mil-lion for his memoirs, putting the money in a London bank account. In another incident the wives of the interior minister and his deputy had returned from

Switzerland with 20 pieces of excess luggage filled with $300,000 of furs, jewellery and watches paid for by Russian businessmen.

Attempts were also made to create parties to support the government, but with little success. It was the restructured Communist Party, the Communist Party of the Russian Federation, that remained one of the biggest parties, albeit with minority support. More disturbing still was the rise of the semi-fascist Liberal Democratic Party under its erratic leader Vladimir Zhirinovsky, though insufficient attention was paid to the way that he supported Yeltsin on key issues (as did the CPRF). Alongside Zhirinovsky's group were other smaller far right parties. Significant right wing tendencies also appeared within the Communist Party, leading to talk of a Red-Brown alliance. The key leaders of the right and far right all had a Communist Party background. The ground-work for this had been laid not only by the crisis of the 1990s, but by the way in which nationalist traditions and thinking had been nurtured within the CPSU more or less unopposed since the late 1920s.

Yeltsin's popularity plummeted. In January 1996 it was at only around 6 percent in the polls. Yet in the summer of 1996 he managed to win the presidential elections against the Communist Party leader. The comeback was remarkable, the explanation less so. Russians saw few alternatives in their squabbling parties. Yeltsin was able to use the resources of the state and media. Above all, what were called the 'oligarchs' – the financial and business leaders who stood at the head of the economy – saw in Yeltsin their protector. They feared that a CPRF government might limit their gains and power, so they threw their weight behind Yeltsin. There was also something else. 'Why risk everything just to have some people put pieces of paper into something called a ballot box?' said Aleksandr Korzhakov. Why indeed, if to the Yeltsin recovery could also be added a little more electoral manipulation and the threat of something worse?[33] Even so, against the odds, the CPRF managed to make a strong showing among those who voted.

But economic turmoil continued. Government financial and economic policy aimed now to reduce inflation and create stability. There was a narrow self-interest here, for this would help protect the transfers of wealth that had been going on. There was also pressure from abroad. Aid, loans and standby credits flowed to support this policy, because Western governments and institutions like the IMF/World Bank believed too that this was the way to salvation. A degree of financial stability did begin to appear from 1995-96. It was based on an illusion of financial manipulation. But Western advisers looked the other way. One of them – Richard Layard, a British economist – co-authored a book that proclaimed *The Coming Russian Boom* and introduced readers to the story of 'how the greatest political-economic challenge of the post Cold War world has become a resounding success and exemplary triumph'. The only problem was that Russia needed more unemployment still. One of Yeltsin's economic advisers said that at the spring 1998 Birmingham G8 meeting he was told: 'We rate your programme very highly, but we'd rate it still higher if you'd just bankrupt something for once'.[34] Yet the situation of the real economy remained dire. As Grigorii Yavlinsky said: 'We have low inflation, a low budget deficit, but we have almost no economic activity'.[35] What positive developments there had been in the 1990s depended on a narrow base of raw material and especially oil sales, financial manipulation, and the ostentatious and quite untypical development of central Moscow. These left the economy vulnerable to changes in world raw material prices and financial movements. When a crisis emerged in East Asia it did not take long for the Russian economy to be hit hard by its wake. The crunch came in August 1998. Amidst financial panic the rouble was devalued, and a large part of the banking system collapsed. For ordinary Russians it meant more poverty, as living standards were pushed down again.

All of this undermined Russia's foreign policy position. Gorbachev had wrongfooted the West from a position of relative strength. With the collapse of the Soviet bloc and then the USSR itself, this disappeared. Russia retained a rusting nuclear threat but, having lost an external and internal empire, it was no longer a superpower challenge to the US. In the first instance this did not seem to matter, as many sections of the ruling class began to look to the West, hoping that economic assistance would be forthcoming and that there would be a longer term recognition of Russia's interests by negotiation and compromise. After 1991 Yeltsin received enormous backing from Washington and the West. But their assumption was that Russia would accept its subordinate position. In the second half of the 1990s some of the negative implications of this became apparent in Russia. This encouraged a less uncritical response and a shift towards a greater concern with Russia's 'national interests'. There was hostility to the expansion of Nato to include some ex Soviet Bloc members. There was concern about the possible weakening of the 1972 ABM treaty. Then in 1999 the bombing of Serbia was viewed with hostility. The then prime minister, Yevgenii Primakov, turned his plane around in midair rather than continue a trip to the West. But trying to assert independence from a position of weakness was a delicate game, although it would be continued under Vladimir Putin as both prime minister and president.

But foreign policy had another dimension. This was the attempt to draw in 'the near abroad' – the republics that had broken away in 1991. Their internal situation was little different from the chaos that ruled in Russia, except that it was perhaps worse. The exception was the Baltic states, though even here there was exaggeration of the extent to which they had escaped the chaos. Russian policy, especially in respect of Belorussia, the southern republics and to a lesser extent Ukraine, was to look benignly on these regimes and support leaders, however unpleasant, who saw the value of links with Russia itself.

The dream of a democratic Russia that would guarantee basic rights was, therefore, far from being realised inside or outside. It was now possible to openly organise, and this was an enormous advance. But in the background human rights abuses continued. They received too little discussion inside Russia and little outside of it. 'The enemy' had become a 'friend', and the West was no longer interested. Yet in 1997 Yelena Bonner, the widow of Andrei Sakharov, said that the situation was 'worse than under Leonid Brezhnev'. Crime flourished. The state itself became semi-criminalised. In 1994 a report of the Presidential Human Rights Commission said that 'the institutions of the Russian penal system continued to be the site of regular and large-scale human rights abuses'.[36]

But the worst situation was in Chechnya. Here the development of a nationalist movement led to demands for independence in the 1990s. Chaos developed as some sections of the population pulled one way and others towards Moscow, which tried to tip the balance in its favour. Criminalisation grew apace, but this should not obscure real grievances (the Chechens were one of Stalin's deported peoples). On 11 December 1994 Yeltsin ordered in Russian troops to quell revolt. Chechnya was 'internal' to Russia and had to be saved. There were economic motives too – vital oil pipelines crossed the territory. The army imagined that its status would be boosted by a 'victorious little war', and Yeltsin's team probably thought he would benefit in the same way. They were wrong. Chechen resistance was considerable. The destruction wielded by nervous and often brutal Russian forces was immense. Perhaps up to 80,000 Chechens died, but resistance was not broken, and in May 1996 a ceasefire had to be negotiated to bring the first Chechen war to an end.[37]

Yeltsin's own constitution prevented him serving more than two terms but, as 2000 approached, Russia remained in crisis. The problem was therefore how to protect himself and his family from growing charges against them, and how to protect the bigger groups at the top whose fortunes he had helped to create. Following the 1998 financial crash the government of Primakov attempted to limit capital flight and use the state to stimulate some recovery. Some did occur, assisted by rising oil prices, but the economy was at such a low level that it made little difference. But Yeltsin was concerned about the bigger issue of social continuity and survival, so Primakov was ditched in favour first of Stepashin and then Vladimir Putin, who had grown up in the KGB and risen to run the post-1991 security services for a time. Whether he could have won an election at this point is an interesting question. Other potential leaders such as Primakov or the mayor of Moscow, Yuri Luzhkov, were trying to build support in the ruling groups for a challenge. But in October 1999 horrific bombings in Moscow killed hundreds and were blamed (too conveniently some said) on 'Chechen terrorists'. Putin seized (or made?) his chance to launch a new war and sweep to the presidency on the wave of popularity (intensified by the now usual electoral manipulation) it created for him. The Chechens were less fortunate. Grozny, the capital, which had once had a population of 400,000 in 1989 was more or less destroyed. Parts of the countryside were subject to carpet-bombing, and by the end of 2000 perhaps another 100,000 had been killed and 300,000 refugees created without anything being resolved.

THE CONVERSION OF POWER

To make sense of these moves at the top it is vital to understand that beneath the turmoil the old ruling class was busily converting itself into the new one. Even before 1989-91 it had seen considerable reinvigoration through the incorporation of younger, less ideological, more technocratic and younger members. Death and retirement were therefore bound to carry off an increasing number. Then there was the attack on corruption and a conscious attempt to bring forward new people. *Perestroika* further widened the opportunities for the newer, more competent and technocratic section of the ruling class that was strategically positioned to capitalise on new opportunities. 'We should not be afraid of the disproportionate representation of various strata of the population,' Gorbachev told the Nineteenth Party Conference. He was rejecting puppet representatives of the workers and peasants in favour of a direct representation of more influential sectors.

The tactical question people here had to deal with, especially after 1989 in Eastern Europe had shown them that those who held power in the old order could survive in the new, was when to move and how far. *De facto* privatisation began in a number of areas in 1989-90, giving rise to what was called '*nomenklatura* capitalism'. This was the Soviet form of the management buyout or giveaway. Parts of the Komsomol proved especially adept at moving in this early period, seizing whatever assets they could. One journalist said that the organisation was now a 'Harvard Business School of the new culture'. The chairman of Entrepreneurs for a New Russia was the former economics secretary for the Komsomol's Central Committee. Komsomol capitalism proved more significant in the newer sectors. In the more traditional cores of the economy movement was slower, and when it came it gave more opportunities to those already directly in charge. The most spectacular example of the conversion of power here was Gazprom, and other raw material and processing companies.

Along with such changes went others. Arkadii Volsky, a Central Committee official and an aide to both Andropov and Chernenko, emerged as a key representative of industrial interests as the head of the Russian Union of Industrial Managers and Entrepreneurs. The coup plotters of 1991 in part wanted to hang on to the old administrative structure, where many of them had positions. But when the coup failed it was not too late for many of them to move too. Yuri Prokofiev, first secretary of the Moscow City party, said: 'You better give me a pistol so I can shoot myself.' He then thought better of it, used his position, and became a successful businessman.[38]

The privatisations of the 1990s were a further stage in this process. That of 1995 was one of the most corrupt, if not the most corrupt, in world history. Firms were effectively given to senior managers and administrators, and finance groups that had sprung up in the first years. Anatolii Chubais, who ran privatisation, had no qualms: 'They steal and steal and steal. They are stealing absolutely everything and it is impossible to stop them. But let them steal and take their property. Then they will become owners and decent administrators of this property'.[39] Nor did his key Western advisers, some of whom were later accused of insider dealing. In fact this privatisation consolidated the power of those running the economy. It boosted the position of the 'oligarchs' – in reality the heads of giant holding companies. It was a further step in the semi-criminalisation of whole areas of economic activity.

What Yeltsin called the 'energetic plant directors' began to play a greater role in local, regional and national politics. Yeltsin saw this as a stabilising factor. He cut straight to the real issue of power at the point of production, and its unity across the supposed divide between Communism and post-Communism, between state and private industry.

> What is a plant director in Russia? First off, he's the man who gives you a job and makes it possible for your family to live, who can fire you or promote you on the career ladder. It doesn't matter whether he runs a government factory that has privatised by forming a joint stock company or a factory still subsidised by the state. The fact is the actual director of the factory is the one who decides your individual fate.[40]

In the end how many members of the old ruling class were able to move? Allowing for natural wastage, the answer seems to be most. One of the largest investigations found that 80 percent of former party *nomenklatura* had moved to either first or second rank positions in the new Russia. More detailed regional studies, studies of industry and plant bosses all pointed strongly in the same direction. The social structure of power was reproduced beneath the political turmoil. Indeed, a surprisingly large part of the top political layers rode the wave of change too.

It has been suggested as a rule of thumb that in the 1990s 10 percent of the Russian population were winners, 40 percent were clear losers, and the 50 percent in between in an ambiguous position.[41] The winners saw their relative wealth and income increase dramatically. Figures are not necessarily precise, but they all point the same way. In 1992 the ratio of the income of the top 10 percent to the bottom 10 percent had stretched to eight to one. By the end of the decade the gap had widened further to 14 to one on one calculation. The UN Development Programme gave a similar picture: 'Russia now has the

❧ 8.2 THE CHAMELEON CAPITALISTS

*In the Russian economy **nachalniki**, bosses of all kinds, always had a degree of autonomy. When Gorbachev introduced more decentralisation in 1986-87 a whole layer of 'bureaucrats' claimed what they could as their own. One commentator likened their actions to a run on a bank. This was not simple state collapse: 'The catalysts…were the agents of the state itself. Once the bank run was on, these officials were not merely stealing resources **from** the state, they were stealing the state itself.' People who were often seen as dull and bureaucratic proved to be clever, adept and unscrupulous at moving from the old to the new. The younger generation of youth officials in the Komsomol were especially nimble, and 'as a consequence many of these former Komsomol officials are now leading Russia's new business elite'.*

Mikhail Khodorkovsky had the most spectacular career. He was a leading Komsomol official at the prestigious Mendeleyev Institute in Moscow. In 1987 encouragement was given to some Komsomol leaders to engage in market business activity. Khodorkovsky was a pet 'experimental capitalist'. He grabbed the chance, and moved from selling advice and research to dealing in computers, setting up the Mentatep Bank and then, in 1996, taking over Yukos oil. Today he is one of the richest men in the world.

But this was no simple climb from rags to riches. Khodorkovsky was well placed to begin with. He needed connections. He needed the prestige of the Komsomol. He needed the trust of the bosses that he was dealing with. He needed the support of the authorities. Some of the party's funds went into his bank, from which they have never reappeared. In 1991 he boasted: 'All the ventures that were started at this time succeeded only if they were sponsored by or had strong connections with high ranking people'.[xxii] Where Khodorkovsky led, others followed: 'Communist Party officials in many regions observed the success of Komsomol officials in transforming their political power and began [the] analogous transfer of party assets into the private sector'.[xxiii]

greatest inequality – the income share of the richest 20 percent is 11 times that of the poorest 20 percent'.[42]

Given the way in which the ruling class was shifting its wealth to its private pocket, the fortunes of some members became enormous, and they began to figure in the lists of the world's wealthiest people. Much of this wealth was in Moscow, where the nouveaux riches were seen at clubs and restaurants. Half the country's mobile phones were located there. Or at least this wealth could be seen in the reconstructed centre of the city, which the mayor, Luzhkov, tried periodically to clear of unwanted 'unfortunates', including black migrants from the south. But in the suburbs of the city, no less than elsewhere, much of the population lived their lives in rotting and crumbling structures on the poverty line. Although only a minority gained, given that Russia had a large population, these new Russians still made up a considerable market bolstering the illusions of Western commentators. Large numbers of Mercedes were imported. Russians with access to dollars went abroad, and could be seen with camcorders and guidebooks to Western capitals that now began to be published in Russian. They shopped in the classiest shops alongside members of the Western ruling class. Their children studied abroad. By 2000 there were said to be 10,000 doing this. Some began to go to English public schools, including Yeltsin's grandson.[43] Holiday homes were bought in Cyprus, Spain and beyond. Western banks were accommodating too. While the situation in Russia was so unstable, it made sense to ensure that money was safe. Alongside the fragile rouble economy was an internal dollar economy. But dollars that came in were also shipped back out again to Western banks. Exports would be paid for in Western currencies that would go straight into Western banks. This was 'capital flight' that swamped incoming investment several times. Some of it was legally done, some illegally. It made little difference to the Russians doing it or the Western banks benefiting from it.

But the capital of the state was not entirely neglected. While production collapsed, while the infrastructure collapsed, and while the poorest scrabbled on rubbish tips to survive, Yeltsin decided that the Kremlin needed a $1.5 billion renovation. Inevitably there were suggestions of corruption, and accusations that Yeltsin's family had benefited from bribery and then salted their gains abroad too.

The nature of these changes was the more perplexing to those who refused to use the concept of class. Revolutions where so little changes, where elites do not even circulate but simply reproduce, remain a great theoretical embarrassment. Fortunately those at the top in Russia had a better grasp of the situation and its implications than some who observed what was happening. 'For more than 30 years now, I've been a boss,' said Yeltsin, 'That's exactly what people of my social class in Russia are called. Not a bureaucrat, not an official, not a director but a boss. I can't stand the word – there's something about it that smacks of the chain gang. But what can you do?'[44] What indeed? Save protect your position and those around you, and then hand it on. As Putin took power Yeltsin said: 'The role of the oligarchs will grow. The term oligarch simply means big capitalist in Russia. And big business is going to play a bigger and bigger role in Russia'.[45]

THE WORKERS

When a popular movement emerged in 1988-89 it was commonplace on the left to predict an explosion of anger that would lead to a mass movement for genuine socialism that would reject both the old state system and the new market one. As we have seen, glimpses of such a movement did develop in 1989, but it was not sustained, and the possibility of really radical change was stolen from the Russian people. The victims of all this were tens of millions of ordinary Russians in the cities and the countryside. 'They expected a paradise on earth, but instead they got inflation, unemployment, economic shock and political crisis,' said Yeltsin with a now hollow tone.[46] The indifference with which the fate of ordinary Russians was treated by policymakers East and West is something that history is unlikely to view kindly. If the price of creation of bureaucratic state capitalism had been paid by an earlier generation of workers, the price of its partial dismantling was paid by their grandchildren and great-grandchildren. Like the economic collapse, the collapse in real wages and collapse of the standard of living was unique in global economic history outside of war and 'natural disaster'.

By the mid-1990s the average level of real wages had fallen by around a half. Many had left the labour force, and unemployment had risen to over 10 percent.[47] But many Russians were kept nominally on the books of firms. Wage payments were often delayed, sometimes for months, as chaos grew. Wages could be paid in kind – food, a TV, a video, perhaps a piece of furniture. Perhaps around a third to a half of the population fell below the poverty line, though in some groups it was much more. The rural situation was usually bad. So too was the situation of many state workers. The young with families also suffered. Survival became a matter of defensive strategies. For the mass of the population savings were destroyed by inflation. According to 1996 data half were now held by the top 2 percent of the population, 72 percent by the top 5 percent, and 97 percent by the top 30 percent. In the 1998 crash more savings were wiped out. What could be sold was sold. The allotment dacha where it existed became more, not less, important. Family members who could help did. Petty trade was tried by some. Some hoped that this might lay the basis for a new entrepreneurialism, but this made no more sense than to see the Western car boot sale as a source of reinvigoration of the capitalist class – less, perhaps, because few Russians had car boots to transport the goods they were trying to sell. Then the devaluation of the rouble in 1998 threw more groups into difficulties. Things were worsened still for many by the collapse of much state social provision. The UN Development Programme, in its report on the first decade of 'transition', said:

> There has been a tragic breakdown in human security with respect to access to social services and social pro-
> tection. There is no longer any secure entitlement to a decent education, a healthy life or adequate nutrition.
> With rising mortality rates, and new and potentially devastating epidemics on the horizon, life itself is increas-
> ingly at risk.

Here was another dark record of the transition. The death rate rose from 11 to 15 per 1,000 between 1990 and 1995. For those of working age it rose by 50 percent. Disease, suicide, injury, stress and the search for relief in alcohol carried off enormous numbers of men in particular. By 1995 life expectancy for males had fallen several years to 58.6. As the 'transition' mounted, what demographers call 'excess mortality' rose to stand, according to the UN, at an astonishing 6 million males in the former USSR as a whole.[48] At the same time the birth rate collapsed. It became a sad joke for the superstitious that a pregnant woman was luckier to see than a black cat. The overall population loss was therefore even greater. The total population of Russia declined even with a net inflow of migrants from the newly independent republics. It is impossible to avoid the comparison with the human cost of Stalinism. And just as then a new group of fellow travellers arrived to sing the praises of what was happening. Whereas George Bernard Shaw in the 1930s was reported to have thrown food away because he refused to believe there was famine when he arrived, now a new generation of Western advisers stepped over the beggars and ignored the street children in the belief that the recipe of the market was really working. Sometimes perhaps they even had to turn away from corpses in the street. Certainly many Russians did. But as one observant journalist put it: 'Public indifference always masks private grief'.[49]

But if the first accounts of the possibility of change from below were over-optimistic, it is easy now to be overly pessimistic. In the years after 1928 Russian workers lost all contact with the idea of independent organisation. In addition, as we have seen, the lies of Stalinism sowed widespread confusion. Overcoming this was bound to take time. This was all the more so given the horrors of the transition. In these terms it is important to recognise, as Stephen Cohen has put it, that 'tales of the Russian people's passivity are considerably exaggerated'.[50] This is not a question of looking for the silver lining in a dismal situation. The problems as we shall see are huge. It is a question, however, of avoiding the 'realism' that is so pessimistic that it becomes self-fulfilling passivity, and it is a question of giving recognition to the struggles that have taken place in conditions of enormous adversity.

Given the new whirlwind that hit them in the 1990s it is understandable that some ordinary Russians should be nostalgic for the stability of the 1970s and early 1980s. It is less so that serious commentators are. Firstly, the fact that workers had instinctively seen through the argument that the old regime was 'their' regime was reflected in the fact that they did not lift a finger to defend it – indeed, it was partly their protests that helped to encourage its dissolution. Secondly, as we have seen, even from the point of view of some of the more backward sections of Russia's rulers there was no possibility of maintaining the old system as it was. To borrow an analogy – to a person on the verge of death the earlier stages of terminal illness look attractive, but they are not a viable place to return to. Thirdly, it was just this weakening of the old regime that gave Russian workers the confidence to begin to act for themselves for the first time for six decades. No longer in fear of automatic repression, they began to reclaim a basic dignity. This was one of the reasons why the miners' strikes of 1989 were so important. For the first time for six decades Russian workers were able to experience the simple dignity of being able to march together in columns, no longer as a ritual, but for themselves: 'Thousands of men still with coal dust under their eyes, in their pit helmets and working clothes'.[51] This points to a fourth crucial point – the problem with the transition is precisely that it has not gone far enough, not that it has gone too far. The issue is not the 'troubles' that democracy brings but the lack of a real democracy, from the bottom up. The problem is the way in which the old order, with the connivance of its Western counterparts, has been able to hang on to power, however hamfistedly, and to milk the system for its own advantage. The way forward is not, therefore, back to some 'golden age' or in the direction of paternalistically welcoming some 'good' leader, but to use the space that exists to build a real alternative from below. But while this is not difficult to see in the abstract, in practice the difficulties are enormous, both because of the legacy of ideological confusion left by the old order and the devastating impact of the worsening crisis.

Developing opposition from the bottom up is more difficult because several problems have to be overcome. There is the dulling impact of the crisis itself which has put such an enormous strain on people. In some workplaces independence is dealt with harshly. One Russian commentator likened conditions of trade union organisation in parts of the country to those in the United States before 1914, with unsympathetic local governments, local judiciaries and managements working together to sack workers, and use violence and intimidation against those who persist in trying to organise.[52] Then there is the organisational confusion. Trade unions under the old regimes were state-run bureaucracies. New trade unions quickly sprang up after 1989 but they struggled to find a space to organise, and many became trapped in the top-down process of transition. Whether as new or reformed old-style unions, therefore, it is taking time for more stable and responsive organisations to emerge, and there are problems everywhere. This has very often thrown workers back on more informal local organisations. The ups and downs of industrial struggle in Russia are set out in the table below.

TABLE 8.1. STRIKING IN THE TRANSITION: THE RUSSIAN STRIKE PATTERN, 1991-99[53]

	NUMBER OF STRIKES	NUMBER INVOLVED (thousands)	WORK DAYS LOST (thousands)	AVERAGE DURATION (days)
1991	1,755	238	2,314	9.7
1992	6,273	358	1,893	5.3
1993	264	120	237	2.0
1994	514	155	755	4.9
1995	8,856	489	1,367	2.8
1996	8,278	664	4,009	6.0
1997	17,007	887	6,001	6.8
1998	11,162	531	2,881	5.4
1999	7,285	238	1,827	7.7

These statistics show that not everything is passive and demoralised. The confusion of 1992-93 can clearly be seen in these figures. So too can the struggle against the devastating impact of the transition, the accumulation of unpaid wages, etc, in 1994-98. But then also the impact of the crash of 1998 is clear. These statistics show the small scale, often guerrilla nature of much industrial conflict. Some conflicts have an edge of desperation as workers go on hunger strike for back pay. Others show more assertiveness.

Perhaps the most important came in the late spring of 1998 in what was known as the 'railway wars'. Miners who had not been paid for months struck and blocked railway lines, disrupting movements of freight and people. The strikes began in the Kuzbass and spread to other areas, and the action lasted several weeks. This 'railway war' began on a small scale, with the miners alone taking action, but it soon attracted wider support in parts of Russia – including from teachers and other white collar workers. One account described these as 'a French revolution style grab your pitchfork and go random spasm of raw underclass [sic] anger'. But for some it was more than this – one telling poster read: 'A hungry miner is fiercer than a Chechen'.[54] We see here protests that can give rise to the possibility of greater social explosions, as what Rob

Ferguson has called 'the bitter fury of broken hopes' can turn outwards.[55] One group of miners camped for four months in Moscow attracting considerable support and visits from a succession of personalities who wanted to associate with what most Russians saw as a positive protest.

Seen from the Kremlin it looked very different. This is how Yeltsin describes it in his memoirs:

> Perhaps few people recall the famous rail wars of the summer of 1998, but I'm sure Kiriyenko [then the prime minister] shudders as much as I do when he remembers the wave of coalminers' strikes. Coalminers' solidarity is a unique thing. One mining district followed another in the protest. Within several days, the miners' action seized almost all the mining regions of Russia. But that wasn't all. The miners began to block the railroad lines. This was a protest of another magnitude.

Some of Yeltsin's supporters wanted the miners jailed, but the state did not have the capacity to act. Indeed, it was at just this point that Yeltsin saw the need to reinvigorate the security forces and a new individual began to make his mark.

> I met with Nikolai Kovalev, then director of the FSB [the successor to the KGB]. He was almost panicking. I understood from our conversation that the situation was new for him and that he didn't know how to handle it. I sympathised — strikes were not technically part of his agency's mandate — but a threat to the country's security was real. A political battle was one thing, but blocking the national arteries of transportation was another entirely.

Yeltsin's sympathy did not extend far. Kovalev's weakness in the face of the miners and his apparent concern to investigate corruption in business and banking led Yeltsin to look for a safer pair of hands for state security. 'The answer was instantly clear – Putin', and on 25 July 1998 in the midst of the protests Putin was appointed head of the FSB. 'We had to restore the Lubianka's authority, which had been so greatly undermined after 1991,' said Yeltsin. But in the meantime there was little that the government could do except try to assuage the anger of the miners. One vice prime minister 'raced from one coal district to another, signing agreements almost without looking at them – anything to come to terms'. But with political perspectives still confused, the miners were unable to capitalise on their position, and then the rouble crash in the summer created even more hardship and difficulties. Yet the memory of this challenge remained a painful one for Russia's rulers, and a reminder that they did not always have things their own way. In the summer of 2000, when Yeltsin replaced the then prime minister, Stepashin, by Putin, a worried Chubais came to him warning that people might not accept it. 'Remember the railway wars?' he said. 'This is something you want to face only once'.[56]

The problem is that workers find it impossible at the moment to generalise from their struggles both in an ideological and an organisational sense.

Ideologically what Stalinism did was to break any connection between the kind of activities that workers engage in on a day to day basis, and the arguments of the socialist and revolutionary tradition about an alternative. At the same time organisationally it is proving immensely difficult for workers to sustain coherent organisation on a broad long term basis. Building an alternative from below in Russia is going to be a long and painful process. Its clarity may in the end depend on successful challenges to capitalism and the market elsewhere, challenges that can destroy the argument that socialism and Stalinism are automatically to be equated with one another, which is one reason why this book has been written.

The Russian contingent on the demonstration against the G8 in Genoa in July 2001

9 CONCLUSION

We began this book by suggesting that the issue of the Soviet Union was of much more than historical interest. Demonstrators across the world, discontented with the existing system, have chanted 'Another world is possible', only to be told that it is not. It has been tried and failed in the Soviet Union. The subsequent chapters have tried to show that this view is false. An opening did occur in 1917, but it was quickly closed down. The subsequent development of the USSR ultimately remained moulded by the same logic, the same imperatives, the same dynamics that operated across the globe in the 20th century and remain dominant today. In the late 19th century, long before the Soviet Union ever developed, William Morris wrote of the dilemma of change in his *A Dream of John Ball* (one of the leaders of the peasant revolt in England in 1381): 'I pondered all these things, and how men fight and lose the battle, and the thing they fought for comes about in spite of their defeat, and when it comes it turns out not to be what they meant, and other men have to fight for what they meant under another name.' Ever since, many critics of the Soviet Union from the left have been struck by the appropriateness of this as a motto for the experience of that society. It could be a motto for this book.

There will be some, no doubt, who will claim that our argument is an excuse. The attempt to remould the world will always end badly, and 'once bitten, twice shy'. To this argument there are several replies. One is that we have tried to show through historical analysis that our explanation of Russia as a form of bureaucratic state capitalism makes better sense of what happened than other accounts. Others have written in a similar vein. Alex Callinicos, for example, early on in the transition after 1989 analysed the shifts in Eastern Europe in terms of regime change rather than qualitative changes in the relations of production.[1] Colin Sparks and Anna Redding made a similar argument in their discussion of the new media in the East, using the analysis to unravel many of the mistaken claims made about civil society and the political transition.[2] We have noted other more detailed contributions at different points in our analysis. Our critics' task is therefore to improve on this analysis by making their theories work and addressing the issues we have discussed here. Here we would venture to suggest that the record of the immediate past does not promise much. There has probably been more written about Russia in the last 10 years than at any time in its history. Library shelves groan with books, and journals bulge with detailed studies. But look for a consistent theory, look for an integrated analysis, and you usually search in vain. What passes for theory is too often the grabbing of a few concepts which are then haphazardly welded together.

But we need to say more. In 1991, we are told, an ideology in power collapsed. As we have seen, it did not. This is wrong not only about what went before. It is wrong about the transition itself. And those with power knew it to be wrong. It was more an idea that could be used to hide other things. Far from believing their own propaganda about the 'Evil Empire', Western policymakers and advisers were desperate to forgive and forget. It would be wrong to have too conspiratorial a view of the transition and see Russia's leaders as simple pawns of the West. Those at the top in both East and West used each other in different ways at different times. But there is a shared complicity. Both sides were knowingly involved, conscious of what they were doing. They were united by a top-down vision of the way in which society had to be run.

They have hardly been successful. Critics of socialism have always tried to tar it with the 'Soviet Union'. 'Get back to Russia' was the riposte to Stalinists and anti-Stalinists alike. Yet in the 1990s Russia was supposed to be the society that would be remoulded by the market. Now the boot is on the other foot – 'Get back to Russia' stands as a rebuke to the illusionists who claim that the market can cure all our ills. It stands as a rebuke to the Western governments, the World Bank, the IMF and the Western advisers. But ordinary Russians cannot be told: 'Get back to Russia.' They are already there – pawns of the system, as their parents and grandparents were pawns of a system over which they had no control.

The failure before and after 1991 has local and global roots that have continually intertwined in the ways we have tried to show. To go beyond this requires a challenge to the global capitalist system that dominates our lives no less than it did in 1917. But we have to do this conscious of the lessons of the past. Here the history of Russia speaks to us in a different way to that which is usually claimed. There is a deeply rooted ambiguity not only in the history of socialism but political thought more generally. This is not the difference between a society run *for* the many or *for* the few. It is the difference between a society run *by* the many or *by* the few. All rulers claim that they are working for us. But we are not trusted to find ways to rule ourselves. 'Politics' is limited in its application. It is not supposed to touch the 'economic'. It is not supposed to touch the great institutions or the state. Indeed, over the past century the separation of the core of the system from wider control has, if anything, grown, despite the gaining of a widened right to vote. In Russia we have the paradox of ordinary Russians gaining basic freedoms only to find themselves victims of another top-down transformation for which the term 'market Stalinism' is entirely appropriate.

But the fact that these basic political freedoms exist and that the old USSR is gone is a major advice. Stalin's counter-revolution was a tremendous defeat. It marked the history of socialism in the 20th century. In the 1930s it combined with the rise of Nazism to produce what Victor Serge called 'midnight in the century'. It is worth remembering how crippling were the conditions produced by Stalinism (and Nazism) to realise the changed potential of our new situation, whatever its immediate difficulties. Towards the end of his life in April 1939 Trotsky, in an interview with C L R James, tried to draw out how disabling both the degeneration of the revolution and the subsequent triumph of Stalin and Hitler had been. The passage is worth quoting at some length to remind ourselves of how dark midnight was at that time:

> We are not progressing politically. Yes, it is a fact, which is an expression of a general decay of the workers' movements in the last 15 years. It is the more general cause. When the revolutionary movement in general is declining, when one defeat follows another, when fascism is spreading over the world, when the official 'Marxism' is the most powerful organisation of deception of the workers, and so on, it is an inevitable situation that the revolutionary elements must work against the general historic current, even if our ideas, our explanations, are as exact and wise as one can demand...
>
> I remember some discussions in 1927 in Moscow after Chiang Kai-shek stilled the Chinese workers. We predicted this 10 days before...and our comrades expressed optimism because our analysis was so clear that everyone would see it and we would be sure to win the party. I answered that the strangulation of the Chinese Revolution is a thousand times more important for the masses than our predictions. Our predictions can win some few intellectuals who take an interest in such things, but not the masses. The military victory of Chiang Kai-shek will inevitably provoke a depression, and this is not conducive to the growth of a revolutionary faction.
>
> Since 1927 we have had a long series of defeats... In Asia and Europe this has created a new desperate mood of the masses. They heard something analogous to what we saw 10 or 15 years ago from the Communist Party, and they are pessimistic. That is the general mood of the workers. It is the most general reason... The current is against us, that is clear...
>
> Our situation now is incomparably more difficult than that of any other organisation in any other time, because we have the terrible betrayal of the Communist International, which arose from the betrayal of the Second International. The degeneration of the Third International developed so quickly and so unexpectedly that the same generation which heard its formation now hears us, and they say: 'But we have already heard this once!'...

We are in a small boat in a tremendous current. There are five or 10 boats and one goes down, and we say it was due to bad helmsmanship. But that was not the reason — it was because the current was too strong. It is the most general explanation.[3]

The fascist states in Europe collapsed in 1944-45, but the state capitalism created under Stalin lived on for another four decades, and its form was spread to other parts of the world. But we have now come a long way from the world that Trotsky described.

History does not move in straight lines. Unlike the rise of Nazism, Stalin's counter-revolution was preceded by a great victory in 1917, which still stands as a testament to the power of a popular movement. We have therefore to learn positive as well as negative lessons. No less, Stalin's counter-revolution eventually produced the circumstances in which it is possible for a much bigger working class to fight back openly.

Winning back the right to form political groups, to create trade unions and to publish opposition papers are all preconditions of any real change, for without them a popular movement cannot be built. Their achievement has been a real gain. The fact that they now exist means that ordinary Russians, whatever their material penury, have the possibility of linking up with wider movements for change around the globe. Their own history should tell them and us not that such movements should not be undertaken, but that the reconstruction of society has to come from the bottom up. This is not simply a moral imperative. It is a social and political necessity if we are to rescue ourselves from a system – East, West, South and North – that has created the potential for real human development even as it denies it to us all. So, far from the end of the Cold War bringing a new world order, the euphoria has given way to a new world disorder which has irrevocably marked the start of the 21st century. When a corruptly elected Russian president, a product of the continuity between old and new, shakes hands with a corruptly elected American president, the product of continuity between the old and the new, we still have a world to win, East and West alike, East and West together.

NOTES

1. INTRODUCTION

1   G Bush, speech to IMF/World Bank annual meeting, 25 September 1990.

2   B Yeltsin, *The View From the Kremlin* (London: Harper Collins, 1994), p41.

3   United Nations Human Development Programme, **Human Development Report 1996** (Oxford: Oxford University Press, 1996), p13.

4   Letter in *Independent on Sunday*, 6 May 1990.

5   M Lewin, *The Gorbachev Phenomenon* (London: Radius, 1988), p3.

6   M Fainsod, **How Russia is Ruled** (Cambridge, Mass: Harvard University Press, 1954), p500.

7   M Malia, *The Soviet Tragedy: A History of Socialism in Russia*, 1917-1991 (New York: Free Press, 1994). Richard Pipes's arguments about the Russian Revolution are summarised in R Pipes, **Three Whys of the Russian Revolution** (Toronto: Vintage Canada, 1995). For his wider discussion see R Pipes, **Communism: The Vanished Spectre** (Oxford: Oxford University Press, 1994).

8   D Volkogonov, *The Rise and Fall of the Soviet Empire* (London: Harper Collins, 1998), p521.

9   D Doder and L Branson, **Gorbachev: Heretic in the Kremlin** (London: Futura, 1990), p217.

10 **Financial Times**, 21 March 1991. G Smith (ed), *The Nationalities Question in the Soviet Union* (London: Longman, 1990), p12.

11 *Newsweek*, 7 May 1990, p4.

12 On the role of the US see S Cohen, **Failed Crusade: America and the Tragedy of Post-Communist Russia** (New York: WH Norton, 2000).

13 On British support for Putin see P Glatter, 'Don't Read My Lips, Especially on Human Rights', **Johnson's Russia List** no 4437, 4 August 2000, http://www.cdi.org/russia/johnson/4437.html##5

14 M Heller and A Nekrich, **Utopia in Power: The History of the Soviet Union from 1917 to the Present** (London: Hutchinson, 1986).

15 *Moskovsky komsomolyets*, 19 April 1995. I am indebted to Dave Crouch for this reference.

16 A Antonov-Ovseyenko, **The Time of Stalin: Portrait of a Tyranny** (New York: Harper, 1980), pxvii. This is not to say that Antonov-Ovseyenko offers a consistent account of Stalinism. Amongst other things his father led the taking of the Winter Palace in 1917.

17 In his editor's introduction to V Serge, **Year One of the Russian Revolution** (London: Allen Lane, 1972), p12.

18 V Serge, 'Reply to Ciliga', **New International**, February 1939, p54.

19 T Cliff, **Russia: A Marxist Analysis** (London: International Socialism, 1964) is the fullest edition).

20 B D Wolfe, **Three Who Made the Revolution** (Harmondsworth: Penguin, 1966), p32. It was probably wartime Germany between 1914 and 1918 that then had the largest state machine.

21 A Maddison, **The World Economy: A Millennial Perspective** (Paris: OECD, 2000), p135.

22 Quoted in N Harris, **Competition and the Corporate Society: British Conservatives, the State and Industry 1945–1964** (London: Methuen, 1972), p144.

23 See N Bukharin, **Imperialism and World Economy** (London: Merlin Press, 1972). For a discussion of Bukharin's work that tries to link his analysis of capitalism to the degeneration of the revolution and eventual development of the Stalinist regime see M Haynes, **Nikolai Bukharin and the Transition from Capitalism to Socialism** (London: Croom Helm, 1985).

24 H Sherman, **Radical Political Economy** (New York: Basic Books, 1972), pp143–144.

25 **Izvestia**, 10 January 1996. For an evaluation of Kryshtanovskaia's research see P Glatter, **Russian Regional Elites: Continuity and Change** (PhD, University of Wolverhampton, 2001).

26 See in particular M Haynes and P Binns, 'New Theories of Eastern European Class Societies', **International Socialism** 7 (Winter 1980), pp18–50; M Haynes, 'Marxism and the Russian Question in the Wake of the Soviet Collapse', **Historical Materialism**, forthcoming.

2. REVOLUTION

1 Until early 1918 the Russians used the Julian calendar, which was 13 days behind the Gregorian calendar in the West. The dates used here for 1917 and early 1918 are the Julian ones.

2 L Trotsky, **History of the Russian Revolution**, vol 1 (London: Sphere, 1967), p109.

3 P A Goluba (ed), **Velikaya Oktyabr'skaya Sotsialisticheskaya Revolutsiya** (Moscow: Sovetskaya entsiklopediya, 1987), p553.

4 T Hasegawa, **The February Revolution: Petrograd 1917** (Seattle and London: University of Washington Press, 1981), p567. On these data 72 percent of the dead and 94 percent of the injured were demonstrators.

5 On the voting for the Constituent Assembly see O H Radkey, **Russia Goes to the Polls: The Election to the All-Russian Constituent Assembly, 1917** (Ithaca: Cornell University Press, 1989).

6 O Figes and B Kolonitskii, **Interpreting the Russian Revolution: The Language and Symbols of 1917** (New Haven and London: Yale University Press, 1997), pp173, 62–68, 58–59.

7 For a brief discussion of the French Revolution that has influenced our discussion here see Robert Darnton, **The Kiss of Lamourette: Reflections on Cultural History** (London: Faber & Faber, 1990), pp3–20. For a detailed discussion of recent conservative trends in writing on the French and Russian revolutions see M Haynes, 'The Return of the Mob in the Writing on the French and Russian Revolutions', **Journal of Area Studies**, no 13 (Autumn 1998), pp56–81; M Haynes, 'Revision or Retreat? Social History and the Russian Revolution', in J Rees (ed), **Essays on Historical Materialism** (London: Bookmarks, 1998), pp57–80.

8 J Keegan, **The First World War** (London: Pimlico, 1999), p4. Churchill quoted in A Marwick, **War and Social Change in the Twentieth Century** (London: Macmillan, 1974), pp2–3.

9 M E Falkus, **The Industrialisation of Russia 1700–1914** (London: Macmillan, 1972), p72; A G Kenwood and A L Lougheed, **The Growth of the International Economy** (London: Allen & Unwin, 1971), p91.

10 R Luxemburg, 'The Junius Pamphlet: The Crisis in German Social Democracy' (1915), in **Rosa Luxemburg Speaks** (New York: Pathfinder, 1970), p257.

11 L Trotsky, **My Life** (Harmondsworth: Penguin, 1975), p257.

12 Tannenberg is at the centre of A Solzhenitsyn's novel, **August 1914** (London: Bodley Head, 1972).

13 On the development of a theory of permanent revolution see J Molyneux, **Leon Trotsky's Theory of Permanent Revolution** (New York: St Martins, 1981).

14 See P Miliukov, **The Russian Revolution** (Gulf Breeze: Academic International Press, 1978-87).

15 Quoted in O Figes and B Kolonitskii, op cit, p163.

16 Peasant quoted in O Figes and B Kolonitskii, op cit, p133. The waiters' radicalism was noted by J Reed, **Ten Days that Shook the World** (Harmondsworth: Penguin, 1977), p39.

17 The issue of popular violence has been much discussed recently. For a review see M Haynes, 'The Debate on Popular Violence and the Popular Movement in the Russian Revolution', **Historical Materialism**, no 2 (Summer 1998), pp185-214.

18 L Tolstoy, **What Then Must We Do?** (Oxford: Oxford University Press, 1925).

19 Quoted in O Figes and B Kolonitskii, op cit, p172.

20 J Reed, op cit, p40.

21 See B Kolonitskii, 'The Press and the Revolution', in E Acton, V Cherniaev and W Rosenberg (eds), **Critical Companion to the Russian Revolution 1914-1921** (London: Arnold, 1997), pp381-390.

22 V Chernov, **The Great Russian Revolution** (New Haven: Yale University Press, 1936), p402.

23 See S Smith, 'Factory Committees', in E Acton et al, op cit, pp346-358; D P Koenker, 'The Trade Unions', in E Acton et al, op cit, pp446-456; R A Wade, **Red Guards and Workers' Militias in the Russian Revolution** (Stanford: Stanford University Press, 1986).

24 N Golovine, **The Russian Army in the World War** (New Haven: Yale University Press, 1931), pp252-256, 272-274.

25 See P Miliukov, op cit.

26 Quoted in T Cliff, **Lenin: All Power to the Soviets** (London: Pluto Press, 1974), p94.

27 L Trotsky, **1905** (London: Allen Lane, 1972), p251.

28 See P Miliukov, op cit.

29 I have attempted to trace some of these in M Haynes, 'Was There a Parliamentary Alternative in Russia in 1917?', **International Socialism** 76 (Autumn 1997), pp3-66, where more detail will be found on a number of arguments made in this chapter.

30 Quoted in M Farbman, **After Lenin: The New Phase in Russia** (London: Leonard Parsons, 1924), p21.

31 Quoted in L Trotsky, **History of the Russian Revolution**, vol 2 (London: Sphere, 1967), p51.

32 V Chernov, op cit, p402.

33 V I Lenin, 'State and Revolution', in **Collected Works**, 5th edition, vol 25 (Moscow: Progress, 1964), p473.

34 V Chernov, op cit, p393.

35 W G Rosenberg, 'The Russian Municipal Duma Elections of 1917: A Preliminary Computation of the Returns', **Soviet Studies**, vol xxi (1969), pp131-163.

36 J Reed, op cit, p254.

37 There is a valuable attempt to set the spread of the revolution in the context of provincial radicalism in M M Hegelson, **The Origins of the Party-State Monolith in Soviet Russia: Relations Between Soviets and Party Committees in the Central Provinces, October 1917-March 1921** (PhD, State University of New York, 1980), pp1-72.

38 I Getzler, **Martov** (Cambridge: Cambridge University Press, 1967).

39 N N Sukhanov, **The Russian Revolution 1917: A Personal Record** (Princeton: Princeton University Press, 1984), pp631-632, 646.

40 S Cohen, **Bukharin and the Bolshevik Revolution** (London: Wildwood House, 1974), p67.

41 V Chernov, op cit, p195.

42 V I Lenin, 'To the population', **Pravda**, 5 November 1917, translated in **Collected Works**, vol 26 (Moscow: Progress, 1972), pp297-299.

43 D Atkinson, **The End of the Old Russian Land Commune, 1905-1930** (Stanford: Stanford University Press, 1983), p209.

44 Calculated from **Sbornik statisticheskikh svedenii po Souzi SSR 1913-1922** (Moscow Trudy Tsentralnogo Statisticheskogo Upravleniia, tom xviii, 1924), pp116-117. The census was a 10 percent sample one.

45 P Gatrell and M Harrison, 'The Russian and Soviet Economies in Two World Wars: A Comparative View', **Economic History Review**, vol 46 no 3 (August 1993), p445.

46 Quoted in O Anweiller, **The Soviets: The Russian Workers, Peasants and Soldiers Councils, 1905-1921** (New York: Pantheon, 1971), p127.

47 D Mandel, **The Petrograd Workers and the Soviet Seizure of Power: From the July Revolution 1917 to July 1918** (Basingstoke: Macmillan, 1984), p284; R Kaiser (ed), **The Workers' Revolution in Russia in 1917: The View From Below** (Cambridge: Cambridge University Press, 1987) summarises much of the most valuable work done in the 1970s and 1980s on the revolution from below and throws further light on these issues.

48 Quoted in S Smith, **Red Petrograd: Revolution in the Factories 1917-1918** (Cambridge: Cambridge University Press, 1983), p220.

49 L Bryant, **Six Red Months in Russia** (London: Journeyman Press, 1982), p134.

50 Quoted in W Bruce Lincoln, **Red Victory: A History of the Russian Civil War** (New York: Simon & Schuster, 1989), p344.

51 Briusov's 1919 poem 'To My Fellow Intellectuals' can be found in J Lindsay (ed), **Modern Russian Poetry** (London: Vista Books, 1960). On Blok see S Hackel, **The Poet and the Revolution: Aleksandr Blok's 'The Twelve'** (Oxford: Clarendon, 1975), pp206-229.

52 Quoted in M M Hegelson, op cit, p105.

53 Quoted in M Farbman, op cit, p101.

3. DEGENERATION

1 Quoted in E H Carr, **The Bolshevik Revolution 1917-1923**, vol 3 (Harmondsworth: Penguin), p128.

2 For a survey of revolutionary crises and forms in the West see D Gluckstein, **The Western Soviets: Workers' Councils Versus Parliament 1915-1920** (London: Bookmarks, 1984).

3 Quoted in A J Ryder, **The German Revolution of 1918: A Study of German Socialism in War and Revolution** (Cambridge: Cambridge University Press, 1967), p155.

4 See C Harman, **Germany: The Lost Revolution** (London: Bookmarks, 1982).

5 Quoted in D Gluckstein, **The Nazis, Capitalism and the Working Class** (London: Bookmarks, 1999), p15.

6 C Wrigley (ed), **Challenges of Labour: Central and Western Europe** (London: Routledge, 1993), takes this view, but as Donny Gluckstein has shown in his review essay it throws up much evidence to support the contrary view argued here, and in Gluckstein's own book noted earlier. See D Gluckstein, 'Revolution and the Challenge of Labour', **International Socialism** 61 (Winter 1993), pp109-122.

7 Quoted in P Frölich, **Rosa Luxemburg** (London: Pluto Press, 1972), pp244-245.

8 For a brief discussion of the history of the Comintern see D Hallas, **The Comintern** (London: Bookmarks, 1985).

9 Quoted in A J Ryder, op cit, p169. Ebert's comment is sometimes translated in a more religious way — 'I hate the revolution like sin.'

10 Quoted in R M Watt, **The Kings Depart: The German Revolution and the Treaty of Versailles** (London: Weidenfeld & Nicolson, 1968), p378.

11   Quoted in C Seton Watson, **Italy from Liberalism to Fascism, 1870-1925** (London: Metheun, 1967), p524.

12   Quoted in A J Ryder, op cit, p183.

13   R Luxemburg, 'The Russian Revolution', in **Rosa Luxemburg Speaks** (New York: Pathfinder, 1980), p394.

14   Quoted in E Mawdsley, **The Russian Civil War** (London: Unwin Hyman, 1987), p59.

15   R Bruce Lockhart, **Ace of Spies** (London: Hodder, 1967), pp90-91.

16   Total rifle production was 3 million, so two thirds were from stock or repairs. D A Kovalenko, **Oboronnaia promyshlennosti sovetskoi Rossii v 1918-1920 gg** (Moscow: Nauka, 1970), p392.

17   For a critique of some of the myths associated with the peasant movement see C Drach, 'The Myth of Nestor Makhno', **Economy and Society** vol 14, no 4 (November 1983), pp524-536.

18   W Bruce Lincoln, **Red Victory: A History of the Russian Civil War** (New York: Simon & Schuster, 1989), p246.

19   The photograph can be found in M Gilbert, **The Holocaust** (London: Board of Deputies of British Jews, 1978), p9.

20   Quoted in D Volkogonov, **Trotsky: The Eternal Revolutionary** (London: Harper Collins, 1996), p175.

21   See, for example, S Brown, 'Communists and the Red Cavalry: The Political Education of the Konarmiia in the Russian Civil War, 1918-1920', **Slavonic and East European Review** vol 73, no 1 (January 1995), pp82-99.

22   These are annual average figures. The fall can be traced through each year.

23   Quoted in V P Stepanov, 'Na zashchite revolutsii', in **Rabochie Leningrada 1703-1975** (Leningrad: Nauka, 1975), p167.

24   O Shkaratan, 'Izmeneniia v sotsialnom strukture fabrichno-zavodskikh rabochikh Leningrada 1917-1928 gg', **Istoriia SSSR** no 5 (1959), pp21-38.

25   E G Gimpelson, **Sovetskii rabochii klass 1918-1920gg. Sotsialno-politicheskie izmeneniia** (Moscow: Nauka, 1974), pp77-78. For more discussion of some of the issues raised here see M Haynes, 'Revision or Retreat? Social History and the Russian Revolution', in J Rees (ed), **Essays on Historical Materialism** (London: Bookmarks, 1998), pp57-80.

26   Quoted in L Lih, 'Bolshevik Razverstka and War Communism', **Slavic Review** vol 48, no 4 (1986), pp678-679. The way that circumstances bent the political structures is explored in great detail for the period from the spring of 1918 to 1921 in M M Hegelson, **The Origins of the Party-State Monolith in Soviet Russia: Relations Between Soviets and Party Committees in the Central Provinces, October 1917-March 1921** (PhD, State University of New York, 1980).

27   V Valentina (ed), **The Struggle for Power: Russia in 1923** (Amherst: Prometheus, 1996), p264.

28   These figures are relatively crude. The important point is that they show the different types of population loss with its sources. See S G Wheatcroft and R W Davies, 'Population', in R W Davies (ed), **The Economic Transformation of the Soviet Union, 1913-1945** (Cambridge: Cambridge University Press, 1994); A Blum, **Naître, Vivre et Mourir en URSS 1917-1991** (Paris: Plon, 1994).

29   N I Bukharin, **Historical Materialism. A System of Sociology** (New York: International Publishers, 1925), pp310-311.

30   Petrograd data taken from A V Gogolevvskii, **Petrogradskii soviet v gody grazdanskoi voiny** (Leningrad: Nauka, 1982), pp191-192. Provincial data from M M Hegelson, op cit, p452.

31   E Goldman, **My Disillusion with Russia** (London: CW Daniel, 1925), p47. In turn Angela Balbanova used her connections to help Goldman when she was seriously ill (p58).

32   For an analysis of the different tribunals operating at the end of the civil war and estimates of the numbers of sentences see D Rodin, 'Revolutsionnye tribunaly v 1920-1922 gg', **Vestnik statistki**, vol 12, nos 1-3.

33   For further discussion of the contested accounts of the level of violence at this time see M Haynes, 'The Debate on Popular Violence and the Popular Movement in the Russian Revolution', **Historical Materialism**, no 2 (Summer 1998), pp185-214.

34   Much publicity was given to the activities of the Cheka at the time. Two 'red books' were published of documents: P

Makintsian (ed), **Krasnaia kniga VCHK, tom 1** (Moscow: 1920); M I Latsis, **Krasnaia kniga VCHK, tom 2** (Moscow: 1922). These were later suppressed, but they were republished in 1989 (Moscow: Polizdat).

35   Mazour endorses a figure of 73,915 camp prisoners in the summer of 1918 and says up to a quarter may have died which would give a still higher figure. He says: 'The most modest estimates were shocking for a nation the size of Finland.' A G Mazour, **Finland Between East and West** (Westport: Greenwood, 1956), p55. Few accounts of the Russian events notice this though it was a crucial issue for the Bolsheviks in 1918. An exception is E Mawdsley, op cit, pp27-29.

36   Hegelson, op cit, p101.

37   V Serge, **Memoirs of a Revolutionary 1901-1941** (London: Oxford University Press, 1967), p80

38   See V Serge, **Revolution in Danger: Writings from Russia 1919-1921** (London: Bookmarks, 1997).

39   In 1923-34 this organisation became the OGPU. In 1934 its name changed to the NKVD. It went through several further changes of initials until it became the KGB in 1954.

40   For some of the ways in which the Polish events were interpreted see D Gluckstein, **The Tragedy of Bukharin** (London: Pluto Press, 1994), pp52-56.

41   P Avrich, **Kronstadt 1921** (Princeton: Princeton University Press, 1970).

42   V I Lenin, **Collected Works**, vol 32 (Moscow: Progress, 1965), p215.

43   R Stites, **Revolutionary Dreams: Utopian Vision and Experimental Life in the Russian Revolution** (Oxford: Oxford University Press, 1989), pp135-140.

44   Quoted in B N Mironov and E V Stepanov, 'Stroiteli sotsializma', in **Rabochie Leningrada, kratkii istoricheskii ocherk** (Leningrad: Nauka, 1975), p188.

45   S W Stoecker, **Forging Stalin's Army: Marshall Tukhachevsky and the Politics of Military Innovation** (Boulder: Westview, 1996), p11; R W Davies (ed), **From Tsarism to the New Economic Policy** (Ithaca: Cornell University Press, 1991), p8.

46   See W Korey, 'Zinoviev's Critique of Stalin's Theory of Socialism in One Country, December 1925-December 1926', **American Slavic Review**.

47   F Engels, **Anti Dühring**, in K Marx and F Engels, Collected Works, vol 25 (London: Lawrence & Wishart, 1987), p154.

48   For detailed statistics of military spending in the 1920s see 'Armaments Supplement', **Economist**, 19 October 1929.

49   Quoted in W Korey, op cit, p257.

50   Quoted ibid.

51   E Preobrazhensky, **The New Economics** (Oxford: Clarendon, 1965); M M Gorinov and S V Tsakunov, 'Life and Works of Evgenii Alekseevich Preobrazhenskii', **Slavic Review** vol 50, no 2 (Summer 1991), p288.

52   On Bukharin at this time see M Haynes, **Nikolai Bukharin and the Transition from Capitalism to Socialism** (Beckenham: Croom Helm, 1985).

53   Quoted in E Preobrazhensky, op cit, pxv. Preobrazhensky was expelled from the party in 1927, made his peace in 1929, was expelled again in 1931, readmitted, expelled in 1934, arrested in 1936 and shot in 1937 after refusing to testify.

54   V I Lenin, **Collected Works** vol 33 (Moscow: Progress, 1965), p65.

55   See M Lewin, **Lenin's Last Struggle** (London: Faber, 1969), which remains invaluable even after the opening of the archives.

56   L Trotsky, 'First letter to the CC', in **The Challenge of the Left Opposition 1923-25** (New York: Pathfinder, 1975), p57.

57   Quoted in M Farbman, **After Lenin: The New Phase in Russia** (London: Leonard Parsons, 1924), p49.

58   Data from J Hough and M Fainsod, **How the Soviet Union is Governed** (Cambridge: Cambridge University Press, 1979).

59 Quoted in J Hough and M Fainsod, op cit, p130.

60 See S Sternheimer, 'Administration for Development: The Emerging Bureaucratic Elite, 1920-1930', in W Pinter (ed), **Russian Officialdom: The Bureaucratisation of Russian Society from the Seventeenth to the Twentieth Century** (London: Macmillan, 1980), p333.

61 G Hosking, **A History of the Soviet Union** (London: Fontana, 1985), p145.

62 Quoted in D Dallin, **The Real Soviet Russia** (New Haven: Yale University Press, 1945), p73.

63 See 'Obrashchenie Oppozitsii Bolshevikov-Lenintsev v TsK, TsKK VKP(b) i ko vsem chlenam VKP(b)', **Bulleten Oppozitsii**, no 17-18 (November-December 1930), p16.

64 This was especially true of a group of intellectuals known as the Smena Vekh Group. See T Kraus, **Sovetskii termidor, dukhovnye predposylki Stalinskogo povorota 1917-1928** (Budapest, 1997).

65 A Bubnov, 'Statisticheskie svedeniia o VKP(b)', **Bolshaia Sovetskaia Entsikolopediia**, vol 18 (Moscow, 1930), pp532-544. The data from 1922 is of members and candidate members.

66 Calculated from the party **stazh** data in A Bubnov, op cit.

67 See M Karpovich, 'The Russian Revolution of 1917', **Journal of Modern History**, vol 2, no 2 (June 1931) for a discussion of early Leninania.

68 M Farbman, op cit, p58. There is a famous Soviet joke that married couples had to buy triple beds because Lenin was always with them.

69 Quoted in M M Gorinov and S V Tsakunov, op cit, p295.

70 Calculated from the data in A Bubnov, op cit, table 13, p537.

71 These data refer to the industrial section of the working class and not the working class as a whole. We still know relatively little of the experience of workers in the widest sense in the NEP years.

72 Soviet commentators, most notably A Rashin, were keen to stress the recovery of the working class and its links to 1917. Their data are reported in J D Barber, **The Composition of the Soviet Working Class, 1928-1941** (University of Birmingham, CRESS Discussion Paper, SIPS, no 16, nd) who supports their conclusion. However the data presented about employment length or **stazh** quoted on p33 point in the direction we have argued in the text.

73 See R Taylor, 'Soviet Cinema: The Path to Stalin', **History Today**, vol 40, no 7 (July 1990), p44.

74 'Labour Disputes in Soviet Russia', **International Labour Review**, (August 1926), pp262-268.

75 S Fitzpatrick, 'The Russian Revolution and Social Mobility: A Re-Examination of the Question of Socials for the Soviet Regime in the 1920s and 1930s', **Politics and Society**, vol 13, no 2 (1984), pp119-141

76 L Trotsky, 'Crisis in the Right-Centre Bloc', in **The Challenge of the Left Opposition 1928-29** (New York: Pathfinder Press, 1981), pp328-329.

77 Quoted in J Barber, 'Working Class Culture and Politics Culture', in H Günther (ed), **The Culture of the Stalin Period** (Basingstoke: Macmillan, 1990), p10.

78 The best short account of Stalin's rise remains R V Daniels, 'Stalin's Rise to Dictatorship 1917-1929', in A Dallin and A Westin (eds), **Politics in the Soviet Union** (New York: Harcourt Brace & World, 1966).

79 J Hough and M Fainsod, op cit; Daniels, op cit.

80 See D Volkogonov, op cit, pp295, 301.

81 See M Reiman, **The Birth of Stalinism: The USSR on the Eve of the 'Second Revolution'** (London: IB Tauris, 1987).

82 K D Slepyan, 'The Limits of Mobilisation: Party, State and the 1927 Civil Defense Campaign', **Europe-Asia Studies**, vol 45, no 5 (1993), pp851-868.

83 J V Stalin, **Works**, vol 12 (Moscow: Foreign Languages Publishing House, 1952), pp52-53.

84 Quoted in S Fitzpatrick, **Everyday Stalinism: Ordinary Life in Extraordinary Times — Soviet Russia in the 1930s** (Oxford: Oxford University Press, 1999), p187.

4. ACCUMULATION

1 J V Stalin, 'The Tasks of Business Managers' (1931), in **Problems of Leninism** (Moscow: Foreign Languages Publishing House, 1947), pp355-356.

2 A Rothstein, **A History of the USSR** (Harmondsworth: Penguin, 1950), p196.

3 L A Gordon and E V Klopov, **Chto eto bylo? Razmyshleniia o predposylkakh i itogakh togo chto sluchilos s nami v 30-40e gody** (Moscow: Polizdat, 1989), p29.

4 M Rubinshtein, **Bolshevik**, no 21 (1937), p70, quoted in J M Cooper, **Defence Production and the Soviet Economy 1929-1921** (CREES Discussion Paper, SIPS, no 3, University of Birmingham, 1976), p7.

5 D Volkogonov, **Stalin: Triumph and Tragedy** (London: Weidenfeld, 1995), p389. See also A Sella, 'Khalkhin-Gol: The Forgotten War', **Journal of Contemporary History**, vol 18, no 4 (October 1983), pp651-687.

6 Litvinov speech, of 27 November 1937, quoted in A Rothstein, op cit, p256; M Werner, **The Military Strength of the Great Powers** (London: Gollancz, 1939), p46.

7 S W Stoecker, **Forging Stalin's Army. Marshall Tukhachevsky and the Politics of Military Innovation** (Boulder Colorado: Westview, 1998), p1934; R W Davies, 'Soviet Military Expenditure and the Armaments Industry, 1929-1933: A Reconsideration', **Europe-Asia Studies**, vol 45, no 4 (1993), pp577-608. See also J M Cooper, op cit; S M Tupper, **The Red Army and Soviet Defence Industry** (PhD, University of Birmingham, 1982).

8 M Harrison, 'Resource Mobilisation for World War II: The USA, UK, USSR and Germany 1938-1945', **Economic History Review**, vol 45, no 2 (May 1988), pp172, 174.

9 M Werner, op cit, pp91, 163-164.

10 S G Wheatcroft, R W Davies and J M Cooper, 'Soviet Industrialisation Reconsidered: Some Preliminary Conclusions About Development Between 1926 and 1941', **Economic History Review**, vol 39, no 2 (May 1986).

11 J V Stalin, 'A Year of Great Change (On the Occasion of the Twelfth Anniversary of the October Revolution)', in J V Stalin, op cit, p291.

12 Data taken from **Narodnoe khoziaistvo SSSR**, various. Sector A crudely refers to the production of the means of production, Sector B to the means of consumption. In fact the division was less clear in practice, and some Sector B production took place in Sector A. But this does not alter the fundamental imbalance shown in the table.

13 **Mirovoe khoziaistvo i mirovaia politika**, no 4 (1930), p128.

14 M Lewin, **The Gorbachev Phenomenon** (London: Radius, 1988), p22.

15 S Webb and B Webb, **Soviet Communism: A New Civilisation** (London: Longman, 1944), p1945. When this book first appeared the Webbs hesitated and added a question mark to the title. They quickly decided to remove it.

16 H Draper, **The Two Souls of Socialism** (Detroit: International Socialists, 1966).

17 M Lewin, **Political Undercurrents in Soviet Economic Debates** (London: Pluto, 1974), pp117, 101. See also M Lewin, **The Making of the Soviet System: Essays in the Social History of Interwar Russia** (London: Methuen, 1985).

18 Quoted in P Temin, 'Soviet and Nazi Planning in the 1930s', **Economic History Review**, vol 44, no 4 (November 1991), p575; E Zaleski, **Stalinist Planning for Economic Growth 1933-1952** (Basingstoke: Macmillan, 1980).

19 V Serge, **Russia Twenty Years After** (New Jersey: Humanities Press, 1996), pp39-40.

20 G Hosking, **A History of the Soviet Union** (London: Fontana, 1985), pp244-245.

21 See S G Wheatcroft et al, op cit, for a comparative evaluation.

22 **Narodnoe khoziaistvo SSSR**, various years. These figures refer to the USSR on the basis of the borders of 1989. The population figure for 1939 is dubious but not the urban share.

23 K Marx, **Capital**, vol 1 (Moscow: Progress Publishers, 1986), p558.

24 A Ciliga, **The Russian Enigma** (London: Inklinks, 1979), p126.

25 Quoted in G Hosking, op cit, p163.

26 Quoted in S Cohen, **Bukharin and the Bolshevik Revolution: A Political Biography** (London: Wildwood House, 1974), p290.

27   S Cohen, op cit, p323.

28   Quoted in J Barber, 'Working Class Culture and Politics Culture', in H Günther (ed), **The Culture of the Stalin Period** (Basingstoke: Macmillan, 1990), p10.

29   J V Stalin, 'Political Report to the Sixteenth Congress' (27 June 1930), in **Leninism**, vol 2 (London: Allen & Unwin, 1933), p334.

30   **History of the Communist Party of the Soviet Union, Bolsheviks, Short Course** (Moscow: Foreign Language Publishing House, 1938), p305.

31   A Maddison, **Economic Growth in Japan and the USSR** (London: Allen & Unwin, 1969), p105.

32   Quoted in S Fitzpatrick, **Everyday Stalinism: Ordinary Life in Extraordinary Times – Soviet Russia in the 1930s** (Oxford: Oxford University Press, 1999), p42.

33   Quoted in R W Davies, **Soviet History in the Yeltsin Era** (Basingstoke: Macmillan, 1997), p191. News of these 1932 strikes leaked out to the West. They also seem to be the strikes referred to by V Serge, op cit, pp15-16, though he dates them to 1931.

34   J Scott, **Beyond the Urals** (London: Secker & Warburg, 1942), pp223.

35   Quoted in D Filtzer, 'Labour and the Contradictions of Soviet Planning Under Stalin: The Working Class and the Regime During the First Years of Forced Industrialisation', **Critique**, no 20-21 (1987), p87.

36   S Fitzpatrick, op cit, p170.

37   R W Davies, op cit, p166.

38   Quoted in D Filtzer, **Soviet Workers and Stalinist Industrialisation** (London: Pluto Press, 1986), pp77-78.

39   A Bergson, 'Income Inequality Under Soviet Socialism', **Journal of Economic Literature**, vol 22 (September 1984), p1082.

40   V Serge, op cit, p18.

41   N S Maslova, **Proizvoditelnost truda i zarabotnaia plata v promyshlennosti SSSR, 1928-1932 gg** (Moscow: Nauka, 1983), p29. The fall reflects an attempt to juggle with the work week that was soon abandoned.

42   A Nove, **An Economic History of the USSR** (Harmondsworth: Penguin, 1972), p207; S G Wheatcroft et al, op cit.

43   **Izvestia**, quoted in A Rothstein, op cit, p260.

44   During the pact 1.5 million tons of grain, 1 million tons of wood, 865,000 tons of oil, crucial key metals like copper, nickel, manganese ore, etc, were supplied to Hitler. Perhaps 800 German and Austrian Communists were handed over to him too. Despicable though this latter act was, ironically their survival rate in Nazi camps was possibly better than it might have been in Stalin's camps.

45   Quoted in D Holloway, **The Soviet Union and the Arms Race** (London: Yale University Press, 1983), p14.

46   Quoted ibid.

47   See J Barber and M Harrison, **The Soviet Home Front 1941-1945: A Social and Economic History of the USSR in World War II** (London: Longman, 1991).

48   Quoted in E Crankshaw, **Putting Up With the Russians, 1947-1984** (Basingstoke: Macmillan, 1984), pp163-164. It is interesting to note that in the West where the Nazis took a more positive attitude to the local population there was perhaps more extensive collaboration.

49   M Sholokhov, 'On the Don' (1941), in M Sholokhov, **One Man's Destiny** (London: Abacus, 1984), p159.

50   M Ellman and S Maksudov, 'Soviet Deaths in the Great Patriotic War: A Note', **Europe–Asia Studies**, vol 46, no 4 (1994), pp671-680. An element of uncertainty still surrounds the figures of Soviet dead, and they may be higher than those quoted here.

51   Quoted in O Ivinskaya, **A Captive of Time: My Years with Pasternak** (London: Collins Harvill, 1979), p80.

52   Quoted in D Holloway, op cit, p104.

53   D Holloway, **Stalin and the Bomb: the Soviet Union and Atomic Energy, 1939-1956** (London: Yale University Press, 1994).

54 A Schlesinger Jr, 'Origins of the Cold War', **Foreign Affairs**, vol 46 (October 1967), pp22-52.

55 Quoted in J Glover, **Humanity: A Moral History of the Twentieth Century** (London: Cape, 1999), p60.

56 W Churchill, **The Second World War: Triumph and Tragedy** (London: Cassell & Co, 1954), pp226-227.

57 See M Haynes and R Husan, 'State and Market in the Eastern European Transition' **Journal of European Economic History**, vol 27, no 3 (Winter 1998), pp609-644 for a discussion of bloc developments.

58 Quoted in D Holloway, op cit, p103.

59 S Alexievich, **Zinky Boys: Soviet Voices from a Forgotten War** (London: Chatto & Windus, 1992), p110.

60 See J Neale, 'Afghanistan: The Horse Changes Riders', **Capital and Class**, no 35 (1988), pp34-48; J Neale, 'The Long Torment of Afghanistan', **International Socialism** 93 (December 2001), pp31-58.

61 C Andrew and O Gordievsky, **Instructions From the Centre: Top Secret Files on KGB Foreign Operations 1975-1985** (London: Hodder & Stoughton, 1991), pp122, 34. See also pp261-276 for a 1976 KGB document 'On Certain National-Psychological Characteristics of the Chinese, and Their Evaluation in the Context of Intelligence Work'.

62 N Khrushchev, **Khrushchev Remembers** (London: Deutsch, 1971), p471.

63 L Polezhaev, **Vpered, na medlennykh tormozakh...** (Moscow: Novosti, 1994), p75.

64 G Ofer, 'Soviet Economic Growth: 1928-1985', **Journal of Economic Literature**, vol 25 (December 1987), p1787.

65 Ibid, p1813; S Brucan, **Pluralism and Social Conflict: A Social Analysis of The Communist World** (New York: Praeger, 1990), pp66-67.

66 S Cohn, **Economic Development in the Soviet Union** (Lexington: Heath Lexington Books, 1970), p84.

67 R Munting, **The Economic Development of the USSR** (Beckenham: Croom Helm, 1982), p200.

68 G Ofer, op cit, p1768.

69 Khrushchev promised a golden future on 17 October 1961 at the Twenty Second Congress: 'In the coming 10 years all the Soviet people will be able to obtain consumer goods in sufficiency, and in the following 10 years, consumer demand will be met in full.' Quoted in A Ledevena, **Russia's Economy of Favours** (Cambridge: Cambridge University Press, 1998), p97.

70 M Mandelbaum, **The Nuclear Question: The United States and Nuclear Weapons 1946-1976** (Cambridge: Cambridge University Press, 1979), pp61-62, 66.

71 M Sholokhov, op cit, p264.

72 See A Maddison, op cit, ppxx, 69.

73 Quoted in C Harman, **Bureaucracy and Revolution in Eastern Europe** (London: Pluto Press, 1976), p254.

74 Quoted in C Andrew and O Gordievsky, op cit, p191.

5. REPRESSION

1 Quoted in A Thorpe, 'Stalinism and British Politics', **History**, vol 83, no 272 (October 1998), p620.

2 Quoted in E A Osokina, **Ierarkhiia potrebleniia o zhizni ludei v usloviiakh Staliniskogo snabzheniia**, 1928-1935gg (Moscow: MGOY, 1993), pp42-43.

3 This was the fate of Riutin, Syrtsov and Lominadze, who tried to break with Stalin in 1930-32.

4 V Serge, **Russia Twenty Years After** (New Jersey: Humanities Press, 1996), p93.

5 Quoted in R W Davies, **Soviet History in the Gorbachev Revolution** (Basingstoke: Macmillan, 1989), p38.

6 Compiled in V Iakobson, 'Naslenie mest zakluchenia v SSSR', **Statisticheskoe obozrenie**, no 5, 1929. There was little secrecy about the prison population in the 1920s. For detailed data on imprisonment by crimes, sex, length of sentence, etc, see 'Faktory repressii za 1928 god', **Administrativnyi vetsnik**, no 4 (1928), pp17-21.

7 To these figures for the Russian Republic (RSFSR) must be added the prison populations of the other republics, which Solomon suggests may have been 70,000 at this time. P Solomon, 'Soviet Penal Policy, 1917-1934: A Reconsideration', **Slavic Review**, vol 31 (June 1980), pp195-217.

8   V Vilkova (ed), *The Struggle for Power: Russia in 1923* (Amherst: Prometheus Books, 1996), pp82–89.

9   V Iakobson, op cit, p103.

10 N Mandelstam, *Hope Against Hope: A Memoir* (London: Collins & Harvill, 1971), pp336, 345.

11 Amnesty International, *Prisoners of Conscience in the USSR: Their Treatment and Conditions* (London: Amnesty International, 1975), p115.

12 Quoted in A Thorpe, op cit, pp619, 623.

13 Quoted in D Volkogonov, *Trotsky: The Eternal Revolutionary* (London: Harper Collins, 1996), p456. Ian Birchall has pointed out to me that just as Trotsky's confidence in the 1930s was boosted by his memory of how quickly the internationalists in the carriages of 1915 became of international significance, so Stalin may have worried that the Trotskyists might achieve a similar feat.

14 O Ivinskaya, *A Captive of Time. My Years with Pasternak* (London: Collins Harvill, 1979), p61; A Larina, *This I Cannot Forget: The Memoirs of Anna Larina, Nikolai Bukharin's Wife* (London: Pandora, 1993), p101; F Raskolnikov, *Kronstadt and Petrograd in 1917* (London: New Park, 1982), pp345–356. Raskolnikov died in mysterious circumstances in September 1939.

15 R W Davies, op cit, p20; Mandelstam, op cit, p13.

16 J A Getty and O V Naumov, *The Road to Terror* (New Haven: Yale University Press, 1999), p456.

17 G Herling, *A World Apart* (Oxford: Oxford University Press, 1987).

18 Former Kolyma prisoner interviewed in *The Hand of Stalin: Kolyma* (October Films/PTV, 1990).

19 A Ciliga, *The Russian Enigma* (London: Inklinks 1979).

20 A Larina, op cit, pp343–344.

21 See A Akhmatova, *Selected Poems* (London: Collins–Harvill, 1989).

22 N Khrushchev, *The Secret Speech* (Nottingham: Spokesman, 1976), p47.

23 G Herling, op cit, pp9, 247, 124.

24 R W Davies, *Soviet History in the Yeltsin Era* (Basingstoke: Macmillan, 1997), pp166, 183; J Barber and M Harrison, *The Soviet Home Front 1941–1945: A Social and Economic History of the USSR in World War II* (London: Longman, 1991), p217. The figures for overall population are the corrected ones published after 1989 on the basis of the archival data.

25 G Herling, op cit, p4.

26 A Larina, op cit, p152.

27 G Herling, op cit, pp138, 136.

28 Anti-Semitism had been rife in Tsarist Russia but was pushed back in the revolution. It came back with a vengeance in the 1930s as conditions worsened and a scapegoat atmosphere developed. Sections of the regime partly encouraged it. Overall it did little to discourage it. Lenin's sister wanted the fact that he had a Jewish ancestor widely published as part of a campaign against anti-Semitism, but this was rejected by Stalin.

29 Such claims were made in the era of *glasnost*. Whether they are prison myth is unclear. Whether as reality or myth they are a sign of the ultimate degradation of the camps or the triumph of human warmth over degradation is an interesting question.

30 A Ciliga, op cit. *The Russian Enigma* combines two books originally published separately.

31 J Arch Getty et al, 'Victims of the Soviet Penal System in the Pre-War Years: A First Approach on the Basis of the Archival Evidence', *American Historical Review*, vol 98, no 4 (October 1993), pp1017–1049. Many of the details figures in this chapter are derived from an analysis of the data in this article.

32 See H Kostiuk, 'The Accursed Year From Lukianivka Prison to the Tragedy at Vorkuta (1935–1940)', *Critique*, no 27 (1995), pp159–180. See also 'Memoirs of a Bolshevik-Leninist', in G Saunders (ed), *Samizdat: Voices of the Socialist Opposition* (New York: Monad, 1974), esp. pp166–181.

33 G Herling, op cit, p192.

34 J Arch Getty et al, op cit, p1041; G Herling, op cit, pp192, 160, 250.

35   For a brief account by an eyewitness see A Nekrich, **Forsake Fear: Memoirs of an Historian** (London: Unwin & Hyman, 1990), p71.

36   A Graziosi, 'The Great Strikes of 1953 in Soviet Labour Camps in the Accounts of Their Participants — A Review,' **Cahiers du Monde Russe**, vol 33, no 4 (October–December 1992), pp419–445.

37   'Forty Days of Kengir', in A Solzhenitsyn, **The Gulag Archipelago**, Volume 3 (London: Fontana, 1978), pp285–331.

38   A Solzhenitsyn, **Stories and Prose Poems** (Harmondsworth: Penguin, 1973), p193.

39   Quoted in A Graziosi, op cit.

40   N Khrushchev, **Khrushchev Remembers** (London: Andre Deutsch, 1970), p301.

41   See D Holloway, **Stalin and the Bomb: the Soviet Union and Atomic Energy, 1939–1956** (London: Yale University Press, 1994).

42   E Crankshaw, **Putting Up with the Russians, 1947–1984** (Basingstoke: Macmillan, 1984), pp190–191.

43   The speech was not published in Russia until the **perestroika** era three decades later. But a Central Committee resolution of 30 June 1956, 'On the Cult of the Individual and its Consequences', legitimised the partial critique of Stalin.

44   Quoted in R W Davies, **Soviet History in the Gorbachev Revolution**, op cit, p102.

45   O Ivinskaya, op cit, pp153, 256.

46   B Yeltsin, **Against the Grain** (London: Cape, 1990), p2.

47   Quoted in D Volkogonov, **The Rise and Fall of the Soviet Empire** (London: Harper Collins, 1998), p275.

48   Amnesty International, op cit, p17.

49   Ibid. Volkogonov quotes figures of 3,488 arrested for anti-Soviet agitation between 1958 and 1966 and a further 1,583 between 1967 and 1975. In 1982 the KGB reported that it had cautioned 15,557 people for hostile activity but it had arrested only 433. D Volkogonov, op cit, pp314, 340.

50   Quoted in R W Davies, 'Soviet History in the Gorbachev Revolution', in R Miliband et al (eds), **Socialist Register 1988: Problems of Socialist Renewal East and West** (London: Merlin, 1988), p71.

51   According to data collected in the West in 1965–1969 8,000 Jews left the USSR; 101,500 in 1970–1974; 112,600 in 1975–1979 and 107,700 in 1980–1989. Before 1975 most went to Israel. In 1975–1979 under half went there and in the 1980s less than a third. E F Sabatello, 'Migrants From the Former Soviet Union to Israel in the 1990s', in H Fassman and R Munz (eds), **European Migration in the Late Twentieth Century** (London: Elgar, 1994), pp261–262. Using different data two Russian demographers suggest that between 1971 and 1990 1,075,700 left the Soviet Union, of which 52.7 percent were Jews and 36 percent 'ethnic Germans'. Calculated from Russian data in A Vishnevsky and Z Zayonchkovskaya, 'Emigration From the Former Soviet Union: The Fourth Wave', ibid, p246.

52   L Kopolev, 'A Lie is Conquered by Truth', in R Medvedev (ed), **Samizdat Register 1: Views of the Socialist Opposition in the Soviet Union** (London: Merlin, 1977), p227.

53   Amnesty International, op cit, pp32, 113, 135.

54   I Ratushinskaya, **Grey is the Colour of Hope** (London: Spectre, 1989), pp96, 19, 21.

6. RULING CLASS

1   A Yanov, **Detente after Brezhnev: The Domestic Roots of Soviet Foreign Policy** (Berkeley: Institute of International Studies, 1977).

2   A S Milward, **War, Economy and Society, 1939–1945** (Harmondsworth: Penguin, 1987), pp42, 59, 67.

3   A Calder, **The People's War: Britain 1939–1945** (London: Panther, 1989), p103; J K Galbraith, **A Life in Our Times: Memoirs** (London: Deutsch, 1981), p164.

4   K Marx, **Capital**, vol 1 (Moscow: Progress Publishers, 1986), p555.

5 For a typical expression of this see S Fitzpatrick, **Everyday Stalinism: Ordinary Life in Extraordinary Times — Soviet Russia in the 1930s** (Oxford: Oxford University Press, 1999).

6 A Sakharov, **Memoirs** (New York: Alfred A Knopf, 1990), p212.

7 R Medvedev, **On Socialist Democracy** (Nottingham: Spokesman, 1977), pxviii.

8 E Mawdsley and S White, **The Soviet Elite from Lenin to Gorbachev: The Central Committee and its Members, 1917-1991** (Oxford: Oxford University Press, 2000), pp285-286.

9 B Moore Jr, 'The Communist Party of the Soviet Union: 1928-44', reprinted in A Inkeles and K Geiger, **Soviet Society: A Book of Readings** (London: Constable, 1961), p127.

10 D Volkogonov, **The Rise and Fall of the Soviet Empire** (London: Harper Collins, 1998), p104.

11 T H Rigby, 'Social Orientation of Recruitment and Distribution of Membership in the Communist Party of the Soviet Union', reprinted in A Inkeles and K Gieger, op cit, p147.

12 In pre-1989 statistics the enterprise manager group was cast so widely as to include some with little or no real power.

13 This was brought out in a US survey of the early 1950s conducted amongst Soviet refugees. See R A Feldmesser, 'The Persistence of Status Advantage in Soviet Russia', **American Journal of Sociology**, vol 59 (1953-1954), pp19-27. Some attacks still took place and in 1933 more foreign workers were put on trial but 'specialist baiting' largely disappeared. In 1933 farm and agricultural officials were tried in secret for their 'failings'.

14 See S Fitzpatrick, **Education and Social Mobility in the Soviet Union, 1921-1934** (Cambridge: Cambridge University Press, 1979).

15 M J Haynes, **Nikolai Bukharin and the Transition from Capitalism to Socialism** (Beckenham: Croom Helm, 1985), p119; O Ivinskaya, **A Captive of Time: My Years with Pasternak** (London: Collins Harvill, 1979), p97.

16 M Gardner Clark, 'The Soviet Steel Industry', **Journal of Economic History**, vol 12, no 4 (Fall 1952), p403.

17 M Tatu, 'Russia's New Class', **New Society**, 7 October 1968, p16.

18 O Anweiller, 'Education Policy and Social Structure in the Soviet Union', in B Meissner (ed), **Social Change in the Soviet Union** (London: University of Notre Dame, 1972), p182.

19 J Gunther, **Inside Russia Today** (Harmondsworth: Penguin, 1962), p115.

20 S Brucan, **Pluralism and Social Conflict: A Social Analysis of the Communist World** (New York: Praeger, 1990), p158.

21 B Yeltsin, **Against the Grain** (London: Cape, 1990), p115; D Volkogonov, op cit, p370. Yeltsin's autobiographical accounts are valuable both for what they say and do not say. He received different degrees of 'help' in writing each of them.

22 Quoted in S Brucan, op cit, p58. See also N A Aitov, 'The Dynamics of Social Mobility in the USSR', **Soviet Sociology**, vol 24, no 1-3 (Summer-Fall-Winter 1985-86), pp254-273.

23 B Kerblay, **Contemporary Soviet Society** (London: Methuen, 1983), p156.

24 J Stalin, 'New Conditions — New Tasks in Economic Construction', in **Problems of Leninism** (Moscow: Foreign Languages Publishing House, 1947), p364.

25 S Fitzpatrick, op cit, pp106-108.

26 A Bergson, 'Income Inequality Under Soviet Socialism', **Journal of Economic Literature**, vol 13 (September 1984), p1065. Death duties were also comparatively minor so that personal inheritance via housing, savings and government bonds was significant.

27 B Kerblay, 'Social Inequality in the USSR', **Problems of Communism**, vol 21, no 1 (January-February 1982), p57.

28 This survey comes from A V Ledeneva, **Russia's Economy of Favours: Blat, Networking and Informal Exchange** (Cambridge: CUP, 1998). My analysis of the material Ledeneva supplies is significantly different from that of the author. See my review in **Russian History**, forthcoming.

29 **Kommunist**, 1989, translated in **Soviet Weekly**, 12 August 1989.

30 In the 1960s Nigel Harris drew attention to the way in which Soviet official ideology incorporated many aspects of

Western conservative thought. See N Harris, **Beliefs in Society** (Harmondsworth: Penguin, 1971).

31 L Brezhnev, **Memoirs** (Oxford: Pergamon, 1982), p13.

32 Quoted in L Kopolev, op cit, p235.

33 **Izvestia**, 14 June 1937, quoted in O Ivinskaya, op cit, p267.

34 L Kopolev, 'A Lie is Conquered by Truth', in R Medvedev (ed), **Samizdat Register 1: Views of the Socialist Opposition in the Soviet Union** (London: Merlin, 1977), p228. The sponsorship of anti-Semitism by sections of the ruling class is extensively illustrated in R Ainsztein, 'The End of Marxist-Leninism', **New Statesman**, 15 December 1978, pp814-818.

35 S Alliluyava, **Twenty Letters to a Friend** (Harmondsworth: Penguin, 1967), pp230-231.

36 D Elliott, 'The End of the Avant-Garde', in **Art and the Dictators** (London: Hayward Gallery, 1996), p198. Nikritin's picture is on p230 of this major work comparing art under Stalin, Hitler and Mussolini.

37 See M Sholokhov, **One Man's Destiny** (London: Abacus, 1984), p270.

38 M Foucault, **The History of Sexuality Volume 1: An Introduction** (London: Allen Lane, 1979).

39 Quoted in J Evans, 'The Communist Party of the Soviet Union and the Woman's Question: The Case of the 1936 Decree "In Defence of Mother and Child", **Journal of Contemporary History**, vol 16, no 4 (1981), p766.

40 Quoted in R Schlesinger (ed), **The Family in the USSR** (London: Routledge, 1949), p393.

41 S Wolfson, quoted in R Schlesinger, op cit, p310.

42 V A Giliarovski, **Psikhiatriia** (Moscow, 1942) quoted in J Wortis, **Soviet Psychiatry** (Baltimore: Williams & Wilkins, 1950), pp61-62.

43 A Sakharov, op cit, p168; Many legends grew up about Beria's sexual exploits. A Knight, **Beria: Stalin's First Lieutenant** (Princeton: Princeton University Press, 1994), argues that most should be discounted.

44 L Coser, 'Some Aspects of Soviet Family Policy', **American Journal of Sociology**, vol 56 (1950-1951), p426.

45 L Trotsky, **The Revolution Betrayed** (New York: Pathfinder, 1972), p238; A V Ledevena, op cit.

46 L Trotsky, p225.

47 B Kerblay, op cit, p199.

48 E Crankshaw, **Putting Up with the Russians 1947-1984** (Basingstoke: Macmillan, 1984), pp83-86.

49 See R Stites, **Revolutionary Dreams: Utopian Vision and Experimental Life in the Russian Revolution** (Oxford: Oxford University Press, 1989), p133.

50 W Campbell, **Villi the Clown** (London: Faber & Faber, 1981), p216. Campbell did eventually manage to sell the statuette and buy a car — a sign of his high status at the time.

51 Quoted in A V Ledevena, op cit, p93.

52 Quoted in A Antonov-Ovseyenko, **The Time of Stalin: Portrait of Tyranny** (New York: Harper & Row, 1981), p185.

53 M Markuzi, 'Soviet Perfumery and Cosmetics', **Economic Survey of the USSR Chamber of Commerce**, vol 3, no 10 (October 1936), pp25-27.

54 L Trotsky, op cit, p120.

55 V Dunham, **In Stalin's Time: Middle Class Values in Soviet Fiction** (Cambridge: CUP, 1976), pp108-109.

56 L Labedz (ed), **Solzhenitsyn: A Documentary Record** (Harmondsworth: Penguin, 1972), p142.

57 Quoted in B Kerblay, **Contemporary Soviet Society**, pp284-285.

58 'The Soviet Joneses are Not Keeping Up', **Economist**, 5 January 1980, p34.

59 M Seton Watson, **Scenes from Soviet Life: Soviet Life Through Official Literature** (London: Ariel Books, 1986), esp. pp32-35, 109-123.

60 See S Davies, **Popular Opinion in Stalin's Russia: Terror, Propaganda, and Dissent, 1934-1941** (Cambridge: Cambridge University Press, 1997).

61 See the discussion of Stalin's speech in R W Davies, **Soviet History in the Gorbachev Revolution** (Basingstoke: Macmillan, 1989), pp80-81.

62 B Yeltsin, op cit, p67.

63 B Kerblay, op cit, p199.

64 R Razaulkas, 'The Kind of Director I Want', *Literaturnaia gazeta*, 25 August 1976. This is translated in J Adams et al, *The USSR Today: Current Readings from the Soviet Press 1975-1977*, 4th ed (Columbus: American Association for Advancement of Slavic Studies, 1977), pp53-54.

65 Like a number of languages, including French, Russian has two forms for 'you'. The **tu** form is used amongst friends but is condescending when used by a 'superior' to an 'inferior'.

66 T Zaslavskaia, 'The Novosibirsk Report', **Survey**, vol 28, no 1 (1984), p106.

7. WORKING CLASS

1   Quoted in E Mandel, **Beyond Perestroika: The Future of Gorbachev's USSR** (London: Verso, 1991), p63.

2   J V Stalin, **Problems of Leninism** (Moscow: Foreign Languages Publishing House, 1947), p544.

3   S Cohn, **Economic Development in the Soviet Union** (Lexington: Heath Lexington Books, 1970), p63.

4   M A Vyltsan, 'Chislennost' i sostav sel'skogo naselenniia SSSR za 50 let', **Voprosy istorii**, no 6 (1967), pp44-51.

5   Compiled from A I Vdovin and V Z Drobizhev, **Rost rabochego klassa SSSR 1917-1940** (Moscow: Mysl, 1976); V S Khorev, **Problemy gorodov** (Moscow: Mysl, 1971), pp215-216; R S Mathieson, **The Soviet Union: An Economic Geography** (London: Heineman, 1975), p50.

6   V A Ezhov, **Rabochii klass — vedushchaia sila vosstanovleniia Leningrada 1943-1950 gg.** (Leningrad: Leningrad University, 1982), pp7, 33-34.

7   S Brucan, **Pluralism and Social Conflict: A Social Analysis of the Communist World** (New York: Praeger, 1990), p64.

8   **Narodnoe khoziaistvo SSSR** v 1988 (Moscow: Finansy i statistika, 1988), p39.

9   J Scott, **Beyond the Urals** (London: Secker & Warburg, 1942), pp223, 80-81.

10 V I Gurev and G P Gorbei, **Nash obraz zhizni** (Moscow: Finansy i statistika, 1990), p12.

11 N Mandelstam, **Hope Against Hope: A Memoir** (London: Collins & Harvill, 1971), p301.

12 L A Gordon and E V Klopov, **Chto eto bylo? Razmyshleniia o predposylkakh i itogakh togo chto sluchilos s nami v 30-40e gody** (Moscow: Polizdat, 1989), p108, 101.

13 Quoted in A Ledeneva, **Russia's Economy of Favours** (Cambridge: Cambridge University Press, 1998), p136.

14 Quoted in S Cohn, op cit, p42.

15 Quoted in M Seton Watson, **Scenes from Soviet Life: Soviet Life Through Official Literature** (London: Ariel Books, 1986), p81.

16 L Kopolev, 'A Lie is Conquered by Truth', in R Medvedev (ed), **Samizdat Register 1: Views of the Socialist Opposition in the Soviet Union** (London: Merlin, 1977), p226.

17 D Lane, **Soviet Society Under Perestroika** (London: Unwin, 1990), p131.

18 V I Gurev and G F Gorbei, op cit, pp42-44.

19 V I Gurev and G F Gorbei, op cit, pp36-38.

20 Quoted in M A Vyltsan, op cit, p60.

21 A Bergson, 'Income Inequality Under Soviet Socialism', **Journal of Economic Literature**, vol 13 (September 1984), p1080. Even under the repressive labour legislation there was some movement — especially if managers connived.

22 **Narodnoe khoziaistvo** (various years).

23 **Narodnoe khoziaistvo** (various years).

24 Data from P Chattopadhyay, **The Marxian Concept of Capital and the Soviet Experience** (Westport: Praeger, 1994), p76.

25 After 1989 the company town nature of many workplaces and even entire cities would help complicate the pattern

of the transition to more loosely integrated forms.

26   The issue of whether or not labour functioned as wage labour has been much debated. The discussion has raised both theoretical questions about what is meant by wage labour and empirical ones about the balance of narrow internal market forces and central direction. Some of these issues are briefly discussed in M Haynes, 'Marxism and the Russian Question in the Wake of the Soviet Collapse', **Historical Materialism**, forthcoming.

27   Data from table 6.5 in A Bergson, **The Economics of Soviet Planning** (New Haven: Yale University Press, 1964), p112.

28   A Bergson, op cit, p1082.

29   Ibid, p1085.

30   From 'Articles of Rules for Plant Trade Union Committees', quoted in B Kerblay, **Contemporary Soviet Society** (London: Methuen, 1983), p185. Note which task comes last. For the Klebanov case see V Haynes and O Semyonova, **Workers Against the Gulag: The New Opposition in the Soviet Union** (London: Pluto Press, 1979).

31   B Yeltsin, **Against the Grain** (London: Cape, 1990), p102.

32   B Kerblay, op cit, p185. Dissident trade union appeal quoted in V Haynes and O Semyonovka, op cit, p33.

33   M T Ivochuk and L N Kogan (eds), **The Cultural life of the Soviet Worker: A Sociological Study** (Moscow: Progress, 1975), pp83, 86.

34   A Bergson, op cit, p1001.

35   V I Gurev and G F Gorbei, op cit, p36.

36   G Arievich, 'Strike', **New Times**, no 31 (1989), p8; **Izvestia**, (27 July 1989), translated in **Current Digest of the Soviet Press**, vol 41, no 30 (23 August 1989), p4.

37   V Kostikov, 'Ne plakatnyi geroi', **Ogonyok**, no 17 (1989).

38   Taken from G Andrusz, **Housing and Urban Development in the USSR** (Basingstoke: Macmillan, 1984), pp22–23; **Narodnoe khoziaistvo v 1989 g** (Moscow: Finansy i statistika, 1989), p165. Andrusz discusses some of the issues raised by the measurement of housing space.

39   B Yeltsin, op cit, p67.

40   The phrase is that of Vladimir Maksimov in his novel, **Seven Days of Creation** (London: Weidenfeld & Nicolson, 1975).

41   Quoted in A Roxbugh, **The Second Russian Revolution: The Struggle for Power in the Kremlin** (London: BBC Books, 1991), p114.

42   E Crankshaw, **Putting Up With the Russians 1947–1984** (Basingstoke: Macmillan, 1984), p8.

43   B Yeltsin, op cit, p94.

44   Quoted in H Defosses, 'Demography, Ideology and Politics in the USSR', **Soviet Studies**, vol 28, no 2 (April 1976), p252; Seton Watson, op cit, p13.

45   E A Osokina, **Ierarkhiia potrebleniia o zhizni ludei v usloviiakh Staliniskogo snabzheniia**, 1928–1935gg (Moscow: MGOY, 1993).

46   V Serge, **Russia Twenty Years After** (New Jersey: Humanities Press, 1996), p184.

47   **Narodnoe khoziaistvo**, various years.

48   B Kerblay, op cit.

49   The word **avoska** itself tells us something about the precarious nature of supplies for the mass of the population. It comes from the Russian **avos** meaning 'perhaps' and **na avos** meaning 'on the off-chance'.

50   This is the figure given by Yeltsin in 1990 for the situation in the mid-1980s. B Yeltsin, op cit, p97.

51   Quoted in A Bergson, op cit, p1058.

52   **Izvestia**, 30 January 1988. Recall again that these average figures hide serious regional variations.

53   Former Kolyma prisoner interviewed in **The Hand of Stalin: Kolyma** (October Films/PTV, 1990).

54   S Fitzpatrick, **Everyday Stalinism: Ordinary Life in Extraordinary Times — Soviet Russia in the 1930s** (Oxford: Oxford University Press, 1999), pp169–170. See also S Davies, **Popular Opinion in Stalin's Russia: Terror, Propaganda, and**

Dissent, 1934-1941 (Cambridge: Cambridge University Press, 1997).

55 Quoted in R W Davies, **Soviet History in the Yeltsin Era** (Basingstoke: Macmillan, 1997), pp191-192.

56 W Teckenberg, 'Labour Turnover and Job Satisfaction: Indicators of Industrial Conflict in the USSR?', **Soviet Studies**, vol 30, no 2 (April 1978), pp193-211; S Malle, 'Planned and Unplanned Mobility in the Soviet Union Under the Threat of Labour Shortage', **Soviet Studies**, vol 39, no 3 (July 1987), pp357-387.

57 S H Baron, **Bloody Saturday in the Soviet Union: Novocherkassk, 1962** (Stanford: Stanford University Press, 2000), pp67-69.

58 Quoted in V Haynes and O Semyonova, op cit, p99.

59 A pioneering and still useful study in English is M Holubenko, 'The Soviet Working Class: Discontent and Opposition', **Critique**, no 4 (Spring 1975), pp5-25. A first post-1991 study in Russian was Y F Lukin, **Iz istorii soprotivleniia totalitarizmu v SSSR** (Moscow: Moscow University, 1992). There is a mass of material in V A Kozlov, **Massoye besporiadki v SSSR pri Khrushcheve i Brezhneve (1953 – nachalo 1980-kh godov)** (Novosibirsk: Sibirskii Khronograf, 1999).

60 T Friedgut and L Siegelbaum, 'Perestroika From Below: The Soviet Miners' Strike and the Aftermath', **New Left Review**, no 181 (May-June 1990), pp5-32.

8. TRANSITION

1   For the different estimates see R C Stuart and P A Gregory, **The Russian Economy: Past, Present and Future** (New York: Harper Collins, 1995), p39. These growth rates refer to total output. Taking account of population growth worsens the picture. The growing divergence of official and real rates of growth was identified in Russia at the time but only revealed after 1985. See, for example, A Aganbegyan, **The Challenge of Perestroika** (London: Hutchinson, 1988), pp1-3, 9-12.

2   For a discussion of the post-war boom from this perspective see M Haynes, 'The Long Boom and the Advanced World 1945-1973', in D Renton and K Flett (eds), **The Twentieth Century Barbarism and Progress** (London: Rivers Oram, 2000), pp183-203.

3   A Aganbegyan, op cit, p142.

4   V Kriuchkov, 'An Objective View of the World', **Mezhdunarodnaia zhizn** (October 1988), translated in C Andrew and O Gordievsky, **Instructions From the Centre: Top Secret Files on KGB Foreign Operations 1975-1985** (London: Hodder & Stoughton, 1991), pp298-299.

5   Quoted in A Brown, 'Gorbachev: New Man in the Kremlin', **Problems of Communism**, vol 34, no 3 (May-June 1985), p9.

6   A Aganbegyan, op cit, p128.

7   Quoted in Alec Nove, 'Agriculture', in M McCauley (ed), **The Soviet Union After Brezhnev** (London: Heinemann, 1983), p97.

8   R Reagan, quoted in Aganbegyan, op cit, p204.

9   Quoted in C Andrew and O Gordievsky, op cit, p296.

10 A popular rhyme of the past was disinterred at this time: 'Moonshine liquor, moonshine liquor, we'll just have to make you quicker'.

11 A Aganbegyan, op cit, pp5, 40.

12 D Volkogonov, **The Rise and Fall of the Soviet Empire** (London: Harper Collins, 1998), pp511-512.

13 **Pravda**, 26 February 1987.

14 G Pavlovsky and M Meyer, 'Public Movements in the USSR', **Moscow News**, no 7 (1990), pp8-9.

15 This was the conclusion of an academic like R W Davies in **Soviet History in the Gorbachev Revolution** (Basingstoke: Macmillan, 1989), as well as many on the left. See also T Ali, **Revolution from Above: Where is the Soviet Union Going?** (London: Hutchinson, 1988).

16 N Shmelev, 'Avansy i dolgi', **Novy mir**, no 6 (June 1987). Translation in **Current Digest of the Soviet Press**, vol

39, no 38 (October 21 1987).

17 Quoted in R Bova, 'Worker Activism: the Role of the State', in J Sedatis and J Butterfield (eds), **Perestroika from Below: Social Movements in the Soviet Union** (Boulder: Westview, 1991), pp31–32.

18 B Eklof, **Soviet Briefing: Gorbachev and the Reform Period** (Boulder: Westview Press, 1989), p124.

19 'Shakhta', interview by P Gutiontov, Vorkuta, December 1989 with Valentin Kopasov, an engineer in the machine section of the Central mine and co-chairman of the Vorkuta strike committee, **Ogonyok**, no 3 (January 1990).

20 R Bova, op cit, p39. In 1981 in the US President Reagan had sacked 12,000 striking air traffic controllers and jailed some.

21 Quoted in A Roxbugh, **The Second Russian Revolution: The Struggle for Power in the Kremlin** (London: BBC Books, 1991), p154.

22 A Gresh, 'Les sentiers escarpés du passage à la démocratie', **Le Monde Diplomatique**, February 1990, p14.

23 **Ogonyok**, no 3 (January 1990).

24 Quoted in **Financial Times**, 20 November 1989.

25 B Yeltsin, **The View from the Kremlin** (London: Harper Collins, 1994), p105.

26 Ibid, pp114–115. At a more personal level the agreement finally eliminated any residual claims that Gorbachev had to a role by destroying his nominal base in the collapsed political structures of the USSR.

27 B Yeltsin, 'Speech to Congress of People's Deputies', **Izvestia**, 28 October 1991, translated in **Current Digest of the Soviet Press**, vol 43, no 43 (27 November 1991), pp1–6.

28 B Yeltsin, **The View from the Kremlin**, op cit.

29 S Cohen, **Failed Crusade: America and the Tragedy of Post-Communist Russia** (New York: Norton, 2000), p130.

30 L Polezhaev, **Vpered, na medlennykh tormozakh...** (Moscow: Novosti, 1994), pp61–62.

31 United Nations Development Programme, **Transition 1999: Regional Human Development Report for Central and Eastern Europe and the CIS** (Geneva: United Nations, 1999).

32 S White, 'From Communism to Democracy', in S White et al (eds) **Developments in Russian Politics 4** (Basingstoke: Macmillan, 1997), p31.

33 Quoted in E Mawsdley and S White, **The Soviet Elite: From Lenin to Gorbachev — The Central Committee and its Members, 1917–1991** (Oxford: Oxford University Press, 2000), pp301–302.

34 R Layard and J Parker, **The Coming Russian Boom: A Guide to New Markets and Politics** (New York: Free Press, 1996); **Observer**, 31 May 1998.

35 **Financial Times**, 15 April 1998.

36 R Sharlet, 'The Progress of Human Rights', in S White et al (eds), op cit, p141.

37 R Ferguson, 'Chechnya: The Empire Strikes Back', **International Socialism** 86 (Spring 2000), pp51–70.

38 B Yeltsin, **The View from the Kremlin**, op cit, p100.

39 **Financial Times**, 1 November 1996.

40 B Yeltsin, **The View from the Kremlin**, op cit, p168.

41 J Millar, 'The De-Development of Russia', **Current History**, vol 98, no 630 (October 1999), p322.

42 UN Development Report, op cit.

43 I Popovic, 'Russian Students Head Abroad for Education', **The Russian Journal**, no 29 (September 1999).

44 B Yeltsin, **The View from the Kremlin**, op cit, p179.

45 A Gentleman, 'The Hard Men Behind Putin', **Observer**, 26 March 2000.

46 B Yeltsin, **The View from the Kremlin**, op cit, p42.

47 This is on the basis laid down by the ILO.

48 UN Development Report, op cit.

49 N Holdsworth, **Moscow The Beautiful and the Damned: Life in Russia in Transition** (London: Andre Deutsch, 2000), p75.

50 S Cohen, op cit, p207.

51 R Ferguson, 'Will Democracy Strike Back? Workers and Politics in the Kuzbass', **European-Asia Studies**, vol 50, no 3 (1998), pp445-468.

52 L Alekseeva, 'Unfree Trade Unions', **Moscow News**, January 15-22, 1995.

53 Compiled from **Russian Economic Trends** (various).

54 On the railway war see RFE/RL Newsline; **The <Moscow> eXile**, 4-18 June 1998. Readers with access to the internet should check the 'Pay us our wages' website (www.icem.org/campaign/no-pay-cc) maintained by the International Federation of Chemical, Energy, Mine and General Workers' Unions, which maintains a list of the bigger industrial actions as well as providing much other useful information.

55 R Ferguson, 'Will Democracy Strike Back? Workers and Politics in the Kuzbass', op cit.

56 B Yeltsin, **Midnight Diaries** (London: Phoenix, 2000), pp169-170, 326-328, 333.

9. CONCLUSION

1 A Callinicos, **The Revenge of History: Marxism and the East European Revolutions** (Oxford: Polity, 1991).

2 C Sparks and A Redding, **Communism, Capitalism and the Mass Media** (London: Sage, 1998).

3 'Discussions with Trotsky', in C L R James, **At the Rendezvous of Victory** (London: Allison & Busby, 1984), pp53-55.

FACT BOXES

i   A G Rashin, **Formirovanie rabochego klassa Rossii** (Moscow: Sotseklit, 1958), pp117, 141, 152, 172.

ii   Data from N N Smirnov, **Tretii Vserossiiskii sezd sovetov** (Leningrad: Nauka, 1988).

iii From **Liberator**, 1918, reprinted in J Newsinger (ed), **Shaking the World: John Reed's Revolutionary Journalism** (London: Bookmarks, 1998).

iv   V I Lenin, **Collected Works**, vol 26 (Moscow: Progress, 1965), p435.

v   Y Zamyatin, **The Dragon and Other Stories** (Harmondsworth: Penguin, 1974), p140.

vi   I Ehrenburg, **First Years of Revolution, 1918-1921** (London: Macgibbon & Kee, 1962), pp139-141, 145-147, 152-154.

vii F King and G Matthews (eds), **About Turn: The British Communist Party and the Second World War. The Verbatim Record of the Central Committee Meetings of 25 September and 2-3 October 1939** (London: Lawrence & Wishart, 1990), pp130-131.

viii A Nove, 'Victims of Stalinism', in J Arch Getty and R T Manning (eds), **Stalinist Terror: New Perspectives** (Cambridge: Cambridge University Press, 1993), p270.

ix   Quoted in M Reiman, **The Birth of Stalinism: The USSR on the Eve of the 'Second Revolution'** (London: IB Tauris, 1987), p22.

x   Quoted in T Cliff, **Trotsky 1927-40: The Darker the Night the Brighter the Star** (London: Bookmarks, 1993), p98.

xi   A Nove, 'Victims of Stalinism', in J Arch Getty and R T Manning (eds), op cit, p269.

xii See M Ilic, 'Soviet Women Workers and Menstruation: A Research Note on Labour Protection in the 1920s and 1930s', **Europe-Asia Studies**, vol 46, no 8 (1994), pp1409-1413.

xiii D Volkogonov, **Lenin: Life and Legacy** (London: Harper Collins, 1994), p4.

xiv R Service, **A History of Twentieth Century Russia** (London: Allen Lane, 1997), p419.

xv   **Iskusstvo**, no 1 (1950), quoted in M Chegodayeva, 'A Double Life? A Double Art', **Moscow News**, no 9 (1989), p16. Picasso quoted in G T Utley, **Picasso: The Communist Years** (New Haven: Yale University Press, 2000).

xvi F J Eroll, 'Industrial Life in Russia Today', **Geographical Magazine**, vol xxvii, no II (March 1955), p585.

xvii See M Haynes, 'Aeroflot: Soviet Airlines', in **International Directory of Business Histories**, (New York and London:

Gale Research Press International, 1993), pp57-59.

xviii   Quoted J Riordan, 'The USSR', in J Riordan (ed), **Sport Under Communism**, 2nd edition (London: C Hurst & Co, 1981), p30.

xix   Compiled from B Yeltsin, **Against the Grain: An Autobiography** (London: Pan, 1991).

xx   N Bukharin, **Imperialism and World Economy** (London: Merlin Press, 1972).

xi   J Cooper, **The Soviet Defence Industry: Conversion and Reform** (London: RIIA Pinter, 1991).

xii   Quoted in D Hoffman, **The Oligarchs: Wealth and Power in the New Russia** (Oxford: Public Affairs Ltd, 2002), p101.

xiii   S L Solnick, **Stealing the State: Control and Collapse in Soviet Institutions** (Cambridge, Mass: Harvard University Press, 1998), pp7, 60-124, 223.

INDEX

RUSSIA - INDEX